LOCAL AREA NETWORKS

and their applications

ony

999

PRENTICE HALL

New York   London   Toronto   Sydney   Tokyo

First published 1988 by
Prentice Hall International (UK) Ltd,
66 Wood Lane End, Hemel Hempstead,
Hertfordshire, HP2 4RG
A division of
Simon & Schuster International Group

Printed and bound in Great Britain by
BPCC Wheatons Ltd, Exeter

Library of Congress Cataloging-in-Publication Data

Tangney, Brendan, 1960–
    Local area networks and their applications/
Brendan Tangney, Donal O'Mahony.
        p.   cm.
    Bibliography: p.
    Includes index.
    ISBN 0-13-539578-X
    1. Local area networks.
    I. O'Mahony, Donal, 1961–
II. Title.
TK5105.7.T36 1987
004.4'8—dc19

British Library Cataloguing in Publication Data

Tangney, Brendan
    Local Area Networks and Their Applicatons.
    1. Local area networks (Computer networks)
    I. Title   II. O'Mahony, Donal
    004.6'8   TK5105.7

    ISBN 0-13-539578-X
    ISBN 0-13-539560-7 (PBK)

---

5 6 7   92 91 90

CONTENTS

Part Two   DISTRIBUTED SYSTEMS

PREFACE

In the early 1970s, a trend began in computing away from large centralized mainframes towards smaller departmental minicomputers. The first micro-processor system was introduced around 1971 and since then cheaper and more powerful machines have appeared on the market. This trend gathered momentum and has developed into a definite movement towards single-user workstations.

One of the disadvantages of this is that facilities that were available on larger, centralized systems were lacking in the new workstation approach. These included the ability to share information, send messages from one user to another, and, most importantly, to share access to peripheral devices, e.g. printers, disks and so on.

While computing devices were getting smaller, cheaper and more powerful, advances were also being made in communications technology. In particular a new generation of networks emerged which operated in a limited geographical area, but much more reliably and at higher data transmission rates than previous networks.

The introduction of these high speed **local area networks** (LANs) opened up the possibility of attaining the advantages of workstations without losing those of centralized mainframe systems. Information could flow between individual workstations at speeds which, to a large extent, hid the fact that they were not working on the same system.

This book examines these two aspects of local networks. Part One discusses the components that go to make up a local network. Part Two looks at the higher level software that is necessary to exploit the capabilities of a 'distributed' computing system, that is one composed of a number of individual machines connected by such a LAN.

The book is suitable for use as a higher level undergraduate and post-graduate textbook. The treatment of LANs is fairly detailed and the second section serves as an introduction to distributed computing. It will also provide valuable, up-to-date knowledge for computer professionals involved in planning and implementing LANs within their organization. No prior knowledge of networks is assumed, but a basic understanding of the field of data communications and computer operating systems will be helpful. The remainder of this preface explains the layout of the book in a little more detail.

Part One of the book begins by defining what exactly we mean by the term 'network', and how a 'local area' network is distinguished from other types. Chapters 2, 3 and 4 will cover the choices available in terms of communications media, the ways in which the machines are connected (topology), and how orderly transmission is carried out (the access method). As an illustration of the techniques covered, Chapter 5 will discuss how some of the better known LANs (e.g. Ethernet, IBM's Token Ring and the Cambridge Ring) are implemented using the previously described techniques. In Chapter 6 the concept of layered protocols is introduced and we examine some of the standards that have been developed in this area.

Part Two of the book concentrates on the details of LAN-based computer systems. It begins in Chapter 7 by analyzing what the essential differences are between running a centralized system and one made up of many interlinked machines. The concept of sharing resources between nodes on a network is introduced. Chapter 8 introduces the notion of the 'client/server' model, a widely used technique for organizing access to resources. Chapter 9 focuses on one very important type of server, namely 'file servers'. This is followed in Chapter 10 by an introduction to the concept of a 'distributed system', it explores some of the issues involved in building one, and looks at some example systems including CMDS, the Newcastle Connection and Locus. We complete the section by discussing how LANs can be used in the office and factory environments.

The following are trademarks: UNIX (A T & T Bell Laboratories); DEC and DECnet (Digital Equipment Corporation); Ethernet (Digital Intel Xerox Corporation); WangNet (Wang Corporation); IBM and SNA (International Business Machines); Apple, AppleTalk and AppleBus (Apple Computer Inc.).

ACKNOWLEDGEMENTS

David Brownbridge, David Hutchison and Les Smith for comments on early versions of the manuscript. Maggie McDougall and Abigail Cooke for editing and production. Stephen and Neville for inspiration, our parents for opportunity. But above all, Tricia and Mary for patience, support, encouragement, etc.

PART ONE

LOCAL AREA NETWORKS

CHAPTER ONE

WHAT IS A LAN?

A concise definition of what constitutes a local area network is difficult to produce. An easier approach is to first define what a computer network is, and then to distinguish LANs as a subset of these. When the term computer network was first used, it described any interconnections between computers. Since that time, three subclasses have emerged that are distinguished primarily by their geographical scope.

The first of these is the *wide area network* (WAN). This network spans a large area – possibly several continents. The second major type is the *local area network* (LAN) and, as the name suggests, it is confined to relatively small areas such as a building or a group of buildings, for example a university campus. A third type, which is just emerging at the time of writing, is the *metropolitan area network* (MAN). The scope of this class of network lies between LANs and WANs, i.e. spanning a small city or a town.

In naming these types of network, the main distinguishing factor would appear to be the size of the area covered. This factor has major effects on the technology used to implement the network, its administration and the type of applications that can be implemented on it. The ramifications of these factors will emerge in the course of this book.

1.1 WHAT IS A NETWORK?

Tanenbaum [1] defines a network as 'an interconnected collection of autonomous computers'. Two computers are said to be interconnected if they are capable of exchanging information. Central to this definition is the fact that the computers are *autonomous*. This means that no computer on the network can start, stop, or control another. This excludes from our definition any system where terminals or other peripheral devices are connected to a central host: for example, an IBM 370 configured with multiple 3270 terminals connected to it.

3

Another type of system that we exclude from our discussions is where two or more processors are connected together via either a common bus or an area of shared memory. While this may conform to the definition above, the problems involved differ significantly from other types of networks.

1.2 WORKING DEFINITION OF A LAN

Having defined what is meant by a network, the next task is to distinguish between LANs and WANs. LANs are different in the following important respects.

- The distance between the nodes is limited. There is an upper limit of approx 10 km, and a lower limit of 1 m.
- While WANs usually operate at speeds of less than 1 mbps, LANs normally operate at between 1 and 10 mbps. Using optical fiber technology, it is possible to achieve speeds of the order of hundreds of mbps.
- Because of the short distances involved, the error rates in LANs are much lower than in WANs. This extra reliability has an impact on both the protocols used in their operation and the range of applications that they can support.
- The distance limitations involved in LANs normally mean that the entire network is under the ownership and control of a single organization. This is in sharp contrast to WANs, where the network typically spans national boundaries. In this case, the network is normally operated by the countries post and telecommunications authorities rather than by its users.

   This fact has no bearing on the performance of the LAN, although it does have a major impact on the way in which it is administered. The localized control of the facility greatly increases flexibility.

It can be seen from the above, that LANs differ from other types of network in that the area they cover is limited. This means they can operate at high speeds and with very low error rates. These two properties are the main distinguishing features of LANs.

   The first local networks were introduced into the academic world in the mid-1970s and, as the technology developed, they were adopted by the major computer manufacturers. By the early 1980s, most major hardware companies were offering LAN-based products. At the time of writing, the lower level aspects of LANs are starting to stabilize. Of the many approaches advocated by the researchers, a select few are becoming international standards, and are being adopted by computer users.

1.3 CLASSIFICATION OF LANS

There are many different network implementations that conform to the above criteria, each adopting a different approach. To distinguish between different types of LAN, one usually examines three things: the media used to connect the nodes, the pattern of connection or *topology*, and the algorithms used to control access to the medium. The next three chapters will examine each of these in some detail before going on to see how companies and researchers have implemented them in Chapter 5.

1.4 REFERENCES

1 Tanenbaum, A.S., *Computer Networks*, Prentice Hall Inc., Englewood Cliffs, New Jersey, 1981.

CHAPTER TWO

TRANSMISSION MEDIA
AND TECHNIQUES

As with any network, LANs must have a connecting medium of some sort to carry the information from node to node. Because wiring a building is a major expense to the potential LAN user, he must ensure that the system he uses fulfills certain criteria before embarking on the work. The medium chosen must be robust, that is, it must be immune to natural and environmental hazards, for example electrical noise, lightning and other forms of *electromagnetic interference* (EMI). For maximum availability of the network, the system must be serviceable. This means that mishaps such as cable breaks and node failures must be easily repairable or bypassed. The final cost of installation of the network will be affected by the cost of the medium, together with the cost of connecting each node to it.

Transmission speed is an important parameter of a network which will depend largely on the range of applications envisaged. These range from *terminal-to-host* traffic, for which speeds of below 1 kilobit per second are adequate, to applications such as graphic image and file transfer which need speeds of the order of megabits per second. The medium chosen will have to accommodate current as well as projected requirements over the system's expected lifetime of 15 years or more.

In order to appreciate the problems involved in medium selection, we must first look at the ways in which information is transmitted.

2.1 DATA TRANSMISSION TECHNIQUES

There are many ways of transmitting digital information through a medium. Making the choice between one technique and another is normally a question of striking a balance between performance, in terms of the speed and accuracy

6

of transmission, and cost. Certain parameters of the system are crucial in determining the former.

The normal way to transmit information through a medium is to vary an electrical signal at the transmitting end by some means, and detect these variations at the receiver. There are two major obstacles to successful reception: *attenuation* and *noise*. Noise can emanate from a variety of sources in the environment and serves to distort the signal. Attenuation is a measure of how much the strength of the signal is reduced in passing through the medium. It is proportional to the distance traveled and will be present to differing degrees depending on the frequency of the signal being transmitted. This dependency on frequency serves to further distort a signal as it passes through the medium.

For a particular medium, there will be a range of frequencies that can be transmitted through it without incurring significant attenuation. If the transmitter strays outside this range, reception will be difficult. In determining how much 'information' can be sent through the cable the most important aspect to consider is the width of this frequency range. This is known as the *bandwidth* of the medium.

Given that the transmission medium has a particular bandwidth, there are a variety of ways of transmitting information through it. In LANs, these are usually divided into *baseband* and *broadband* transmission. The details of these two methods will be described in the following sections.

2.1.1 Baseband transmission

When transmitting digital information, the simplest scheme is to have two voltage levels to represent 1s and 0s. Figure 2.1 shows how a number of bits have been encoded in this manner. More sophisticated schemes such as Manchester encoding (see Appendix A) can be used.

In baseband transmission, this voltage-encoded signal is applied directly to the medium. The signal is attenuated in its passage through the medium, causing the quality of the received signal to decrease with distance traveled.

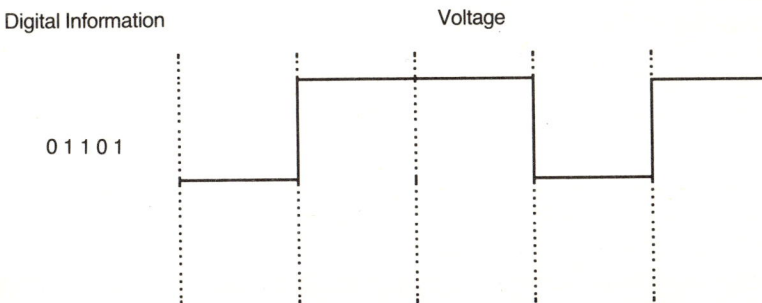

Figure 2.1 Digital information represented as a voltage

The implications of this for LANs are that baseband networks are limited to fairly low transmission speeds, and if long distances are involved, some form of amplifier must be inserted into the medium.

2.1.2   Modulated transmission

A more sophisticated way to transmit data is called *modulation*. Here, one starts off with a simple *carrier wave*. One of its qualities i.e. *amplitude*, *frequency*, or *phase* can be varied to reflect the data being transmitted. Figure 2.2 shows how a sequence of bits looks as a frequency modulated signal. This modulated signal is sent through the medium and demodulated by the receiver. Normally, a computer using this technique will be equipped with a device to carry out transmission and reception called a *modulator/ demodulator* abbreviated to *modem*.

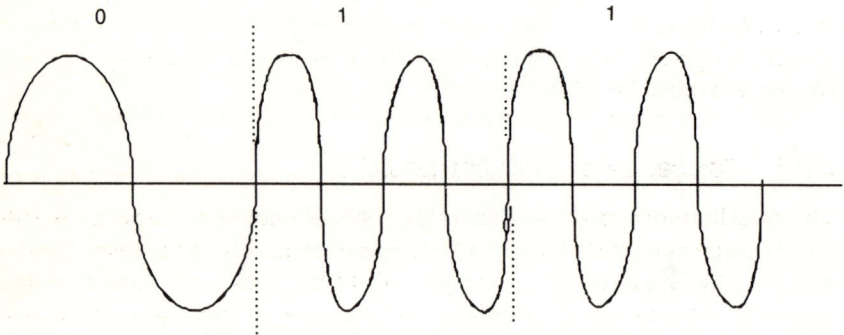

Figure 2.2   Frequency modulated signal

The modulation process alters the mix of frequencies present in the signal to one more suited to the medium through which it is to be transmitted. Because of this, attenuation is not as great a problem as with baseband transmission, and longer distances can be achieved. However the disadvantage of this approach is that each device must be equipped with a modem. This imposes a severe cost penalty, and tends to make network connection more expensive than the simple baseband method.

2.1.3   Broadband transmission

A signal that has been modulated as described above will have a fixed bandwidth requirement. This is often considerably less than is provided by the medium in use. In order to make more efficient use of the cable, it is possible to divide its bandwidth up into channels, each of a predefined bandwidth. For example, a coaxial cable can accommodate frequencies between 10 and 300 mHz. This could be split up into bands with a width of 12 mHz, each of which would be capable of carrying digital information at a rate of 10 mbps and leave provision for a 1 mHz 'guard' band on either side of the channel. Thus a single cable could have more than 30 of these channels operating simultaneously.

It is more common, however, to use the excess capacity to carry other forms of information. Some examples of these services include digitized voice, TV and video signals and so on. The ability of broadband networks to carry a wide variety of different types of information simultaneously has led to an increase in their popularity, and examples of their use can be seen in Chapter 5.

2.2 CHOICE OF MEDIUM

In LANs, many different types of media are in use. Copper conductors in the form of twisted pair or coaxial cable are by far the most common. More recently, very serious consideration has been given to the use of optical fiber technology in LANs. Other media e.g. microwave transmission, infrared, telephone lines, etc. are used and will be dealt with at the end of this chapter. Firstly though, it is worthwhile to compare the relative merits and demerits of copper and optical media.

2.2.1 Copper versus optical media

The usefulness of copper as a conductor has been known for many years. This fact alone gives it two significant advantages over newer technologies. Firstly, the processes involved in its use, from all stages of its production up to the mechanics of cable installation, are well understood. Over the years a large amount of supporting technology in the form of connectors, ducting and other wiring accessories have been developed. Also, because of its wide use, economies of scale have come into play, making it a very low-cost option. It is a mature medium which means that it is unlikely that its price will drop further to any significant extent.

Optical fiber, on the other hand, is a fledgeling technology which is currently the subject of much research and development. In essence, it involves transmitting a modulated light beam through a glass fiber from source to destination. The major problem with this medium is that no reliable, low-cost, low-loss method has been devised to join two fiber fragments together. Also the technology of light sources and detectors are still in their infancy and are subject to rapid change. The raw material for fiber production (silica) is present in abundance and, given the appropriate technological developments, there is every reason to expect it to become a low-cost mature medium.

2.2.2 Suitability for data traffic

The *attenuation* of a medium is an important characteristic. Figure 2.3 shows a graph of the attenuation of both copper and optical media over a range of

Attenuation

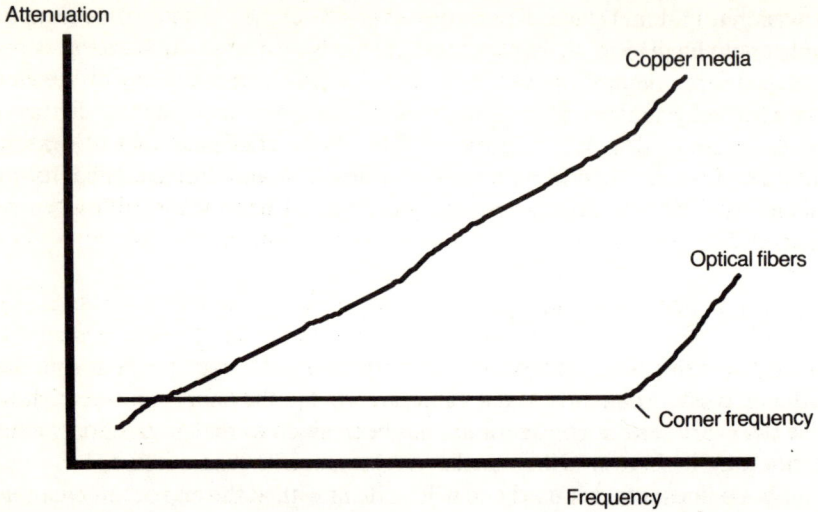

Figure 2.3   Graph of attenuation versus frequency for copper and optical media

frequencies. It can be seen from the graph that the attenuation of copper is strongly frequency-related whilst that of optical fibers is relatively constant over the full range up to its so-called *corner frequency*. This severely limits the usefulness of copper for either long distances or for high frequencies. Distances can be extended by the use of *repeaters* to amplify the signal placed at regular intervals on the line. These components, however, increase the cost of the network and can introduce intolerable delays in signal propagation. In LANs, copper has been found useful (and cheap) for applications involving short distances with data transfer rates of between 1 and 10 mbps.

With current technology, optical fibers have bandwidths of 100–400 mHz. This provides sufficient capacity for several high-speed data channels with ample bandwidth remaining for use in other applications. Traffic along the fibers is essentially monodirectional and this imposes some limitations on the type of network topology with which it may be used.

2.2.3   Noise problems

One of the major problems associated with data transmission of any kind is electrical noise. This problem has two aspects. Firstly, noise emanating from the environment can enter the medium and corrupt the signal being carried. This is usually caused by sources of electromagnetic radiation in the vicinity. Typical sources would be heavy electrical equipment, lightning strikes, and radiation from neighboring cables.

The second noise-related problem is that of radiation emanating from the cable itself. This can interfere with other equipment and is the subject of strict controls by national standards institutes worldwide. An additional reason for minimizing radiation is that of security. If the transmitted signal is being radiated from the medium, it is often possible to detect and decode the signal using listening equipment.

A length of copper cable has similar characteristics to that of a radio antenna. This means that it picks up outside noise and radiates signals quite efficiently. The main method of avoiding this is to surround the cable with one or more copper shields. This alleviates the problem but imposes additional cost.

Optical fibers, on the other hand, use light as the carrier. This is not subject to the influence of electromagnetic radiation. In hostile environments, for example in networking a factory using high-voltage equipment, this is a major advantage. The leakage involved in optical fibers is extremely low and does not pose any environmental problems. Security is ensured by the difficulty of detecting the signal without disrupting the medium.

Having examined the pros and cons of copper versus optical media, we will now examine in more detail the common forms of copper cable, i.e. twisted pair and coaxial cable.

2.3 TWISTED PAIR CABLE

The most common form of wiring in data communication applications is the *twisted pair cable*. As a *voice grade medium* (VGM), it is the basis for most internal office telephone wiring. It consists of two identical wires wrapped together in a double helix. Both wires in the pair have the same impedance to ground, making it a *balanced* medium. This characteristic helps to lower the cable's susceptibility to noise from neighboring cables, or external sources..

Problems can occur due to differences in the electrical characteristics between the pair (e.g. length, resistance, interpair capacitance). For this reason, LAN applications will tend to use a higher-quality cable known as *data grade medium* (DGM). In order to achieve uniformity of both wires in the pair, they are usually taken from the same production run. Capacitance problems are minimized by using a high quality insulation material and external noise can be combated by surrounding the cable with a shield made of copper foil or wire braid.

The main advantages of twisted pair cable are its simplicity and ease of installation. It is physically flexible, has a low weight and can be easily spliced or connected. These advantages are present to a lesser extent when using DGM but are still significant when compared with coaxial cable.

The data transmission characteristics are not so good. Because of high attenuation, it is incapable of carrying a signal over long distances without the use of repeaters. Its low bandwidth capabilities make it unsuitable for broadband applications and its susceptibility to noise makes it an impractical choice for electrically harsh environments (e.g. factories). Despite these disadvantages, it is a perfectly adequate medium for low-speed (up to 10 mbps) applications where the distances between nodes are small.

2.4 COAXIAL CABLE

This type of cable consists of a solid wire core surrounded by one or more foil or braided wire shields, each separated from the other by some kind of plastic insulator. The inner core carries the signal, and the shield provides the ground. While it is less popular than twisted pair, it is widely used for television signals. In the form of *community antenna television* (CATV) cable, it provides a cheap means of transporting multichannel television signals around metropolitan areas. It is also used by large corporations in building security systems, closed circuit television systems, etc.

Physically, coaxial cable varies from the quite light and flexible CATV cable to heavily shielded, low-loss cable that is very rigid and quite heavy. The type used has a major impact on the ease and cost of installation. Signals may be transmitted and received from the cable by using coaxial cable taps, which involves drilling into the cable and clamping on the connection. This technology is relatively new and a certain amount of expertise is required to carry out the installation of a coaxial cable network.

The data transmission characteristics of coaxial cable are considerably better than those of twisted pair. When used in conjunction with broadband transmission techniques, it can offer up to 300 mHz of bandwidth. This opens the possibility of using it as the basis for a *shared cable* network, with part of the bandwidth being used for data traffic, and the remainder being dedicated to the transmission of other information such as TV signals or digitized voice. It has a lower attenuation than twisted pair (especially at higher frequencies) which means less need for repeaters. Because the shield in the cable is part of the signal circuit, grounding it can introduce noise. A second shield solves this problem but at additional expense.

2.5 OPTICAL FIBERS

Optical fibers consist of thin strands of glass or glass-like material which are so constructed that they carry light from a source at one end of the fiber to a detector at the other end. The light sources used are either *light emitting diodes* (LEDs) or *laser diodes* (LDs). The data to be transmitted is modulated onto the light beam using frequency modulation techniques. The signals can then be picked up at the receiving end by a *pin field effect transistor* (pin FET) and demodulated. The bandwidth of the medium is potentially very high (up to 5 gHz) and tends to be limited by the maximum modulation rate of the light source. For LEDs, this ranges between 20 and 150 mbps and higher rates are possible using LDs. The technology is continually being developed and the speeds achievable can be expected to rise.

The major problems with optical fibers are associated with installation. They are quite fragile and may need special shielding to make them sufficiently robust for an office environment. This problem is being alleviated by the advent of all plastic or glass/plastic fibers. Connecting either two fibers together or a light source to a fiber is a difficult process. Thicker fibers make this job easier, but these tend to have a higher attenuation and a smaller bandwidth. Special equipment is usually required to align the fibers before joining them.

If the nodes in a LAN are connected in a ring configuration by optical fibers and one node becomes defective, it must be bypassed. In systems using copper media, this can be done using a simple and inexpensive relay switch. Fiberoptic bypass switches however are still under development and are currently very expensive.

One of the major advantages of optical fibers over other media is their complete immunity to noise. Because the information is traveling on a modulated light beam, electromagnetic interference, no matter how severe, has no effect on it. This means that interbuilding connections do not need lightning protection and it also makes it an ideal choice for industrial environments. Because of its essentially monodirectional mode of operation, it is useful where ring topologies are used. In those cases, it can be used for segments of the ring which are susceptible to noise (e.g. sections operating near heavy electrical machinery).

A side-effect of this noise immunity is that optical fibers are virtually impossible to tap. In order to intercept the signal, the fiber must be cut and a detector inserted. This device must be capable of both receiving the signal and repeating it so that it continues its path along the network. This makes the network very secure over those sections where optical fibers are used.

Despite its shortcomings, optical fiber is an important technology for LANs. If, and when, the technology matures, its advantages of high speed, low attenuation and total noise immunity will make it a very attractive transmission medium indeed.

2.6 OTHER MEDIA

The necessity of high speed and reliable data transmission in LANs tends to restrict the choice of medium to those covered above. Others are in use in systems that provide similar functions to LANs. The system most used in this regard is the telephone system.

The majority of existing, as well as all new office buildings, are equipped with a telephone system. This, in effect, is a communication network using voice grade twisted pair cable as the transmission medium and having a star topology. At the hub of the system is a *private (automatic) branch exchange* (PBX or PABX). This device has the capability to connect any two lines of the network together or any line to an external telephone line. Recent PABXs have been enhanced to cope with rapid switching of digital information streams as well as traditional voice streams. While this situation does not constitute a LAN, it is sometimes used to answer interoffice data communication needs.

Because telephone systems use cable of voice grade, they are seldom used for speeds in excess of 1 mbps. This speed precludes the use of the network for advanced applications, but may be adequate for simple interoffice communication. The PABX system does, however, offer the advantages of using existing wiring and allows easy access to wide area networks through the public telephone networks. This topic is covered further in Chapter 11.

An alternative to transmitting the information over cables is to transmit it using either *infrared* or *microwave* radiation. This system depends for its operation on there being a clear line of sight between transmitter and receiver and is subject to interference from smoke, passing objects and so on which makes it impractical in the usual office situaton. It is however quite a useful system for communicating between buildings or in large open plan offices and factories. High transmission rates are possible with no associated cabling cost.

2.7 SUMMARY

The two mainstream technologies in use for LANs are copper media (twisted pair and coaxial) and optical fibers. Of the two, copper is at present the cheaper. It is a well-understood medium that is easy to install. Transmission speeds range from 1 to 10 mbps for baseband transmission up to approximately 300 mbps for coaxial cable using broadband. Optical fibers are, at present, a developing medium which offers high speed with no interference, with the promise of low cost systems combined with very high speed.

Telephone lines can be used for interoffice data transmission. They offer the capability of low speed communication with little or no extra wiring cost. Further possibilities are the use of infrared or microwave systems to give high speed communication between nodes having a clear line of sight with each other.

2.8 REFERENCES

1 Abrahamson, P. and Noel, F. E., Local Area Network Media Selection for Ring Topologies, Proceedings of COMPCON Fall '82; Washington DC, September 1982.
2 Vikland, B., Optical Fibres in Local Area Networks, Communications/ Communications International; October 1985, pp. 18–24.
3 Squibb, N., Broadband vs Baseband – The choice for Ethernet, August 1985, DEC User Journal pp. 43–45.
4 Tanenbaum, A.S., Computer Networks, Prentice Hall Inc., Englewood Cliffs, New Jersey, 1981.

CHAPTER THREE

NETWORK TOPOLOGIES AND WIRING CONSIDERATIONS

In the previous chapter, we discussed the range of possible transmission media that are available to connect nodes in a network. The next step is to decide on how the nodes are to be connected together. The pattern of interconnection of nodes in a network is called the *topology*.

The selection of a topology for a network cannot be done in isolation as it affects the choice of media and the access method used. Because it determines the strategy used in wiring a building for a LAN, it may represent the greatest single cost to be faced, and accordingly deserves some study. There are a number of factors to consider in making this choice, the most important of which are set out below.

1 **Cost** Whatever transmission medium is chosen for a LAN, it has to be physically installed in the building. This may be a lengthy process involving the installation of cable ducts and raceways. Ideally, it is carried out before the building is occupied and should be able to accommodate foreseen growth requirements. For a network to be cost effective, one would strive to minimize installation cost. This may be achieved by using well-understood media and also, to a lesser extent, by minimizing the distances involved.

2 **Flexibility** One of the main benefits of a LAN is the ability to have the data processing and peripheral nodes distributed around a given area. This means that computing power and equipment can be located close to the ultimate user. Because the arrangement of furniture, internal walls etc. in offices is often subject to change, the topology should allow for easy reconfiguration of the network. This involves moving existing nodes and adding new ones.

15

3 **Reliability**   Failure in a LAN can take two forms. Firstly, an individual node can malfunction. This is not nearly as serious as the second type of fault where the network itself fails to operate. In the second case, although the individual nodes can function, any software making use of the facilities of the LAN will be rendered useless. The topology chosen for the network can help by allowing the location of the fault to be detected and to provide some means of isolating it.

Many topologies have been developed to cope with communications over a limited geographical area, but three major ones have influenced LAN design and implementation. These are:

- the *star* or *radial* topology;
- the *bus*;
- the *ring* or *loop*.

There are also a number of hybrid network topologies which combine features of the above. The following sections will evaluate each of these topologies and their hybrids in turn.

3.1   THE STAR OR RADIAL TOPOLOGY

This topology consists of a central node to which all other nodes are connected by a single path (see figure 3.1a). It is the topology used in most existing information networks involving data processing or voice communications. The most common example of this is in IBM 370 installations. In this case, multiple 3270 terminals are connected to either a host computer system or a terminal controller. The connection is achieved via a single length of coaxial cable per terminal. Another example is the office PBX. In this case, each telephone is connected to a central PBX by a single dedicated voice grade twisted pair cable.

In many cases, when a building is wired with a star network, feeder cables radiate out from the center to intermediate concentration points called *wiring closets* (see figure 3.1b). This allows sufficient connection points to be provided for one subarea (e.g. a floor of an office building), while providing flexibility in their allocation within that area.

The two examples cited above would not qualify as LANs because in both cases, a central intelligent node is controlling the operation of all of the others. The pure star topology is seldom used in LANs, but is worthy of study because of its prevalence in more traditional data networks and its influence on the star-ring topology which is covered later in the chapter.

3.1.1   Advantages of the star

- **Ease of service**   The star topology has a number of concentration points, i.e. at the central node or at intermediate wiring closets. These provide easy access for service or reconfiguration of the network.

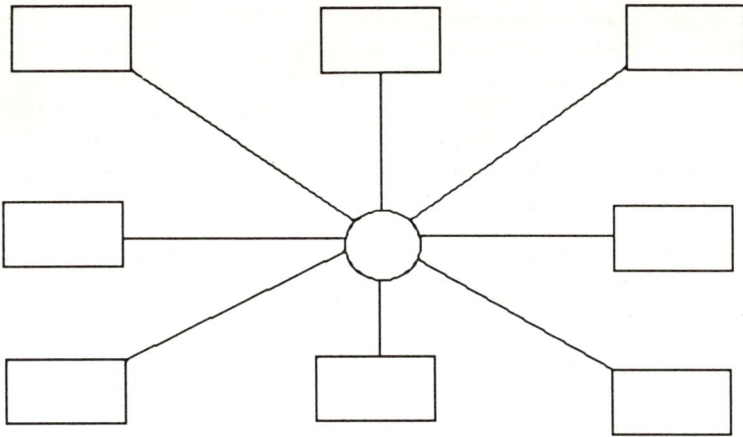

Figure 3.1a   The star topology

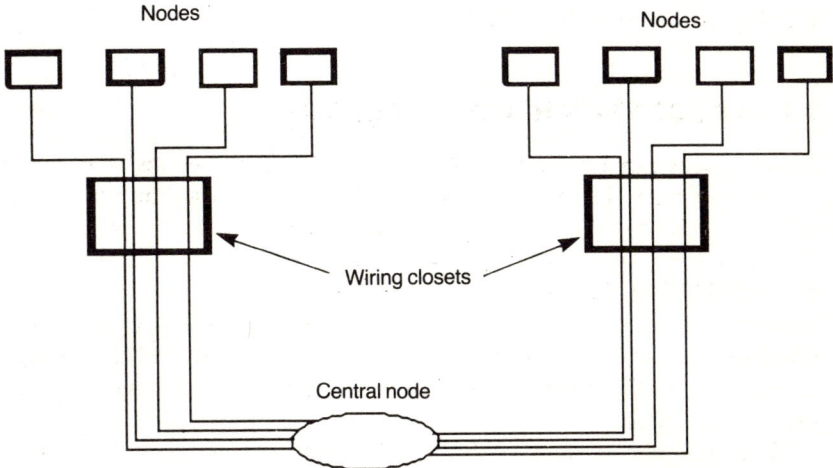

Figure 3.1b   The star topology using wiring closets

- **One device per connection** Connection points in any network are inherently prone to failure. In the star topology, failure of a single connection typically involves disconnecting one node from an otherwise fully functional network.
- **Centralized control/problem diagnosis** The fact that the central node is connected directly to every other node in the network means that faults are easily detected and isolated. It is a simple matter to disconnect failing nodes from the system.
- **Simple access protocols** Any given connection in a star network involves only the central node and one peripheral node. In this situation, contention for who has control of the medium for transmission purposes is easily solved. Thus in a star network, access protocols are very simple.

3.1.2   Disadvantages of the star

- **Long cable length**   Because each node is directly connected to the center, the star topology necessitates a large quantity of cable. Whilst the cost of the cable is often small, congestion in cable ducts and maintenance and installation problems can increase costs considerably.
- **Difficult to expand**   The addition of a new node to a star network involves a connection all the way to the central node. Expansion is usually catered for by providing large numbers of redundant cables during the initial wiring. However problems can arise if a longer cable length is needed or an unanticipated concentration of nodes is required.
- **Central node dependency**   If the central node in a star network fails, the entire network is rendered inoperable. This introduces heavy reliability and redundancy constraints on this node.

The star topology has found extensive application in areas where intelligence in the network is concentrated at the central node. The tendency in recent computer systems is away from host-based computing power, and the advent of microprocessor-based systems where all nodes possess a high level of processing power has led to a falloff in the use of this topology. Nevertheless, the technology is well understood and, because it is currently the dominant configuration in traditional data communications, it is likely to be with us for many years to come.

3.2   THE BUS

Another popular topology for data networks is the *bus*. This consists of a single length of the transmission medium (normally coaxial cable) onto which the various nodes are attached (see figure 3.2). This topology is used in traditional data communications networks where the host at one end of the bus communicates with several terminals attached along its length. This configuration is known as a *multidrop line*. It is also the topology used in the Ethernet [1] LAN described in Chapter 5.

3.2.1   Advantages of the bus

- **Short cable length and simple wiring layout**   Because there is a single common data path connecting all nodes, the bus topology allows a very short cable length to be used. This decreases the installation cost, and also leads to a simple, easy to maintain, wiring layout.
- **Resilient architecture**   The BUS architecture has an inherent simplicity that makes it very reliable from a hardware point of view. There is a single cable through which all data propagates and to which all nodes are connected.

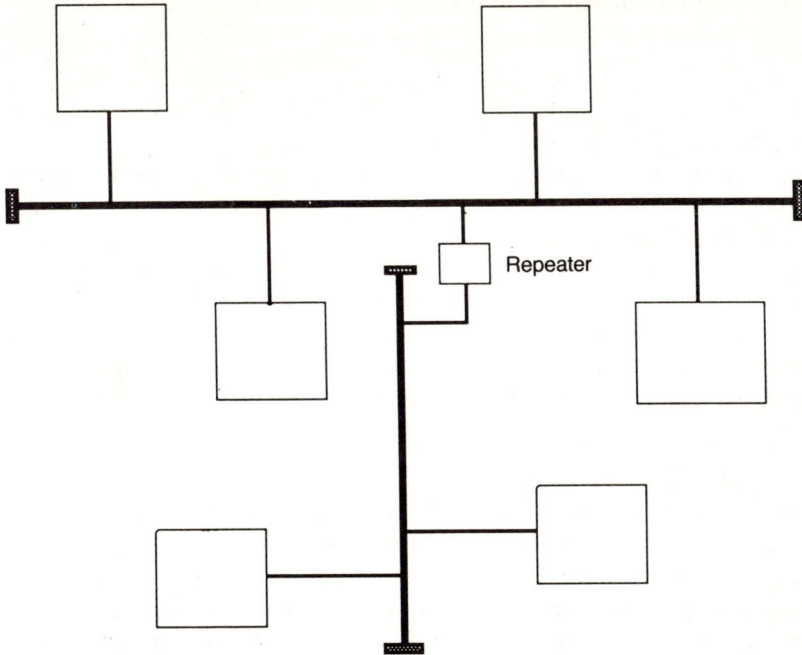

Figure 3.2 The bus topology

- **Easy to extend** Additional nodes can be connected to an existing bus network at any point along its length. More extensive additions can be achieved by adding extra segments connected by a type of signal amplifier known as a *repeater*.

3.2.2 Disadvantages of the bus

- **Fault diagnosis is difficult** Although the simplicity of the bus topology means that there is very little to go wrong, fault detection is not a simple matter. In most LANs based on a bus, control of the network is not centralized in any particular node. This means that detection of a fault may have to be performed from many points in the network.
- **Fault isolation is difficult** In the star topology, a defective node can easily be isolated from the network by removing its connection at the center. If a node is faulty on a bus, it must be rectified at the point where the node is connected to the network. Once the fault has been located, the node can simply be removed. In the case where the fault is in the network medium itself, an entire segment of the bus must be disconnected.
- **Repeater configuration** When a BUS-type network has its backbone extended using repeaters, reconfiguration may be necessary. This may involve tailoring cable lengths, adjusting terminators, etc.

- **Nodes must be intelligent**   Each node on the network is directly connected
  to the central bus. This means that some way of deciding who can use the
  network at any given time must be performed in each node. It tends to
  increase the cost of the nodes irrespective of whether this is performed in
  hardware or software.

3.3   THE RING

The third topology that we will consider is the *ring* or *loop*. In this case, each
node is connected to two and only two neighboring nodes. Data is accepted
from one of the neighboring nodes and is transmitted onwards to another (see
figure 3.3). Thus data travels in one direction only, from node to node around
the ring. After passing through each node, it returns to the sending node,
which removes it.

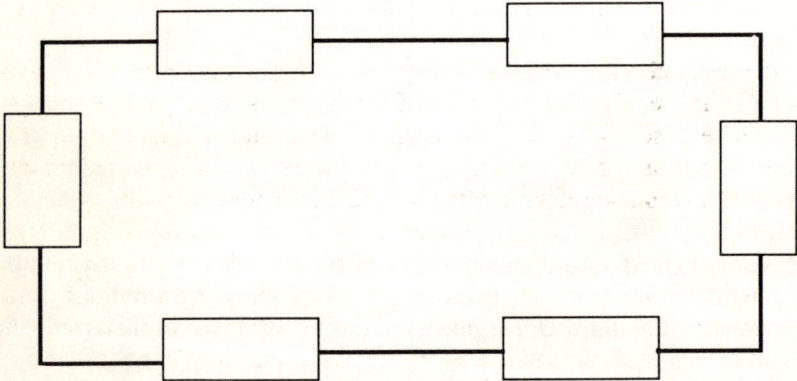

Figure 3.3   The ring topology

It is important to note that data 'passes through' rather than 'travels past' each
node. This means that the signal may be amplified before being 'repeated' on
the outward channel. It is a simple matter for the recipient to mark a message
as read before resending it. This means that when the message arrives back at
the sender, this mark can serve as an acknowledgement that the message was
correctly received.

3.3.1   Advantages of the ring

- **Short cable length**   The amount of cabling involved in a ring topology is
  comparable to that of a bus and is small relative to that of a star. This means
  that less connections will be needed, which will in turn increase network
  reliability.
- **No wiring closet space required**   Since there is only one cable connecting

each node to its immediate neighbors, it is not necessary to allocate space in the building for wiring closets.

- **Suitable for optical fibers** Using optical fibers offers the possibility of very high speed transmission. Because traffic on a ring travels in one direction, it is easy to use optical fibers as a medium of transmission. Also, since a ring is made up of nodes connected by short segments of transmission medium, there is a possibility of mixing the types used for different parts of the network. Thus, a manufacturing company's network could use copper cables in the office area and optical fibers in the factory areas, where electrical interference may be a problem.

3.3.2 Disadvantages of the ring

- **Node failure causes network failure** The transmission of data on a ring goes through *every* connected node on the ring before returning to the sender. If one node fails to pass data through itself, the entire network has failed and no traffic can flow until the defective node has been removed from the ring.
- **Difficult to diagnose faults** The fact that failure of one node will affect all others has serious implications for fault diagnosis. It may be necessary to examine a series of adjacent nodes to determine the faulty one. This operation may also require diagnostic facilities to be built into each node.
- **Network reconfiguration is difficult** The all or nothing nature of the ring topology can cause problems when one decides to extend or modify the geographical scope of the network. It is not possible to shut down a small section of the ring while keeping the majority of it working normally.
- **Topology affects the access protocol** Each node on a ring has a responsibility to pass on data that it receives. This means that the access protocol must take this into account. Before a node can transmit its own data, it must ensure that the medium is available for use.

3.4 HYBRID TOPOLOGIES

By modifying or combining some of the characteristics of the 'pure' network topologies, a more useful result may be obtained. These combinations are called *hybrid* topologies.

3.4.1 The tree

The tree topology is a variant of the bus. The shape of the network is that of an inverted tree with the central root branching and sub branching to the extremities of the network (see figure 3.4). It is normally implemented using coaxial cable as the transmission medium and broadband transmission tech-

Headend

Nodes

Nodes

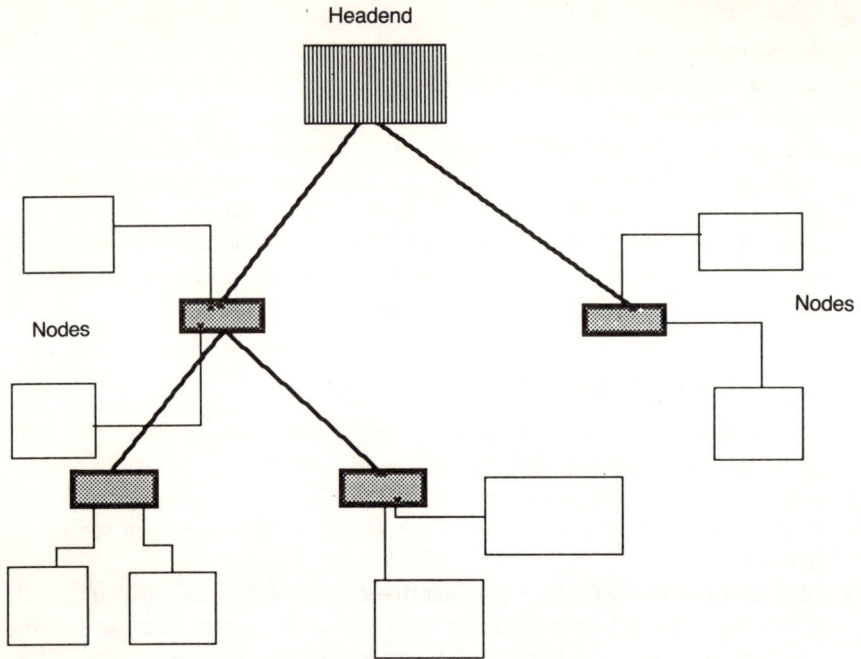

Figure 3.4   The tree topology

niques. The best known example at the time of writing is IBM's Personal
Computer Network.

The main difference between this type of network and one made of several
bus segments is the presence of a 'root' to the tree. When a node transmits, the
root (or 'headend' as it is sometimes called) receives the signal and rebroad-
casts it through the entire network. In this way, repeaters are no longer
necessary.

The pros and cons of the tree are very much the same as those of the bus,
but there are some extra advantages and disadvantages.

3.4.1.1   Advantages of the tree
- **Easy to extend**   Because the tree is, of its very nature, divided into
  subunits, it is easier to add new nodes or branches to it.
- **Fault isolation**   It is possible to disconnect whole branches of the network
  from the main structure. This makes it easier to isolate a defective node.

3.4.1.2   Disadvantages of the tree
- **Dependent on the root**   If the 'headend' device fails to operate, the entire
  network is rendered inoperable. In this respect, the tree suffers from the
  same reliability problems as the star.

3.4.2 The star-ring topology

We have seen that all of the 'pure' network topologies have associated advantages and disadvantages. In the *star-ring*, two topologies have been combined with the aim of achieving the best of both.

The configuration consists of a number of concentration points connected together in a ring. These concentration points would, in practice, consist of wiring closets located on each floor of a building. From each closet, nodes are connected in a star configuration with some or all of the connection points used up.

Electrically, the star-ring operates in the exact same way as a normal ring. The difference is that the physical wiring is arranged as a series of interconnected stars. Because of this, this topology is sometimes more descriptively called the *star-shaped ring*.

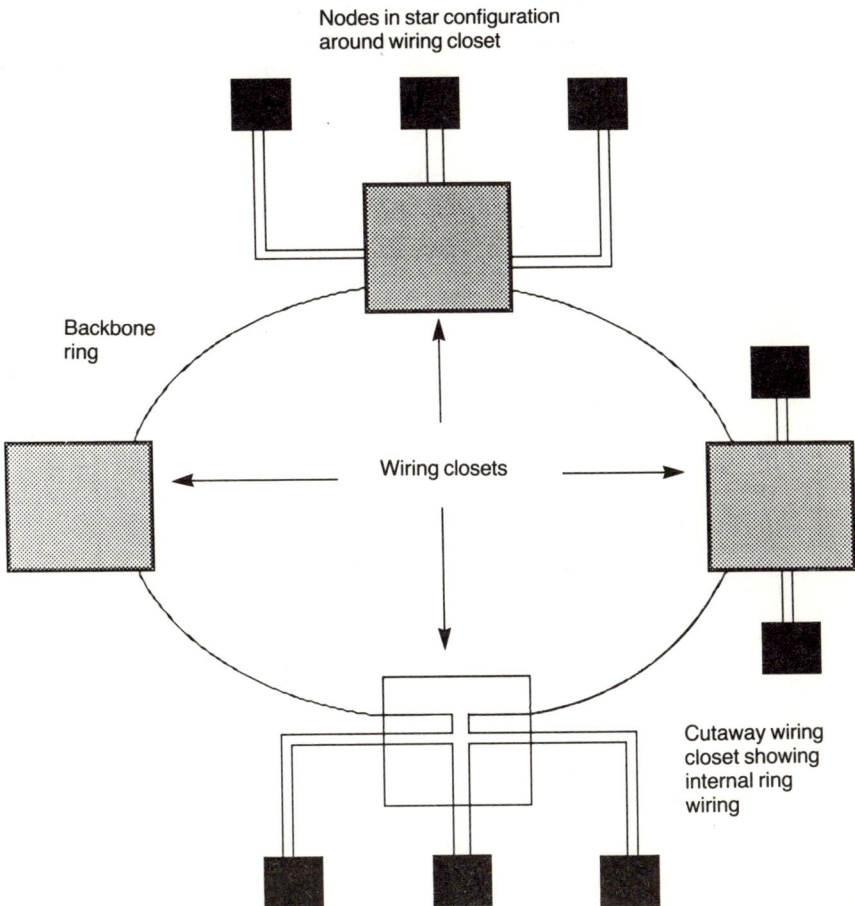

Figure 3.5   The star-ring or star-shaped ring topology

3.4.2.1   Advantages of the star-ring

- **Fault diagnosis and isolation**   The presence of concentration points in the network greatly eases fault diagnosis. If a fault is detected on the network, the initial problem is to find out which concentration point in the ring is to blame. The fact that this ring is quite small in relation to the total size of the network makes this problem more manageable. The offending concentration point can be isolated easily, leaving the network in a fully functional state while further fault diagnosis is carried out.

- **Ease of expansion**   The modular construction of a star-ring network means that new sections may be easily added. When designing the network originally, each concentration point can have extra, unused, lobes which can be called upon later, if needed. The next growth step involves adding a new concentration point and wiring it into the ring.

- **Cabling**   The concentration points in a star-ring are connected via a single cable. This simplifies wiring between areas in an installation and cuts down on the congestion of cable ducts. Also, the wiring practices involved are very similar to that of telephone system installation. These techniques are well understood by building engineers and lend themselves well to the prewiring of buildings.

3.4.2.2   Disadvantages of the star-ring

- **Intelligent concentration points required**   Depending on the implementation used, the concentration points may need to have built in intelligence/processing ability. This will be necessary if it is to assist in network fault diagnosis, node isolation, or conversion from one form of transmission medium to another.

- **Cabling**   The intercloset cabling in a star-ring is critical to its operation. This may mean that redundant cabling in the form of one or more back up rings may be necessary to meet reliability requirements. The largest section of the network (i.e., between the concentration points and the nodes) is laid out in a star. This means that a considerable amount of cable may be required.

3.5   CONCLUSIONS

In choosing a topology for a local area network, many factors must be considered. It must be easy to install both in existing buildings and those that are being prewired. Once installed, it must be able to cope with growth requirements. These may be sporadic and not well distributed geographically. It should be possible to carry out extensive changes to the network without completely depriving current users of service.

As with any other equipment, breakdowns in a LAN are to be expected. It is desirable to have a system where faults can be detected quickly and subsequently isolated, leaving the main section of the network operating normally.

The choice of topology can affect the range of possible media and the access method used to share it. Both of these can in turn affect the complexity and speed of operation of the individual nodes.

We have examined three pure topologies: the *star*, the *bus* and the *ring*, and two hybrids: the *tree* and the *star-ring*. The star topology is of most interest from a historical point of view, and also because it is the topology against which the others are measured. It is more appropriate for terminal-host configurations than for LANs. The remaining two 'pure' topologies both have good and bad points, some of which can be improved by combining them with other topologies. Some examples of networks using these topologies are given in Chapter 5.

3.6 REFERENCES

1 Saltzer, J.H., Pogran, K.T. and Clark, D.D.: 'Why a ring?' in *Computer Networks* 7, pp. 223–231, Rotterdam: North-Holland, 1983.

2 Metcalfe, R.M. and Boggs, D.R.: 'Ethernet: Distributed packet switching for local computer networks' *Communications of the ACM*, **19**, no. 7, pp. 395–405, 1976.

3 Watson, I.: 'The integrated services local network', *British Telecom Technology Journal*, **2**, no. 4, pp. 26–33, 1984.

4 Viklund, B.: 'Optical fibers in local area networks', *Communications International*, **12**, no. 10, pp. 19–24, October, 1985.

CHAPTER FOUR

NETWORK ACCESS CONTROL

In our discussion on network topologies in the previous chapter, we saw that in all except the star, the transmission medium was shared between a number of nodes. In bus and tree networks, all nodes are connected directly to a common medium, while in the ring and star-ring, the transmitted data flows through all of the nodes.

This common access to the medium raises two problems. Firstly, there must be a mechanism for making sure that one node's transmission does not interfere with any others, i.e., a means of sharing access to the medium must be provided. Secondly, we must establish a means of transferring chunks of data from one node to another. This is a matter of extending the capability provided by the transmission technique to transmit and receive signals from the medium. The first topic of sharing will be returned to later in the chapter after we have covered the principles of *packet switching*.

There are a number of ways in which nodes can communicate over a network. The simplest is to establish a dedicated link between the transmitting and receiving stations. This may be achieved either with a direct link, or by a technique known as *circuit switching*. In the topologies outlined in the previous chapter, this would involve dedicating the medium to communication between two of the nodes (see figure 4.1). Circuit switching is extensively used in the public telephone network, with each conversation between users traveling over a dedicated path from one telephone, through the central switch, to the other party.

The requirements for data communication are, however, quite different from those of voice traffic. Computers tend to communicate with each other in 'bursts'; i.e., periods of high information transfer, followed by lulls. During this period of inactivity, precious bandwidth capability is being wasted. A

26

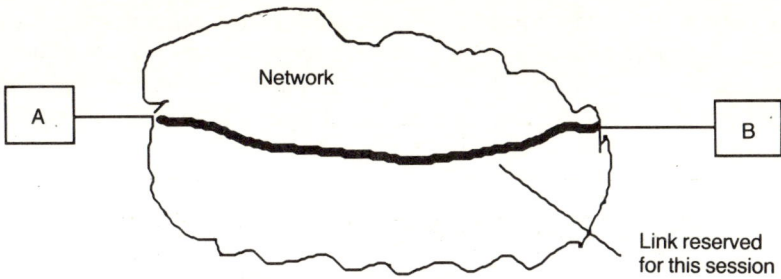

Figure 4.1 Circuit switching

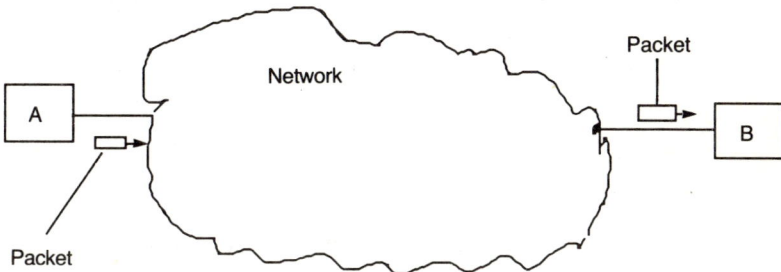

Figure 4.2 Packet switching

more efficient way of utilizing the communications channel is to use a technique known as *packet switching*.

In this scheme, no dedicated path is reserved between source and destination. Rather, the data to be sent is 'wrapped up' in a packet and launched into the network (see figure 4.2). Using this mechanism, maximum use can be made of the available bandwidth. Stations only have exclusive access to the medium while they are sending a packet. During the intervening period, other nodes will have an opportunity to transmit. The problem of sharing access to the network can now be reduced to providing some rules that will periodically, and in a fair manner, allow each node on the network to launch a packet.

4.1 PACKET FORMAT

The exact format of the packets used in a local network varies widely. It is, however, possible to isolate the common elements that make up a typical packet (see figure 4.3) and examine their uses.

4.1.1 Preamble or start-of-packet indicator

This field serves to inform all other nodes on the network that a packet is being transmitted. It usually consists of some transmission sequence that never occurs in normal data (e.g. a particular bit sequence or a code violation in Manchester encoding – see Appendix A). In some systems, this field is also used as a means of synchronizing the clock speeds in the transmitting and receiving nodes.

4.1.2   Addressing information

Nodes on the network identify each other by means of a fixed *address*. This address is unique to the station and is normally set by some form of hardware switch. In order to send a packet to a particular node, its address must be placed in the appropriate position in the packet. Typically in LANs, a node 'sees' all traffic passing by or through it, but only copies those packets containing its own address in the destination field.

The sender's address is included so that nodes can recognize where a packet came from. This information can be used by either the sender or the recipient. The receiver can use it to send acknowledgements, while the sender may use it to remove a packet that it has sent from the network.

Most networks also allocate certain addresses to be used for special purposes. For example, it may be possible to use a broadcast address to cause the packet to be received by all nodes on the network.

4.1.3   Control information

This field is used to state the purpose of the packet. In some cases, packets may be sent for network management purposes. These special packets may be used to discover the status of either individual nodes or sections of the network. Again, this information is placed before the data field to give the nodes the choice of ignoring the packet or not.

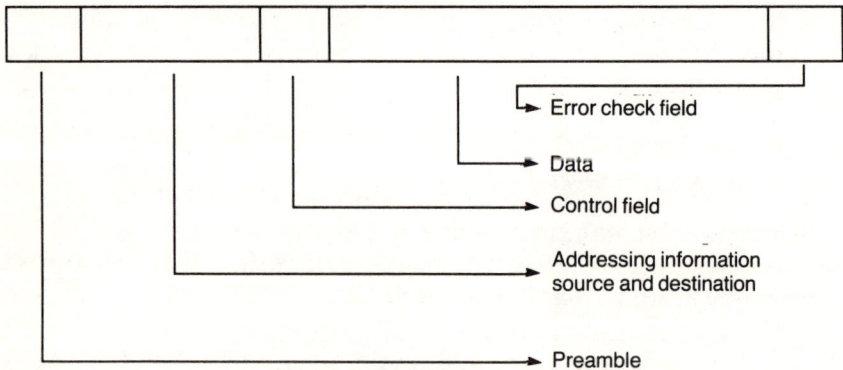

Error check field

Data

Control field

Addressing information
source and destination

Preamble

Figure 4.3   The format of a packet

4.1.4 Data field

This field contains the actual data to be transferred between nodes and may be either fixed or variable in length.

4.1.5 Error check

The error rate in local area networks is typically very low. For this reason, the amount of error checking done is limited, compared with that performed in wide area networks. Nevertheless, packets usually contain a field to allow the network hardware to detect transmission errors. This may take the form of a simple parity bit, or may be the more extensive **cyclic redundancy check** (CRC) (see Appendix B).

4.2 SHARING THE MEDIUM

The packets described above must be sent through the network to arrive at their destination. Many nodes may wish to send data simultaneously, and, in order that transmission proceeds in an orderly manner, some mechanism must exist for controling access to the medium. In traditional data communications, a single line was shared between several communicating pairs of nodes by a device known as a *time division multiplexor* (see figure 4.4). This device allocates the link exclusively to each communicating pair for a fixed proportion of the time available. Thus pair 1 would have exclusive use of the medium for time slot 1, pair 2 for time slot 2 etc. One disadvantage of this method is that the medium is allocated to a pair of nodes whether or not they

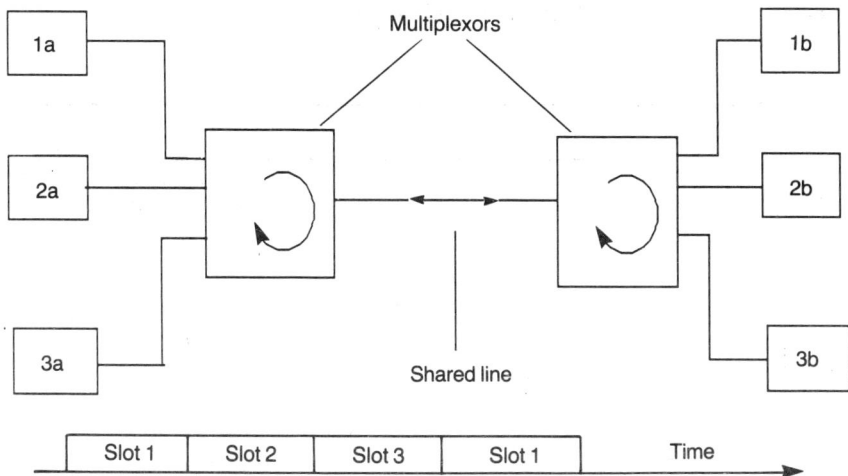

Figure 4.4   Time division multiplexing

have data to send at that particular time. A better way would be to arrange the system so that the link was given only to those nodes which wish to exchange data. Another important goal of such a system would be to distribute time fairly among those nodes waiting to communicate.

In local area networks, the same problem of media sharing exists. The burden of solving this problem however, is normally distributed among the nodes. By agreeing on a common access method, all nodes on the network will observe certain procedures in order to send data. These procedures or access methods can be divided into two types: contention and noncontention. As the name suggests, in the contention case, a node will wait for an opportunity to transmit. When the network becomes idle, it will seize the opportunity and begin transmitting. In some cases, this can lead to more than one node transmitting at the same time. The access method must provide techniques to recover from this.

Noncontention access, on the other hand, is much more orderly. If a node wishes to transmit in one of these networks, it must wait to receive 'permission'. Again the access method must provide procedures for passing this permission from one node to the next.

4.3   CONTENTION-BASED ACCESS METHODS

4.3.1   Multiple access

One of the earliest contention-based networks was the Aloha system [10] at the University of Hawaii. This allowed users in seven campuses spread over four islands to use the central computing facility on the island of Oahu. The method of transmission involved forming the data into packets and sending it by radio from source to destination. Two radio channels were provided; one for terminal-to-host, and the other for host-to-terminal traffic.

In the case where the host sent data to terminals, no sharing problems existed. Data was simply placed into addressed packets to which all terminal stations listened. The terminal with a matching address received its packet while all others ignored it.

When a terminal wanted to send data to the host, it would simply send the packet. Occasionally, two terminals would send data simultaneously. This is called a *collision* and causes both packets to be destroyed. In order to recover from this, the station starts an interval timer as soon as it begins transmitting its packet. If the station has not received an acknowledgement from the host within a specified time, it knows that its packet has been destroyed. It then waits for a random period before retransmitting it.

4.3.2   Carrier sense multiple access (CSMA)

An improvement on the above technique is for a node to check the status of the network *before* transmission. This is called *carrier sense* and is done by

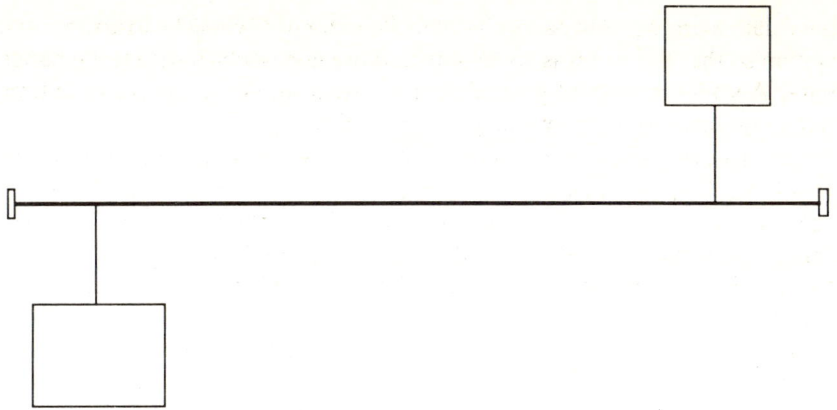

1 Both nodes listening – network quiet

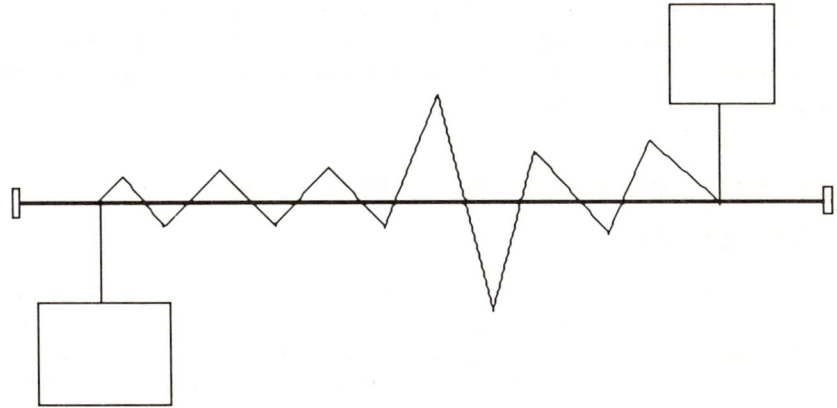

2 Both nodes transmit – collision

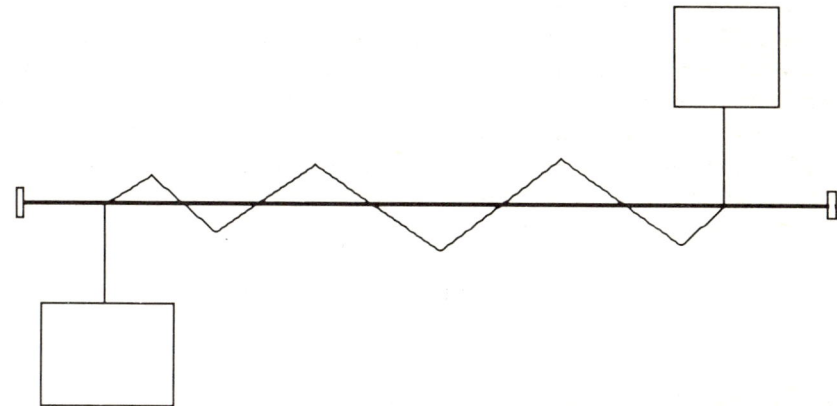

3 After some time, one node begins to transmit – the other node waits for a lull.

Figure 4.5   Carrier sense multiple access with collision detect (CSMA/CD)

listening to the network before sending a packet. In this case, collisions can only occur when two or more nodes begin to transmit at exactly the same time.

4.3.3   Carrier sense multiple access with collision detect (CSMA/CD)

A further improvement can be achieved by enabling the node to continue to listen to the network *while* it is transmitting. If a collision occurs, all transmitting nodes will detect a garbled signal on the network.

If the collision only lasts a short time, it is possible that some nodes on the network would not detect it. In order to avoid this, the colliding nodes adopt a procedure known as *collision consensus enforcement* which means that they transmit a number of bytes of random data (called a *jam*). This lasts long enough to propagate to all nodes on the network so that there is no doubt that a collision has taken place. The time spent in carrying out this procedure depends on how long it takes for the signal to travel from one end of the network to the other (called the *end-to-end propagation delay*). In order to avoid wasting bandwidth, this should be as short as possible.

If a number of nodes collide, they 'back off' without transmitting their packets. Each will try again after a suitable *retransmission delay* which is computed in each individual node. The algorithm used is known as *truncated binary exponential backoff* and is designed to minimize the amount of collisions that take place. After a fixed number of retries, no further attempts will be made to transmit. The precise details of this process are described fully in [1, 5].

An analogy has been made between this network access method and a conversation at a cocktail party. At the party, a group of people are gathered together, some of whom would like to say something. Each person listens to the conversation until a lull is perceived. At this point, they start speaking while at the same time hearing what they say. If two or more people start simultaneously, all conversation stops momentarily and people try again at a later time.

4.3.4   Register insertion

In the case of CSMA/CD, we had a number of nodes in contention for the shared medium. In ring topologies, the closest approximation to this technique is that of *register insertion*. Each node on the network contains two shift registers. The first of these is normally in series with the ring. Data arriving on the input line is shifted into this register. The address of the packet is decoded and if it is destined for this station, it is received. If not, it is shifted onto the output line so that it may travel on to the next node.

A second register called the *output buffer* is used when the station wants to transmit. The packet is loaded into this register where it waits until conditions are right for transmission. Firstly, the shift register must complete the trans-

Shift Register

Outgoing   Incoming

Packet being   Empty   Packet being
transmitted   space   received

Packet waiting   Output buffer (shift register)
for transmission

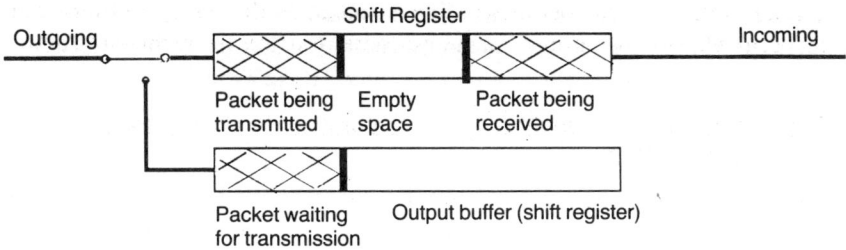

1 Packet waiting for transmission – station must finish transmitting current packet

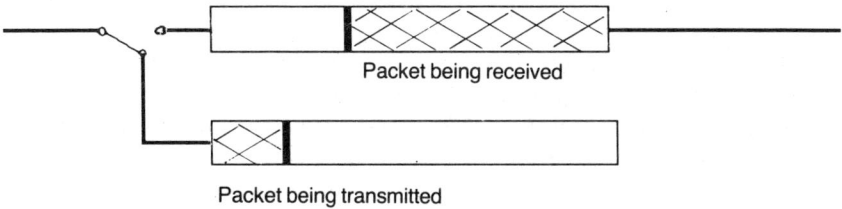

Packet being received

Packet being transmitted

2 As soon as transmission is complete – insert output buffer into ring and begin transmitting waiting packet

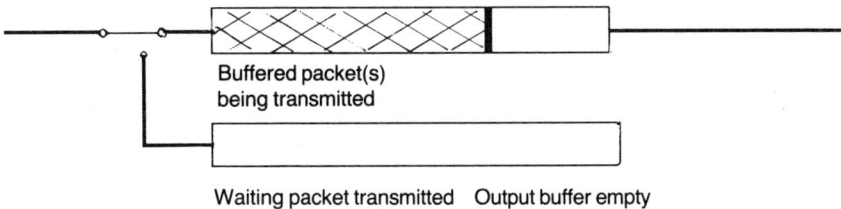

Buffered packet(s)
being transmitted

Waiting packet transmitted   Output buffer empty

3 Finished transmitting packet – switch output buffer out of ring. Packets that arrived during transmission are buffered.

Figure 4.6   Register insertion

mission of the current packet. Secondly, there must be a sufficient number of empty bit slots in the input register to contain any bits that should arrive while the output buffer is being transmitted. At this point, the output line is switched from the input register to the output buffer, thus *inserting* it into the ring. This buffer is now shifted out a bit at a time onto the network. Any traffic arriving during this interval is shifted into the input buffer. When the new packet has been launched, the switch moves back to the input buffer.

The second condition for transmission is that the input register must have as many free slots as there are bits to transmit. This has beneficial effects for load sharing. If the network is lightly loaded, there is little traffic passing through the input register. Thus, it is likely that, when a packet is to be transmitted, this condition will be fulfilled.

As the load rises, however, it becomes more and more likely that the input register will be relatively full. In this case, all nodes intending to transmit must wait until the load falls before they can begin transmission. Thus the protocol stops any individual node from swamping the network under high load conditions.

This access method has similar advantages to the CSMA/CD method in that it allows very fast transmission times under low load conditions. It also maintains 'fairness' under high load conditions. As with CSMA/CD, the response time is statistical rather than deterministic.

4.4 NONCONTENTION ACCESS METHODS

In both of the above cases, stations wishing to transmit a packet must wait until an opportunity arises before they can transmit. In this way, nodes are competing or 'contending' for available network bandwidth. *Slotted rings* and *token passing* are alternative access methods that involve the nodes waiting to receive *permission to transmit*.

4.4.1 Slotted rings

A slotted ring is a ring which is carrying a number of fixed length slots. Each slot is marked as either empty or full. A full slot contains a packet of information in transit from one node to another. On ring startup, one of the stations on the ring must generate at least one empty slot and transmit it. This slot will circulate around the ring until it reaches a node with data to transmit. Seeing that the arriving slot is marked as empty, the transmitting node will mark it as full and copy its data into it. This filled packet will travel onwards through the network being ignored by all intervening nodes until it reaches its destination. The addressed node will recognize the destination field in the packet and copy it. It then sets a 'received' indicator in the trailer of the packet to indicate successful reception.

Eventually, the packet will return to the sender where the 'received' indicator will be inspected before marking the packet as empty and sending it on its way. Fairness is ensured by requiring the sender to relinquish the slot after a single transmission. Under heavy load conditions, the next node to use this would be the nearest downstream node with data to transmit. If all nodes wish to transmit, they will each get a single slot in turn in a *round robin* fashion.

Each station in the ring will impose a delay in the transmission of the

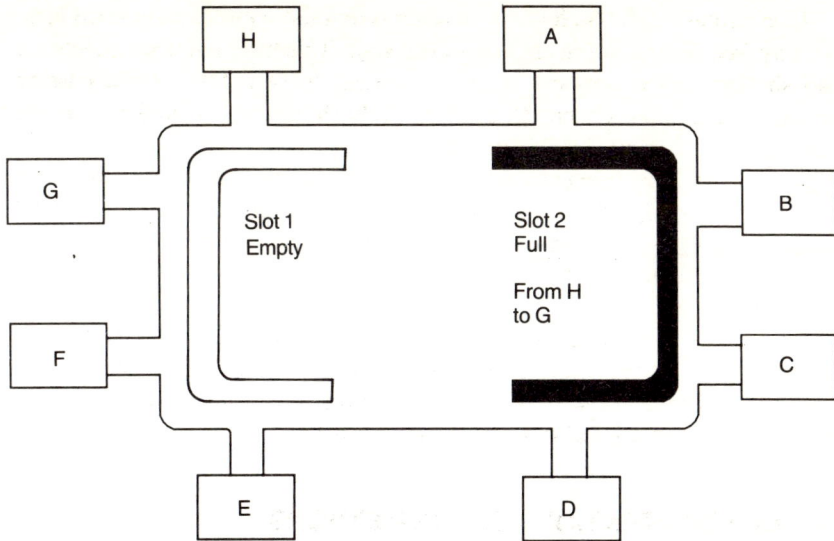

Figure 4.7   The slotted ring

signal. It is important that the sum of all of these delays will be at least as long as a packet transmission time. Otherwise, the beginning of the packet will return to the sender before it has finished transmitting it. Normally, a delay buffer is inserted into the ring to avoid this.

One potential problem with the slotted ring is that of a permanently full slot. This could occur if a station transmitted its data and then failed to remove it and mark the slot as empty. In this case, the slot would continuously circulate around the ring preventing further transmission. In practice, one of the nodes on the network is given the responsibility of removing any packets that pass by more than once. This is usually the station that started up the network. The failure of this node is a similar problem to the failure of the central node in a system with a star topology. A solution to this is to give all nodes the capability to monitor the network in this way. At any given time, only one node is the *active monitor*, while the remaining nodes are *passive monitors* ready to take over in case the primary monitor fails.

4.4.2   Token passing

Another noncontention-based access method is that of token passing. This works by passing a unique transmission sequence called a *token* from one node to another. When a node has taken possession of this token, it has permission to transmit a packet of information, after which it must pass it on to the next node in sequence.

The access method can be used with any of the topologies described in the previous chapter, but we will only consider its use in connection with the ring and the bus.

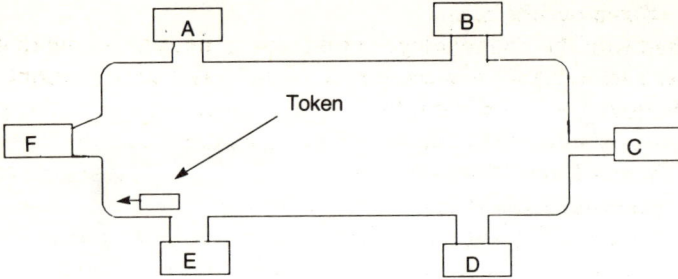

1   Token circulating – F has data for D

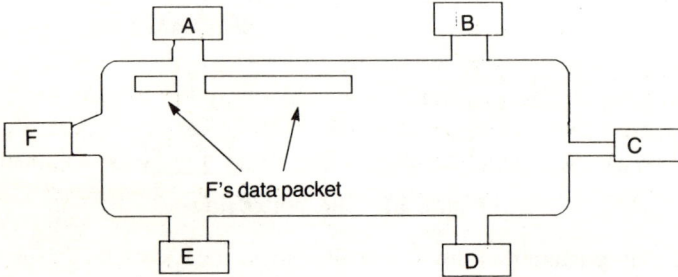

2 : F seizes the token and transmits its data packet

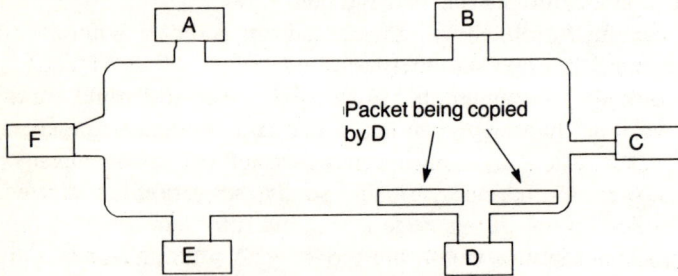

3   D copies the packet and marks it as received

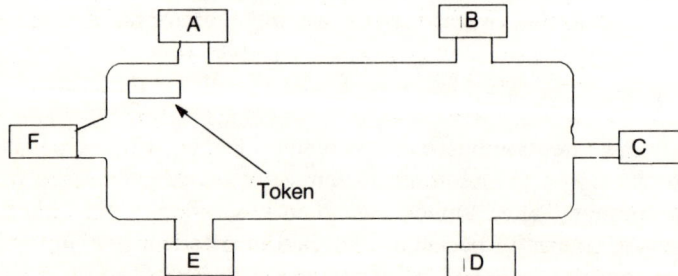

4   F removes its packet and releases the token – transmission and acknowledgement are complete

Figure 4.8   The token ring

4.4.2.1 Token-passing ring

When used with the ring topology, a token circulates around the ring being passed by each node to its successor. If a node has data to transmit, it will 'seize' the token (i.e. remove it from the network) and transmit its packet. This process is illustrated in figure 4.8 where node F has data to be sent to node D. When F receives the token, it transmits its data packet, which is passed through nodes A, B and C until it reaches its destination node, D.

D will receive the packet by copying the data, mark it as 'correctly received' and send it on to the next node. When the packet returns to node F, it must remove it and release a new token. If a node has a packet waiting for transmission, it removes the token and sends out its packet. The data packet will travel on the ring through to its destination node. Here its contents will be copied and it will resume its journey, eventually arriving back at the sending node where it is removed from the ring.

As with the slotted ring, fairness is achieved by forcing a node to give up the token after transmitting a single packet. This means that under conditions of heavy load, the circulating token will give each node the opportunity to send one packet before passing the token on to its successor in the ring.

4.4.2.2 Token-passing bus

In the case of the token-passing ring, the token is continuously passed from each node to its successor. Because there is only one incoming and one outgoing connection to each node, no addressing information is required. This is called an *implicit token*.

When using this access method on a bus, where all nodes are physically adjacent, each node must explicitly transmit the token to its successor. This *explicit token* is formed by adding addressing information before transmission. Each participating node must, therefore, be equipped with the address of the next station in the sequence. In this way, the nodes on a *token bus* are ordered into a *logical ring*.

Normal operation in a token-passing bus is very similar to that of the token-passing ring. The token, constituting permission to transmit, is circulated from node to node around the logical ring. If a node wishes to transmit, it seizes it, transmits a packet addressed to the destination, and on completion, releases the token to the next node in the sequence.

It is important to note that the ordering of nodes in the logical ring need not, in any way, reflect their physical arrangement. Similarly, nodes may be physically connected to the bus, but not be a part of the logical ring. This characteristic may be used to advantage for specialized applications, but leads to problems in adding/removing nodes from the system.

When the network is first activated, no transmission can take place due to the absence of a token. Before the network can operate, one, and only one of the nodes must generate a token. The choice of which node carries out this function is based on the station's address. In simple terms, each station initializes a timer whose value depends on its address. When this timer expires, and providing the network is still silent, the station will generate a token. In this competitive situation, the node with the 'highest' address wins.

At this stage, the logical ring is initialized, and contains a single node. The remaining nodes become part of the ring in response to a form of 'invitation' issued by this node at periodic intervals. This process is also used to add new nodes to the logical ring during normal operation.

The use of the token-passing technique in a bus topology allows the provision of a more sophisticated service than would be possible with CSMA/CD. However, the method of explicit token passing imposes a severe transmission overhead which causes greater transmission delays and affects throughput.

4.4.2.3   Priority traffic

In some system configurations, it may be necessary for certain nodes to have a higher priority than others. This situation can be accommodated within the token-passing access method by the provision of a priority indicator in the packet header. The majority of nodes on the network would be operating at priority 000. A node wishing higher priority can set the priority indicator in a passing packet to its own level. When the currently active sending node receives its own packet back with the priority altered, it must carry out the following actions. Firstly, it retains the current priority for later use. It then issues a token with the requested (higher) priority. Only those nodes operating at that level or higher are allowed to seize this token.

When the original sending node receives a free token at the higher priority, this indicates that all traffic at the higher level has been completed. At this stage, it issues a new token at the original (low) priority.

4.4.2.4   Synchronous traffic

Some communication requirements cannot be satisfied by the essentially asynchronous nature of token passing. An example of this would be digitized speech. Transmission of this type of information requires that the transmitting node be guaranteed to send a packet at predefined time intervals. This can be accommodated by extending the priority access scheme described above.

An additional node called a *synchronous bandwidth manager* is present on the network. This node maintains an internal timer which will, at predefined intervals, cause it to request priority access at a certain level. The high priority token will pass around the ring giving each node operating at that level (or higher) an opportunity to transmit. The net result is that, at regular intervals, normal traffic is halted leaving the total bandwidth of the network to be divided between the high priority nodes. This allows token networks to be used for real time traffic e.g. digitized speech. It is important, however, to regulate the number of nodes offering synchronous traffic to ensure that there is sufficient bandwidth to go around.

4.5 COMPARISON BETWEEN CSMA/CD AND TOKEN PASSING

As a network access method, CSMA/CD has several attractive features. The algorithm involved is very simple and as such as easily implemented in hardware. This is an important factor for the design of network adapter cards and, since these are required at each node on the network, there are 'knock on' effects for the cost of the network as a whole. The algorithm also ensures that 'fairness' is maintained under conditions of heavy load. It has been shown in practice [2] that when the network is busy, the available bandwidth is divided evenly among those nodes with data to send.

A disadvantage of this rigid 'fairness' is that it is impossible to give priority access to selected nodes. Furthermore, because the access time (and therefore the response time) is statistical rather than deterministic in nature, it is impossible to quote a guaranteed minimum response time. This makes the scheme unsuitable for real time applications.

When a collision occurs in a CSMA/CD network, all nodes transmitting must back off and try again after a period of time. For the collision to be detected however, the node must allow for its signal to propagate to the furthest extreme of the network, collide with another node's packet and to return for detection. The objective after a collision is to schedule each station to retransmit its packet at points in time quantized in steps at least as large as the collision interval. This time quantization is called the *retransmission slot time*. In order to achieve maximum use of the available bandwidth, this should be as short as possible, so it is usually chosen to be a value just over the end-to-end round trip delay. The IEEE (see Chapter 6) have standardized on a value of 51.2 microseconds for a 10 mbps baseband CSMA/CD system. This means that the network's geographical span must be carefully engineered so that end-to-end round trip delay must never exceed this maximum.

The network's slot time is an important parameter when considering its overall efficiency. From a performance point of view, time spent in the handling of collisions represents channel bandwidth wasted. For this reason, it is important that the proportion of time spent in this activity is minimized. When a node begins transmission, it is exposed to the risk of a collision occurring for the duration of one slot interval. Thus the ratio of frame transmission time to slot length should be maximized. Unfortunately, the slot time is fixed by physical and electrical considerations. Thus, the only way to improve network efficiency is to increase the packet length or to decrease the transmission speed. The latter solution is ruled out because it would decrease overall system throughput.

It has been shown in practice [2] that the efficiency of a heavily loaded Ethernet can vary between 97% with a packet size of 512 bytes to 54% with a 4-byte packet. An important implication of this is that the extent to which the throughput of a CSMA/CD network can be improved by increasing the transmission speed is severely limited.

These problems only arise in situations where the network is operating with a load which is heavy in relation to capacity. It is normal to engineer CSMA/CD networks so that they will run with a sustained load of no more than 50% of available capacity. This means that the access method provides reliable transmission with very low delay periods.

When discussing the CSMA/CD access method, we saw that time spent in handling collisions represented wasted bandwidth. The token-passing method avoids this by requiring the nodes to gain possession of the token *before* transmitting. On the other hand, if we consider a token ring with only one station active, we can clearly see that this access method also has inherent inefficiencies.

When a node transmits its packet and receives it back, it is compelled to give up the token. This ensures that all nodes receive a fair share of the bandwidth. If we consider the case where no other node on the network has any data to send we will see that the token will circulate the ring incurring a single bit delay in each station, before returning to the active station. This traversal of the ring by the token represents wasted bandwidth. The more evenly the load is spread over all stations in the network, the less time is wasted. Thus, it can be seen that a token-passing network will achieve its maximum throughput when it is heavily loaded, and that load is spread evenly among the connected nodes. This is in sharp contrast to the CSMA/CD case, where best performance is achieved when the number of collisions is minimized, i.e. when the load is concentrated in a single node.

The token-passing access method is inherently prone to two related error conditions. The first of these is that a node may seize the token, transmit a message and then fail to remove it. This packet would continuously circulate around the ring making further communication impossible. The second type of error is where the token is destroyed. Both of these conditions are handled by a node called the *token monitor*. There must be one of these nodes active on every ring. Every time a packet travels past the monitor, it sets a bit in the packet header. If a packet with this bit set arrives on the input line of the monitor station, then an error has occurred. This is easily corrected by removing the packet and issuing a new token. Normally, every node on the network has the capability to be a monitor node and another can take over if the original fails.

The active monitor also maintains a timer which is reset by the passing of either a full data packet or a token. If the token is lost due to either interference or noise, then the timer expires and the ring is reinitialized by issuing a free token.

4.6   CONCLUSIONS

In this chapter, we have examined a number of popular access methods in some detail. The IEEE standardization effort (see Chapter 6) concerns itself with three of these: the CSMA/CD bus, the token ring and the token bus and because of this, merit close study.

The CSMA/CD bus involves a very simple algorithm which is amenable to being implemented in VLSI (very large scale integration) technology. Connection to the network is simply achieved using taps into a passive coaxial cable. It performs well at low loads, and will continue to offer good performances as the load increases, provided that the packet size is kept reasonably large. There are some question marks over its future applicability at higher speeds, using optical fibers, etc.

The token-passing method is more complex to implement and thus involves more expensive interface. Its performance at low loads is reasonable and will give best results with heavy loads which are well distributed over the stations on the network. The basic technology does not place any limitations over either the geographical span of the network or the transmission speed used. When used in conjunction with the ring topology, it can easily use optical fibers, or a mixture of different media.

The ability to allow priority access to the network may be an important selection criterion in certain applications. Also, the synchronous traffic capability may allow the network to be used to carry many different types of real time information.

4.7 REFERENCES

1 Metcalfe, R.M. and Boggs, D.R.: 'Ethernet: Distributed packet switching for local computer networks' *Communications of the ACM*, **19**, no. 7, pp. 395–403, 1976.

2 Shoch, J.F. and Hupp, J.A.: 'Measured performance of an Ethernet local network' *Communications of the ACM*, **23**, no. 12, pp. 711–721, 1984.

3 Bux, W.: 'Performance issues in local area networks' *IBM Systems Journal*, **23**, no. 4, pp. 351–374, 1984.

4 Saltzer, J.H., Pogran, K.T. and Clark, D.D.: 'Why a ring?' in *Computer Networks* 7, pp. 223–231, Rotterdam: North-Holland, 1983.

5 Shoch, J.F., Dalal, Y.K., Redell, D.D. and Crane, R.C.: 'The Ethernet' in *Local Area Networks: An Advanced Course*, eds. D. Hutchinson, J. Moriani and D. Shepherd, Springer Verlag Notes in Computer Science, No. 184, Berlin: Springer Verlag, 1985.

6 Dixon, R.C., Strole, N.C. and Markov, J.D.: 'A token ring network for local data communications' *IBM Systems Journal*, **22**, nos. 1 and 2, pp. 47–62, 1983.

7 Strole, N.C.: 'A local communications network based on inter-connected token-access rings: a tutorial' *IBM Journal of Research and Development*, **27**, no. 5, pp. 481–496, 1983.

8 Watson, I.: 'The integrated services local network' *British Telecom Technology Journal*, **2**, no. 4, pp. 26–33, 1984.

9 Tanenbaum, A.S.: *Computer Networks*, Englewood Cliffs: New Jersey, 1981.

10 Abramson, N.: 'The Aloha system – another alternative for computer communications networks' *Proceedings*, Fall Joint Computer Conference, 1970.

CHAPTER FIVE

LAN IMPLEMENTATIONS

5.1 INTRODUCTION

In the preceding chapters the following important aspects of LANs have been covered:

- the different types of communication medium;
- techniques for transmitting data;
- network topologies;
- techniques for controlling access to the network.

These are the distinguishing features of a network and this chapter describes a number of existing local area networks in terms of these features.

In the course of this discussion references are made to certain 'higher level protocols' and 'standards'. These are topics covered in detail in the following chapter, but are mentioned here for completeness.

5.2 ETHERNET

Ethernet [1, 2, 5] is one of the oldest LANs. It was announced as a product in 1980 but the development work dates back to the early '70s [3]. Many of the original ideas came from the Aloha wide area network used in the University of Hawaii. Ethernet is marketed jointly by three large corporations: Digital; Intel and Xerox. The original product announcement was an attempt by them to establish a *de facto* industrial standard in the then emerging field of local area networks.

Briefly, Ethernet is a baseband network, with a bus topology and a data transmission rate of 10 mbps. The access method used is CSMA/CD.

The original specification of Ethernet [1], and the version described here, divides it into two components or layers: the *physical layer* and the *data-link layer*. The physical layer, as its name suggests, describes the physical characteristics of the network, these include the topology, transmission medium, transmission technique and the data transfer rate. The data-link layer deals with higher level aspects like the packet format and the access method. The description of Ethernet and of the other LANs described in this chapter covers each of these layers in turn. (These two layers correspond directly with the bottom layers of the I.S.O. *open system interconnection* model which is described in the following chapter.)

The interface presented to users of Ethernet is a facility to transmit and receive variable length packets between any two nodes on the network.

5.2.1 Physical layer

The medium used is *shielded coaxial cable*, and the transmission mechanism is *baseband* with *Manchester encoding*, as described in Appendix A. The physical connection to the network is made using a device called a *transceiver* (see figure 5.1). The transceiver contains the electronic circuitry to perform the following functions:

- transmit and receive data bits;
- monitor the network and detect if a packet is being transmitted;
- detect the occurrence of collisions.

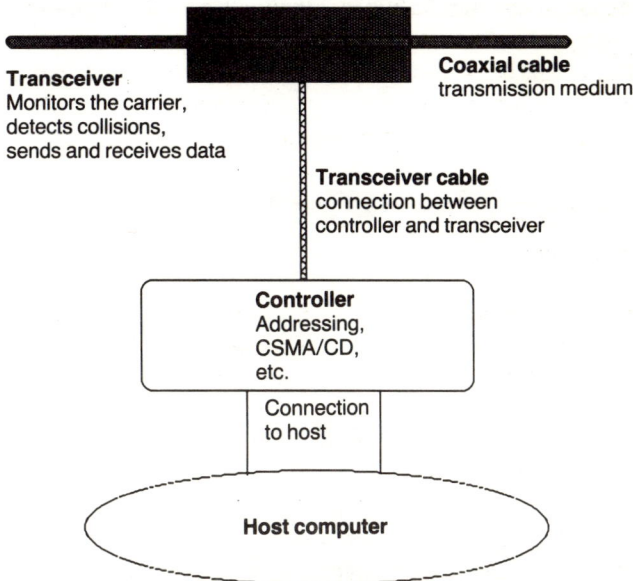

Transceiver
Monitors the carrier, detects collisions, sends and receives data

Coaxial cable
transmission medium

Transceiver cable
connection between controller and transceiver

Controller
Addressing, CSMA/CD, etc.

Connection to host

Host computer

Figure 5.1   Ethernet components

All other functions including the interface to the host computer are implemented on a separate controller board which is connected to the transceiver using transceiver cable, made up of four twisted pairs.

Once a node starts transmitting, the signal propagates to all parts of the network without any retransmission by intervening transceivers. This differs from ring networks where each node propagates the signal. For this reason the failure or removal of any individual transceiver does not affect the rest of the network.

5.2.1.1   Topology

In the simplest case, Ethernet uses a bus topology, as shown in figure 5.2a. A single piece of cable is known as a *segment*. Individual segments of an Ethernet can be connected together using *repeaters* (see figure 5.2b).

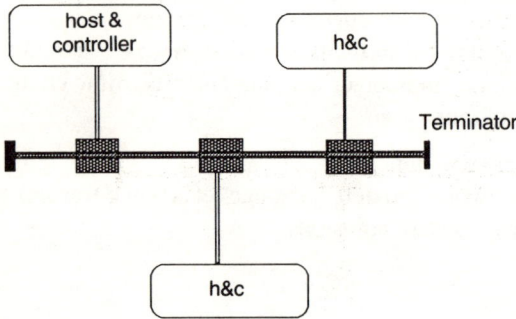

Figure 5.2a   Simple bus topology with a single segment

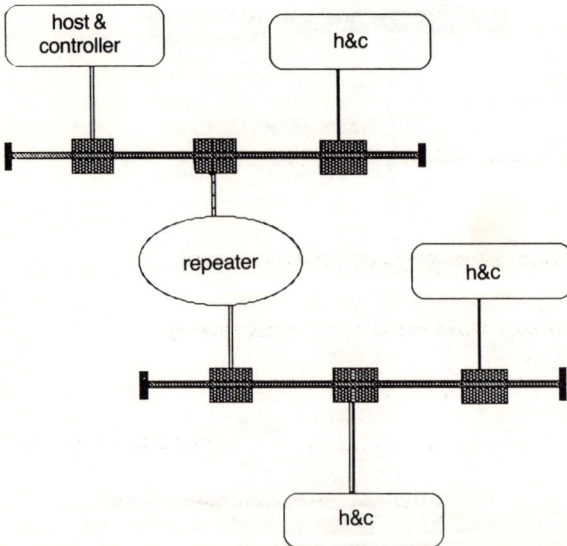

Figure 5.2b   Two segments connected using a repeater

Repeaters allow an Ethernet to be expanded in what is called a *branching tree* topology. Figures 5.2a to 5.2d show a number of different Ethernet configurations. Because no segment has precedence over another, and the network can be extended in any direction, this topology is also known as an *unrooted tree*. Loops however, as shown in figure 5.2c, are not allowed, there can only be one path between any two nodes on the network.

This topology makes Ethernet very flexible and easy to expand. The geographical area covered by a single network can be extended by using a

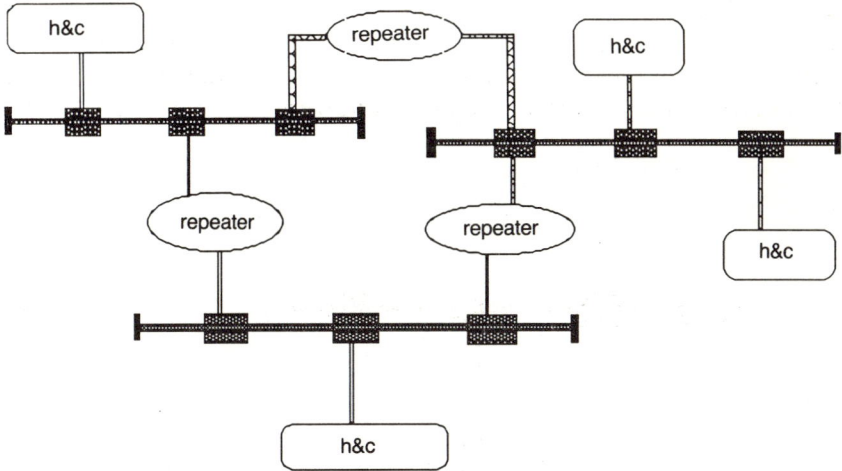

Figure 5.2c Illegal Ethernet topology – there is more than one path between nodes

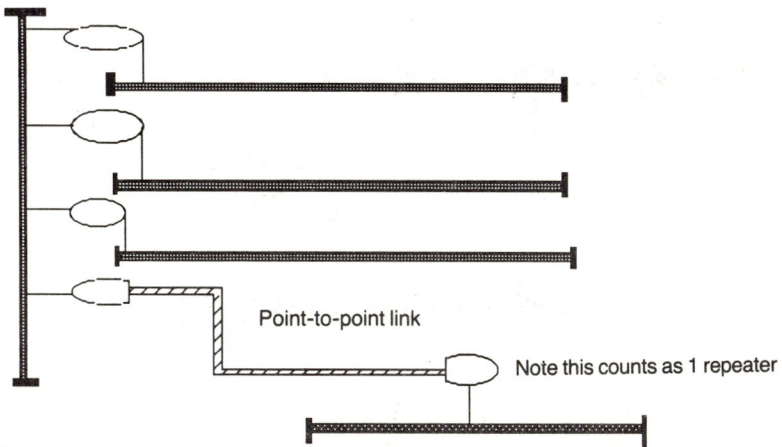

Figure 5.2d A large number of segments can be connected to a single backplane segment

point-to-point link between segments, e.g. two segments can be connected using a dedicated fiberoptic cable, this is useful to connect segments in different buildings or in different parts of a large factory.

5.2.2 Data-link layer

The data-link layer defines the packet format, the access control mechanism and the interface presented to users. These are implemented on top of the facilities provided by the physical layer, i.e. the ability to transmit and receive data and to monitor the network.

5.2.2.1 Packet format

The format of a packet, or *frame* to use Ethernet terminology, is shown in figure 5.3. It consists of a variable number of 8 bit bytes.

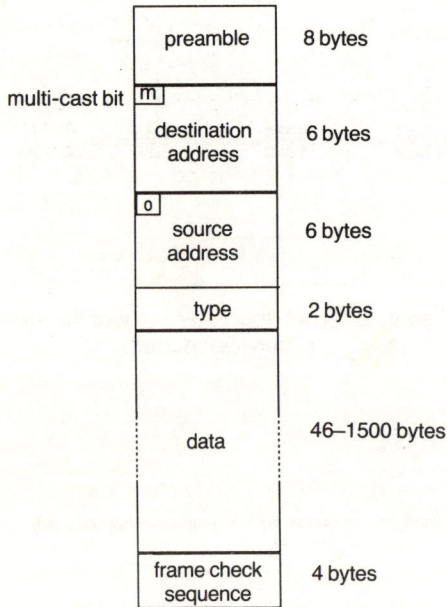

Figure 5.3   Ethernet packet format

The fields that go to make up a frame are as follows:

1 **Preamble** (8 bytes): All transmissions begin with a fixed 64 bit preamble. This is included to allow all nodes to recognize that a frame is being transmitted and to synchronize with the transmitter.
2 **Destination address** (6 bytes): The address of the destination node.
3 **Source address** (6 bytes): The address of the node sending the frame.
    Addresses in Ethernet are 48 bits long, 47 of which are used for addressing individual stations. The first bit in the destination address field is

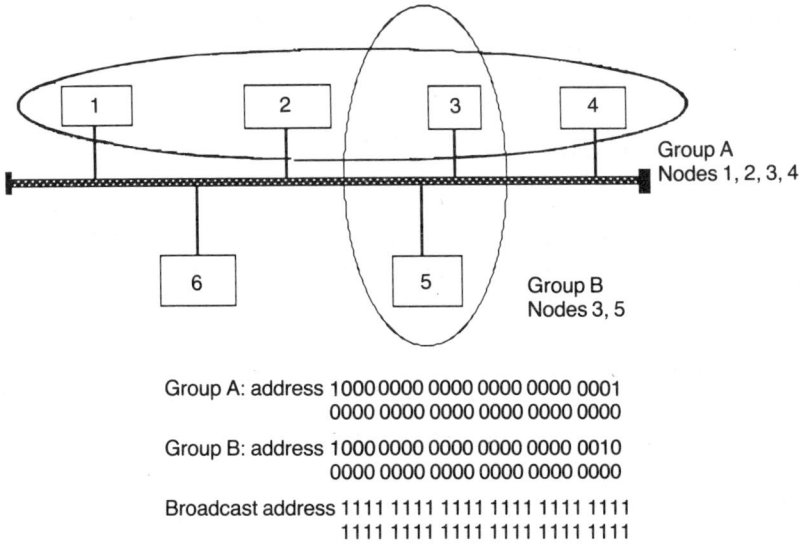

Group A: address 1000 0000 0000 0000 0000 0001
0000 0000 0000 0000 0000 0000

Group B: address 1000 0000 0000 0000 0000 0010
0000 0000 0000 0000 0000 0000

Broadcast address 1111 1111 1111 1111 1111 1111
1111 1111 1111 1111 1111 1111

Figure 5.4   Multicast addressing in Ethernet
Note: Packets addressed to group A are received by nodes 1, 2, 3, 4. Packets
addressed to group B are received by nodes 3 and 5. Broadcast packets are received by
all nodes

special and is called the *multicast* bit. Multicasting allows a frame to be sent to a *group* of stations in a single transmission. If the multicast bit is clear, the remaining 47 bits give the unique address of the destination node. If the multicast bit is set, then the rest of the address is used to specify not an individual node but a group number. Nodes can belong to any number of groups and a group can contain any number of nodes. A frame addressed to a group is received by all its members. If all the bits of the destination are set to 1 then that indicates that the frame is a *broadcast* one, to be received by *all* nodes (see figure 5.4).

4 **Frame type** (2 bytes): This field is included for the convenience of high level protocols. It can be used to indicate to the destination how the data in the data field is to be interpreted. (This is explained further in the following chapter.)

5 **Data** (46–1500 bytes): This field contains the user data. The network places no restrictions on the contents of the data field. The only constraint is that it cannot be smaller than 46 bytes or greater than 1500.

6 **Frame check sequence** (4 bytes): Error checking takes the form of generating a cyclic redundancy check (CRC) (see Appendix B) for each frame based on the contents of the address, type and data fields.

Excluding the preamble, the smallest valid frame size is 64 bytes and the largest is 1518. Frames received with sizes outside this range, or with a fractional number of bytes, are rejected as being 'framing errors'.

5.2.2.2 Access method

The network access method used is CSMA/CD as described in Chapter 4.

The minimum packet size of 64 bytes is a direct result of the nature of the CSMA/CD protocol. Transmitting stations monitor the status of the network for collision only *while* they are transmitting. Therefore, for a station to detect a collision of one of its own packets, it must still be transmitting when the first bit of the frame returns to it.

The length of time between a station transmitting data and the signal propagating to the end of the network and returning is called the *end-to-end propagation delay* (or round trip propagation delay). Its value depends on the length and the transmission speed of the network. On a 10 mbps Ethernet, of maximum length, the end-to-end propagation delay is slightly less than the time taken to transmit 64 bytes, hence the figure for the minimum packet size.

5.2.2.3 User interface

The interface presented to the user is the ability to transmit a variable length packet between nodes on the network. Once a packet is accepted for delivery, Ethernet does not guarantee that it will be received correctly. If the channel is very busy, the packet may not be successfully transmitted within the specified number of retries. In this case the user is informed. Even if the packet was successfully sent, it may be received at the other end with a CRC or framing error. In the worst case the destination station may not even be in operation.

Thus the service offered by Ethernet is what is known as a *datagram*. A single message is sent with a very high, but not 100%, probability of being successfully received. Higher levels of reliability can be achieved at the user level. This topic is discussed in more detail in the next chapter.

5.2.3 System parameters

There are defined numerical limits for various aspects of the network to which all implementations must adhere. These are:

- The cable running from the transceiver to the controller must not exceed 50 m.
- A segment can be up to 500 m in length.
- There should be no more than two repeaters, i.e. three segments, in the path between any two nodes.
- There is an upper limit of 1000 m on the length of point-to-point connection within a single network.
- The minimum length of coaxial cable between two nodes is 2.5 m and the maximum is 1500 m. Thus the overall maximum separation is 2800 m, which is made up of 1500 m coaxial cable, 1000 m of point-to-point links and 300 m of transceiver cable. This latter figure is made up of 50 m for each node and 100 m for each of the two repeaters.

- A 47 bit station address gives a range of 140 million million. This may at first seem a little excessive but it is used because station addresses are required to be unique across *all* Ethernets. This simplifies connecting Ethernets together. All addresses, and use of the type field, are assigned by a centralized authority to ensure uniqueness. The maximum number of addresses allowed on a single Ethernet is restricted to 1024.

5.2.4 Broadband Ethernet and other developments

Although it was previously stated that Ethernet is a baseband network, an alternative *broadband* version has recently been announced. There is trade off between the relative merits of broadband and baseband Ethernet [4]. Early baseband transceivers were too large and cumbersome for many office wiring ducts, although the situation is improving. The taps used to connect to a broadband cable are easily installed. The maximum length of cable that can be used with broadband is much longer: about 3800 m.

Perhaps the greatest advantage of broadband Ethernet is that it uses only 20% of the available cable bandwidth. The remainder of the bandwidth is free to be used by other systems, e.g. other broadband networks, voice or video transmission.

Other Ethernet developments include 'thin wire' Ethernet, which uses a cheaper and lighter cable. It is much easier to install and handle than the more rigid standard cable. Normal baseband transmission is used, but the distances that can be covered are less than with the standard cable. Devices also exist, e.g. a DELNI (digital local network interconnect), which make it possible to connect a number of nodes, with different addresses, to a *single transceiver* on a conventional Ethernet. Thus it is possible to have a small Ethernet configuration, within a machine room for example, where there is no coaxial cable, all the nodes being connected to a DELNI.

5.3 THE CAMBRIDGE RING

Work started on developing a local area network at the computer laboratory in Cambridge University in 1974. This is the same time as work was beginning on Ethernet, but the system development at Cambridge followed a very different path. The Cambridge network, or Cambridge Ring [6, 7, 8] is an empty slot ring, using standard telephone twisted pair cable with a transmission speed of 10 mbps. The packet format is similar to that used in Ethernet, i.e. address, data, control and error checking fields. The packet size is however much smaller, 38 bits in all.

The ring, and variations of it, is widely used within the UK academic community and some commercial products based on the Cambridge design have been put on the market. The particular version described here is the

original one used at Cambridge University, as part of the Cambridge Model
Distributed System which is discussed in the second part of this book. The
differences between it and the *CR-82* standard are described in the next
chapter. The network consists of a number of components, as shown in figure
5.5.

- The transmission medium.
- The *repeater*, which connects sections of cable together and handles the low
  level functions to do with the transmission and reception of data bits.
- The *station*, which handles the access method, etc.
- The *access box*, which is the interface between a station and the attached
  device.

These and the other components are examined in the process of explaining
the physical and data link layers of the network. It should be noted that the
distinction in functionality of the layers is not as clear cut as in the case of
Ethernet.

5.3.1 The physical layer

As its name suggests, the Cambridge Ring uses a ring topology. Data bits
travel around the ring in one fixed direction. Sections of cable are connected
using *repeaters*, in a point-to-point fashion. The basic transmission medium is
twisted pair cable, using baseband signaling with a raw data transmission
speed of 10 mbps. It is however possible to use different media in different
sections of the ring. The original ring at Cambridge University had one
fiber optic section (see figure 5.5).

5.3.1.1 Repeaters

The repeaters used on the ring differ from those used in Ethernet. In fact,
'repeater' in this context is a slightly misleading name, the corresponding
component on other LANs is called a 'tap' or simply 'network connection'. As
well as passing data bits between sections of cable, the repeater allows the
station to send and receive data bits. Each repeater has a switch to set its
network address, and there is a recommended maximum of 100 m between
two repeaters. The distance is longer if optical fiber is used.

There is a delay of 3 bit times in each repeater and roughly 5 bit times in
100 m of twisted pair cable [9]. These figures are important because the sum
of the individual bit delays in a complete circuit of the ring determines how
many slots can be in circulation. The effective length of the ring can be
increased by inserting extra shift registers to increase the overall delay.

Power for the repeaters comes from the ring and not from the attached
station or device. There are a number of repeaters around the ring which act
as power input points. These repeaters do not have stations attached to them.
The advantage of this scheme is that repeaters, and, therefore, the ring,
function independently of the stations and devices attached to them. A
number of power points can be used for enhanced reliability.

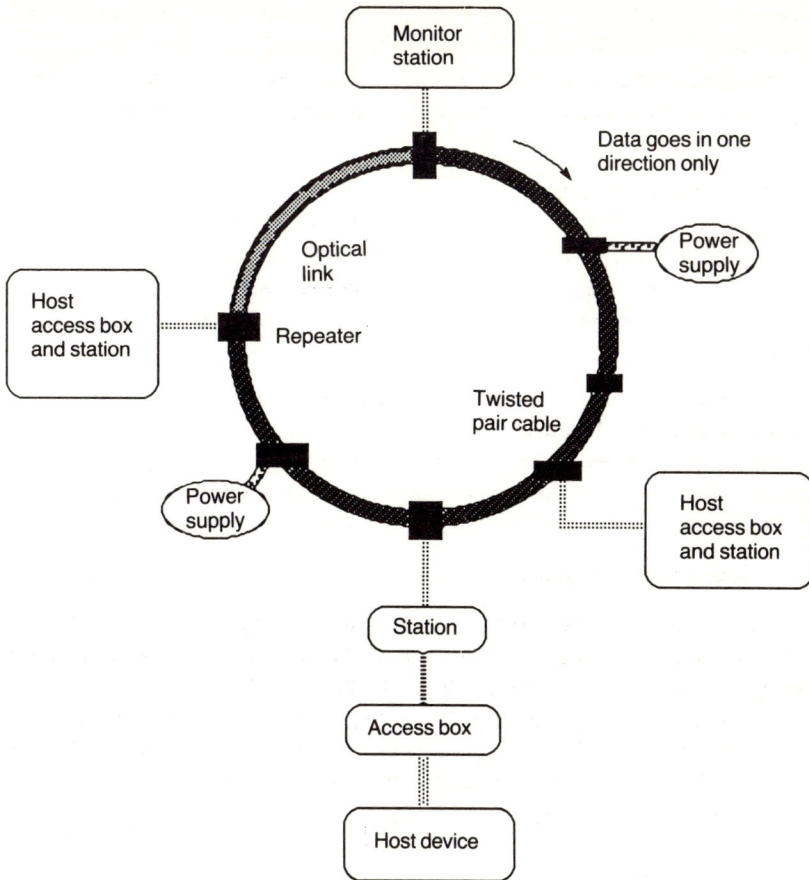

Figure 5.5   Ring components

5.3.1.2   Transmission technique

The Cambridge Ring is a baseband network but uses four wires or two channels to carry the signal. A '1' bit is represented by a transition on both channels while a '0' bit is represented by a transition on one channel only. Thus there is always at least one transition in each clock pulse (see figure 5.6).

5.3.2   The data-link layer

The data link functions of the ring are implemented in the station, using the facilities provided by the repeater. The access mechanism is 'empty slot'. There is one special station on the network, known as the *monitor*. It resides at address 0 and is responsible for error handling and starting up the network. The next section gives the exact slot format.

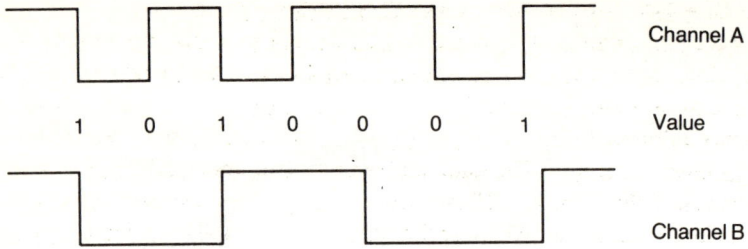

Figure 5.6   Two channel signaling

Note: A transition in both channels represents a '1' while a transition on one channel only represents a '0'

5.3.2.1   Minipacket format

Packets, or minipackets as they are called in the Ring, have a format as shown in figure 5.7. The total delay time in a single bit circulating the ring determines the number of such minipackets that can be in circulation at one time.

1 **Start bit**   Interslot gaps are represented by at least two 0 bits. Thus, the start of a packet is indicated by a 1. As in Ethernet the start of packet indicator is used for synchronization and framing purposes.

2 **Full/empty bit**   If this field is 0 the slot is empty and may be used to transmit data.

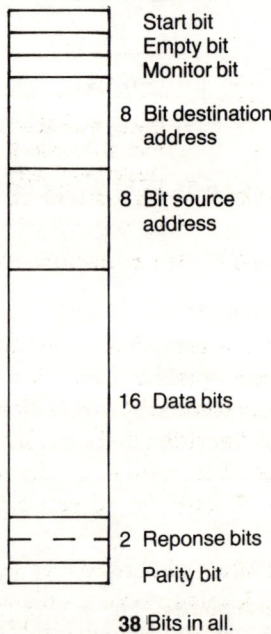

Start bit
Empty bit
Monitor bit

8 Bit destination
  address

8 Bit source
  address

16 Data bits

2 Reponse bits
Parity bit

38 Bits in all.

Figure 5.7   Minipacket format

3 **Monitor bit** Used by the monitor station for error detection.
4 **Destination address** (8 bits) If the destination address is set to all 1s, i.e. 255, then the packet is a broadcast one. Multicasting, or group addressing, is not supported.
5 **Source address** (8 bits)
6 **Data field** (16 bits) The data field is of a fixed, and small, size.
7 **Response field** (2 bits) These are used by the destination station, to indicate to the sender whether the packet was actually received or not.
8 **Parity bit** This is used as part of the error handling mechanism on the ring, see Appendix B.

5.3.2.2 The empty slot access method

As previously stated the basic access method used is empty slot, as described in Chapter 4. There are a few features of the Cambridge implementation worth noting.

1 A station wishing to transmit waits for the start of packet indicator. It then reads and sets the 'empty' bit in one operation. If the value read was a 0 then the packet was empty and it fills it with data. On the other hand if the value read was a 1, indicating a full slot, it does nothing. Setting the empty bit in this case has no effect.
2 When transmitting a packet, the station sets the response bits to 11. The destination sets the response bits according to the table shown in figure 5.8. If the destination is not operational, the original value set by the transmitter will be returned.

Value	Meaning
11	Destination Absent
01	Packet Accepted
10	Destination Deaf
00	Destination Busy

Figure 5.8   Packet response bits

Each station has a *source select register*. This allows nodes to select which stations they wish to accept packets from. A value of 255 means that it is accepting packets from all sources. A station sets the response field to 10 if it is not accepting the packet addressed to it. If a station is still processing a recently received packet when another arrives it sets the response to 00 to indicate that it is busy. Finally, the response is set to 01 for a correctly received packet.

The ability to select which stations to receive from is particularly useful for implementing higher level protocols. A high level packet is made up of a number of minipackets, and a node may decide to ignore minipackets from all other sources until the entire high level packet is received. This however causes problems with 'broadcasting', as a station, although active, may be 'deaf' to the broadcasting node.

3 If a transmitter station, on getting back its own minipacket does not mark the slot empty it can reuse it and effectively monopolize that slot. The Cambridge implementation prevents this by forcing each transmitter station to mark returned slots empty before passing them on. Thus every other station on the ring will have the opportunity to use that slot before it returns to the original transmitter.

4 If a station receives back a packet with the response bits set to indicate that the destination is deaf, the higher levels (i.e. the access box) may direct it to retransmit it immediately. To prevent such a 'busy wait' wasting bandwidth the station introduces a delay before informing the access box that the destination is currently deaf to it. For each unsuccessful transmission the delay is increased.

5 Having sent a packet, a station must wait for it to return. On return, the slot must be marked 'empty' and the response bits must be checked. The most obvious way for a station to recognize its own packets is to read the source address field, but this is not done in practice for the following reason. Within a slot the 'empty' bit comes before the address fields, so it cannot be reset until the source address has been read. This would introduce a considerable delay at each station. A second scheme, and the one used on the ring, is to have each station use its knowledge of the number of slots in circulation to keep track of the ones it sends. As the 'empty' bit can be set, or cleared, 'on the fly', this greatly reduces the delay at each station.

The raw transmission rate on the ring is 10 mbps, shared out fairly between all stations. The actual bandwidth available to stations will depend on the number of stations on the ring and on the number of slots. Unlike with CSMA/CD, it is possible to calculate the effective bandwidth available to each node.

On the ring, a station can use only one slot at the time. If there are n slots, then ignoring interslot gaps and assuming only one station wishes to transmit, the bandwidth available to it is $1/n$ of the total. When it is taken into account that a station cannot reuse the slot it has just used, the fraction available to it becomes $1/(n + 1)$. It can be seen from this that increasing the number of slots decreases the bandwidth available to each node but improves the utilization of the total ring bandwidth, as more than one station can be transmitting simultaneously.

The figure of $1/(n + 1)$ holds if only one station wishes to transmit. If there are m stations on the network, all trying to transmit at the same time, the fraction available to each is less. Once a station has used a slot all the other $(m - 1)$ stations will use it before the first can reuse it, i.e., the fraction of bandwidth available to each is $1/(n + 1 + (m - 1))$ or $1/(n + m)$. Given that only 16 bits of each 38 bit slot actually carries data, the effective data bandwidth on a 10 megabit ring is $16 \times 10/38(n + m)$ megabits or roughly $4.2/(n + m)$ megabits per station.

The above figures assume that the number of stations is greater than the number of slots, and that the number of stations is at least 2 [6]. The actual bandwidth available in the trivial case of single station transmitting is $1/(n + 2)$. This is because a station is not able to use the slot immediately following one it has just marked empty. In the more general case of m nodes wishing to transmit, this slot will be in use anyway so the fraction available per node is still $1/(n + m)$.

As an example, take a ring with 8 stations, each separated by 100 m of twisted pair cable. The delay at each is 3 bits plus 5 for each length of cable giving a total delay of $8(5 + 3) = 64$ bits. Extra shift registers can be introduced to bring the delay time to over 80 bits so that 2 slots can be used (38 bits per slot and at least 2 bits for each interslot gap). The guaranteed minimum bandwidth available to each node is then $4.2/(2 + 8)$ which equals 0.42 megabits per station.

5.3.2.3   The station

The station is responsible for framing, sending and receiving packets and implementing the access protocol. As well as the source select register, each station contains both *receive* and *transmit* packet shift registers. The latter is circular to ease the retransmission of packets. Stations have the ability to set packet bits 'on the fly', e.g. to set and test the 'empty' bit.

Stations also implement parity checking. As packets circulate around the ring, the parity bit at the end of the minipacket is computed and set at *every* station. If the new value does not equal the old one, an error must have occurred since the last upstream station. On detecting an error, the station sends a notification packet to the monitor.

5.3.2.4   The monitor station and error handling

The monitor performs a very important role in the network. It injects the initial slots into the network on startup. Errors are reported to it and it can also be used to gather information on performance. There is no device connected to it and it resides at address 0.

If a station fails to clear the empty bit on a packet it transmitted or if the empty bit gets corrupted due to noise, then that packet will continuously circulate around the ring. The monitor prevents this happening as follows.

- It sets the monitor bit on each packet as it passes.
- Stations transmitting packets set the 'empty' bit and *clear* the monitor bit.

Thus, when a full packet first reaches the monitor it will have its empty bit set and the monitor bit clear, i.e. 10, the packet is sent on its way with the monitor bit set, 11. On detecting a packet reaching it with both bits set, 11, the monitor will mark it empty because that value can only occur due to an error.

5.3.2.5   The access box

The access box or access control circuitry is the interface between the station and the attached device. Its complexity varies depending on the device it is interfacing with. It can range from a simple 'polled' interface to faster, more complicated, direct memory access (DMA). Some sophisticated access boxes implement the packet protocol, as described in the following section.

5.3.3   The packet protocol

The basic facility provided by the ring is the ability to transmit minipackets between devices. Unlike in Ethernet where the packet can be quite large, a minipacket contains just 16 data bits. This is too small for many applications. Accordingly, the designers at Cambridge defined a higher level protocol, called the *packet protocol*. This protocol, although not actually part of the ring itself, is used by most applications running on it at Cambridge University. (The packet protocol is a network layer protocol in terms of the OSI model.) A brief description is given here but the reader is referred to [6] for further details.

In the packet protocol, a packet is made up of a number of minipackets. The minipackets that go to make up a packet are defined as follows.

- **Header**   (1 minipacket) This contains a start-of-packet indicator and a count of the number of minipackets in the data field, as well as some other state information.
- **Route**   (1 minipacket) This is used to identify the destination process on the device.
- **Data**   (1 to 1024 minipackets) These contain the actual data.
- **Checksum**   (1 minipacket) This is used for error checking, similar to the frame check field in an Ethernet packet.

The first part of the packet sent is the header. If the receiver gets it correctly and decides it wants to receive the entire packet it sets the source select register to be the address of the sender. The sender then transmits the rest of the minipackets. If any errors occur during the transmission the sender stops sending minipackets, i.e., the packet transmission is aborted. There is no acknowledgement at this level.

High level protocols are discussed in detail in the next chapter. This description is included for completeness as the packet protocol is an important part of using the Cambridge Ring.

5.4   IBM'S LOCAL NETWORKS

As the dominant manufacturer in the computer marketplace, IBM's choices of technology tend to become *de facto* standards throughout the industry.

They were relatively late entrants into the market for LANs, introducing them as products for their personal computer range in the first instance. The first product introduced was a low speed bus network called the PC Cluster. This was followed by a broadband tree network called the PC Network. The final product introduced was the Token Ring network. This is a full function network that will allow connection of a wide variety of machines in the company's product line. In terms of long term significance, the PC Network and the Token Ring network are probably the most important, and will be discussed below.

5.4.1   The PC Network

In 1984, IBM launched the PC Network for use with machines from its personal computer family. It was intended to provide a simple network that would allow up to 72 machines to share peripheral devices and exchange information. Users of the Network would have the option of linking to the Token Ring network when it became available.

5.4.1.1   PC Network physical layer

The PC Network is based on standard CATV cable, arranged in a tree topology. The transmission technique employed is broadband using the *midsplit method*. This works by installing a device called a *translator unit* at the root of the tree. Nodes wishing to transmit do so on one frequency. This signal radiates through the network until it reaches the translator where it is amplified and sent out again using a different frequency (see figure 5.9). All nodes on the network listen to this frequency, and thus the signal will eventually be picked up at all nodes.

Cabling components   The cable used in the PC Network is CATV coaxial cable, identical to that used in the television industry. This has a usable bandwidth of 300 mHz divided into 50 channels, each 6 mHz wide. Only two of these are used by the network: transmission is carried out at 50.75 mHz and all nodes receive at 219 mHz. Within these channels, PCs transmit and receive data at a speed of 2 mbps. This leaves 48 channels to be used for other applications, e.g. video, voice, etc. In cases where a building is already wired for broadband devices, this feature may be an important cost saver.

Normally, the installation of a broadband network requires careful planning and tuning of cable lengths and components. The PC Network, however, can be made up of precut cable segments. The translator unit provides eight basic connections for use with PCs. A base expander is used to provide eight connections to this. These connections may be occupied by either PCs or lengths of cable of fixed sizes called long, medium and short distance kits each of which provides a further eight connections for PCs. Thus using these special cabling components, the network can be extended to a maximum of 72 nodes spanning a radius of 1000 feet from the translator unit.

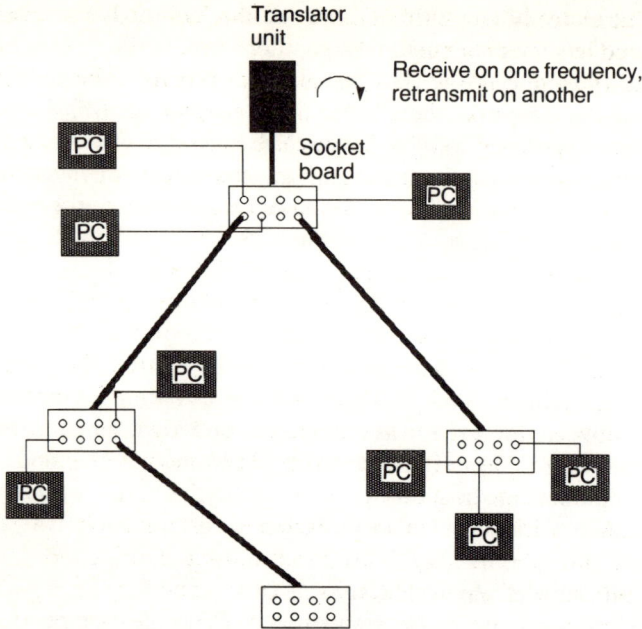

Figure 5.9   The IBM PC Network

By using a custom built cable network and more sophisticated translator unit, the network can be built up to 1000 nodes within a 5 km range of the central unit.

5.4.1.2 PC Network data-link layer

All nodes on the network transmit on the same frequency. Arbitration between them is handled using the CSMA/CD access technique. Because of this, the network is at its most efficient when handling larger packet sizes. On the positive side, a lightly loaded network will impose very small delays on a node wishing to transmit.

The Network adapter   Each node on the network must be equipped with a network adapter card. This card provides support for a layered architecture up as far as the session layer. The card contains a radio frequency (RF) modem operated by a serial interface controller. An Intel 82586 Communications Controller packages the data in HDLC format and feeds it to the serial interface controller, while applying the CSMA/CD protocol conventions. It is the combination of the coaxial cable and the above components that provides the physical and datalink layers of the system.

The card is also equipped with an Intel 80188 16 bit microprocessor chip with supporting 16K RAM and 32K ROM. These provide the network, transport and session layers. A user interface is provided by the Network

Basic Input Output System (NETBIOS) ROM. This higher level access will be described in a later chapter.

Rather than setting switches to configure a card to be at a particular address on the network, the PC Network adapter card has a unique ID encoded into a special ROM chip on the card. Each card manufactured is given its own unique address. (This feature is likely to be used in software protection schemes to ensure that only registered users may execute programs residing on a file server).

Fault diagnosis in a tree network can be difficult. To assist in this, the adapters are equipped with a range of self-diagnostic capabilities. When the node is first switched on, the card carries out a complete *power on self test* (POST). Failure of any part of this test will prohibit the adapter from participating in the network. In the special case where the problem is in the interface between the card and the computer, the PC will be informed, but the adapter will participate in the network. This allows other nodes on the network to interrogate its status.

The CSMA/CD process involves each node listening to the network, first for a pause and subsequently to itself transmitting. During this process, two error conditions can be detected: missing carrier and 'hot' carrier. In the first of these conditions, an adapter having started to transmit cannot 'hear itself'. This indicates a fault either in the cable or in the transmit/receive circuitry of the card. In this case, the adapter simply signals an error to the driving software. In the latter case, a node wishing to transmit is waiting for a pause and, after waiting a certain amount of time, concludes that either itself or another node is permanently imposing the signal. In order to detect which condition is occurring, the station broadcasts a packet to itself. If the packet arrives correctly, the card will report a 'hot carrier here', otherwise it will conclude that some other node is causing the problem and report a 'hot carrier elsewhere' error. In this way, hot carrier problems on the network can be solved by the culprit node 'owning up'.

The adapter card assists in other network management functions by keeping statistics, e.g. collision count, transmission error count, etc. This information can be accessed by the node itself, or remotely by another network user.

5.4.2 The Token Ring Network

In announcing the PC Network, IBM also issued statements to the effect that that product was intended for use within the PC product line only. Communications between other products in the range were served by communications hardware/software conforming to the SNA architecture. The intention was to later launch a major local network which could be used with the majority of its computing products. In order to allow customers to prepare for its arrival, they announced a cabling system which would cater for its needs. This allowed large computer users and building companies to adopt a wiring strategy for new buildings in the knowledge that it would eventually form the basis for a corporate network.

In October 1985, IBM launched the Token Ring Network for release in early 1986. The hardware comprised a token ring adapter for PCs as well as a unit called a multistation access unit. Software support was provided in the form of a NETBIOS interface and an SNA Advanced Program-to-Program Communications interface, both of which will be described in a later chapter.

The token ring product was based on the experimental Zurich Ring developed at IBM research laboratories in Zurich, Switzerland. Due to lack of hard technical information at the time of writing, the information below is supplemented by the results of that research.

5.4.2.1   Token Ring Network physical layer

Transmission medium   The transmission medium used by IBM in the Token Ring Network is copper twisted pair cable. The main influence involved in this choice is its widespread use in office telephone systems. This means that it is a well-understood, mature medium that has a large installed user base. It is however susceptible to noise. This problem can be combated, at an increased cost, by using data grade twisted pair with a suitable shield. In order to allow customers to use existing telephone wiring, IBM specified that the network can work with cable of different qualities, each imposing its own restrictions on distance covered and number of nodes attached. When using data grade cable, the network can handle up to 260 nodes. This reduces to 72 if the cheaper cable is used.

The fact that nodes on the network are connected in a ring means that the transmission medium is naturally segmented. This opens up the possibility of mixing media in the future. An example of this would be to use optical fibers for segments of the ring where there was a high level of electrical noise.

Transmission technique   The method of signaling used is baseband at 4 mbps. Because baseband is used, the adapter cards do not have to be equipped with radio frequency modems which keeps costs down. Data is encoded using the technique of *Differential Manchester Encoding*. This method of electrically encoding data offers a number of advantages which are fully explored in Appendix A.

Topology   The network topology involved in the Token Ring Network is a star-ring, or star-shaped ring. Electrically, the nodes in this form of network are wired in a ring configuration, with each node having connections to its successor and predecessor. Physically, however, the nodes are clustered around boxes called wiring concentrators. The signal flows out of the concentrator, through the node and back to the wiring concentrator again. The path traced by the signal is called a 'lobe' of the star-ring, and a network is made up of a number of wiring concentrators, each with a ring-in and a ring-out connection.

The concentrator is made up of a unit containing a ring with a number of sockets to which nodes can be attached. When a node, attached in this manner, becomes active, it supplies power to a relay inside the box, which extends the ring to encompass the new node. This insertion process can be carried out while the ring is operating with only temporary upset to any transmission in progress.

The quality of cable used determines the maximum number of wiring closets per ring, as well as the distance between nodes and closets. If using telephone grade, unshielded cable, the ring may consist of up to two closets versus 12 in the case of data grade media. Connections between wiring closets must be made with data grade media.

In traveling around the network, the signal is regenerated at each station. This means that limitations apply to the distance between both the nodes and the closets, and to the intercloset distance. Table 5.1 sets out these restrictions. The maximum area that can be covered by a single network is shown in figure 5.10. This involves the installation of a complete wiring system consisting of the relatively expensive data grade twisted pair cable. A lower cost alternative that may make use of existing installed telephone cable is shown in figure 5.11.

In cases where one network is insufficient, several networks may be connected together by means of *bridges* [11]. These nodes have normal network connections to two rings and provide logical routing of packets between them, based on the destination address. Because the bridge has two independent connections, it may perform speed conversion between net-

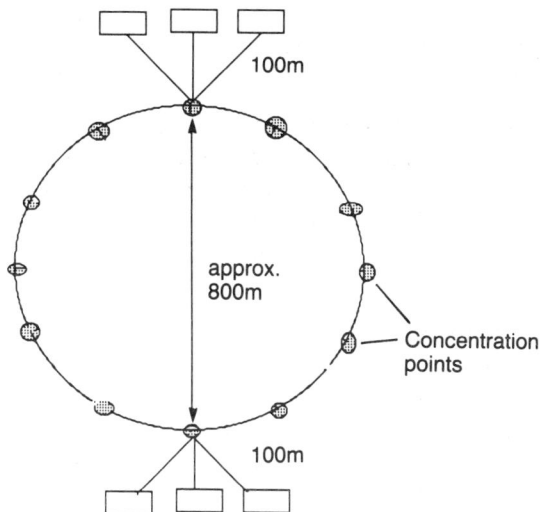

Figure 5.10   Maximum network configuration: 260 nodes connected to 12 wiring closets. Data grade cable is used throughout

Table 5.1   Distance limitations for different media types on a token ring system

	Data-grade media	Voice-grade media
Max Closets per Ring	12	2
Max Node-Closet Distance (only one closet in ring)	300m	100m
Max Node-Closet Distance (multiple closets in ring)	100m	45m
Max Closet-Closet Distance	200m	120m

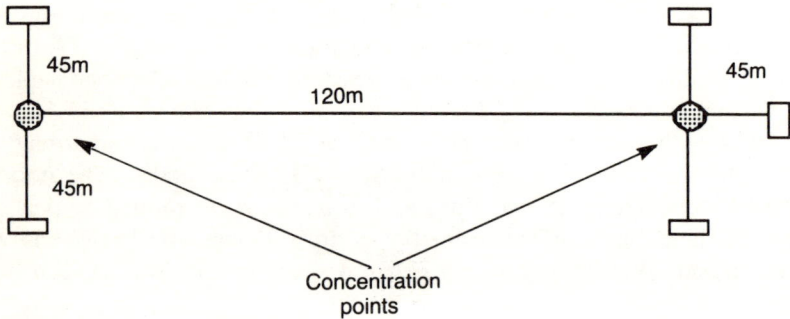

Figure 5.11   Maximum network configuration using telephone grade cable. 72 nodes connected to 2 wiring closets

works in future. Further expansion would be possible by connecting several networks via bridges to a high-speed ring called a *backbone*. This could be a high speed optical fiber-based token ring, or a channel on a broadband CATV cable.

5.4.2.2   Data-link layer

The protocols used in accessing the medium conform to those specified in IEEE 802.5 (see Chapter 6). Briefly, a special packet called a token passes from node to node around the ring giving permission to each node to transmit a packet. On completion of this transmission, the node must release a free token before attempting to transmit again. Thus permission to use the network passes from node to node around the ring.

By including a number of control bits in the packet, the basic mode of operation can be extended to enhance the functionality of the system in terms of data transfer and network management facilities.

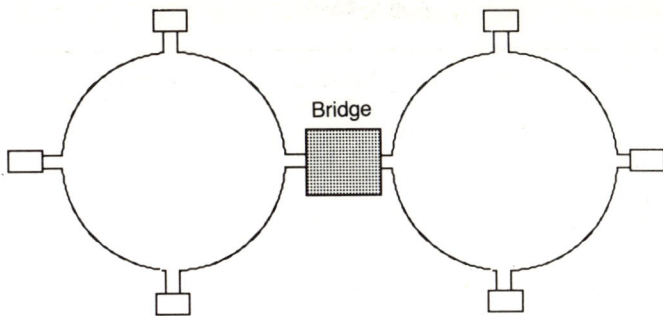

Figure 5.12   Bridge connecting 2 token rings

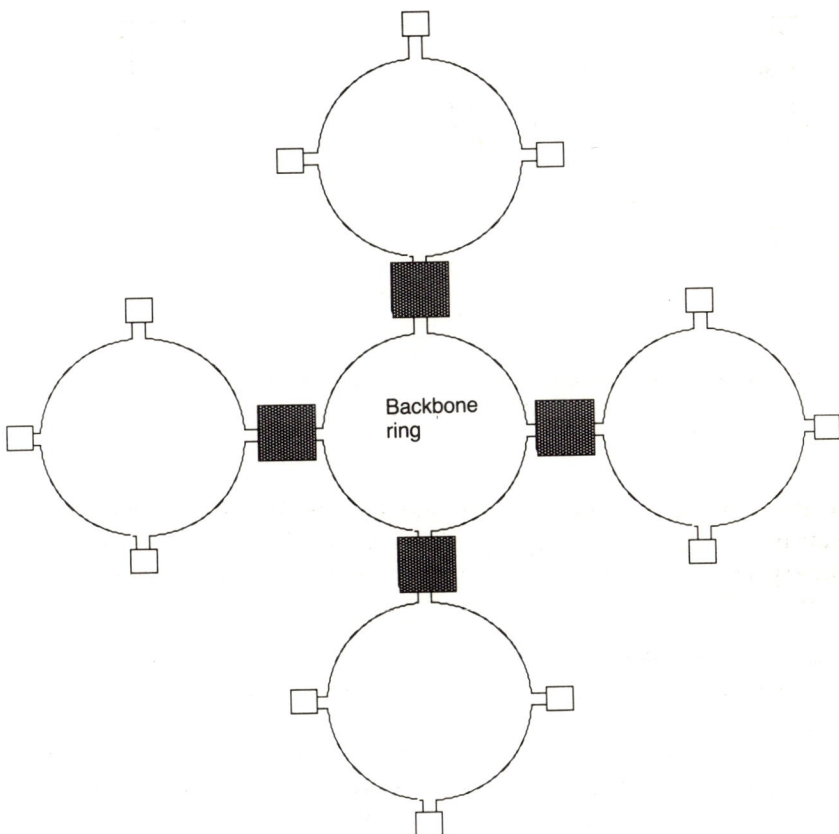

Figure 5.13   Multiple rings connected through a backbone ring

Packet/token format   A normal data packet, as illustrated in figure 5.14, is made up of a chunk of data surrounded by a physical header and trailer. This section of data will contain user information together with data-link information used by higher level software.

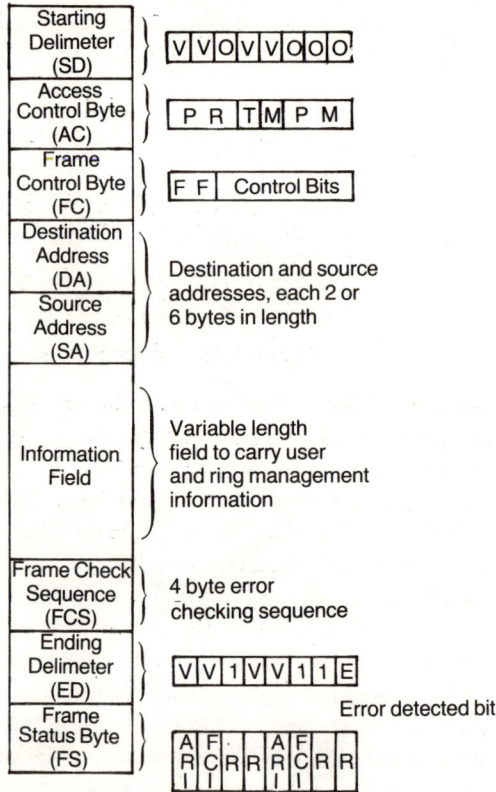

Figure 5.14   Token ring packet format

The physical header begins with an 8 bit *starting delimiter* (SD) that marks the start of a packet. Rather than being a discernible bit pattern, it is made up of violations in the Manchester encoding scheme (see Appendix A). This is followed by two bytes used for access and control purposes called the access control (AC) byte and the frame control (FC) byte respectively. The functionality of each of the bits in these control bytes will be discussed below. The final two entries consist of the destination (DA) and source (SA) node addresses. The length of these addresses is fixed at either 2 or 6 bytes depending on the way the network is configured.

The data field is followed by a physical trailer which includes a frame checking sequence (FCS) for error detection, an ending delimiter (ED) and an 8 bit frame status (FS) byte. Certain bits in the access control and frame status bytes can be changed by any node on the ring as the packet passes through them and thus are not included in the calculation of the frame checking sequence. Thus the FCS refers only to the frame control byte, the source and destination addresses, and the information field.

When data is not being transmitted, a token is circulated. This is a subset of the above consisting of the starting delimiter, followed by the access control byte and terminated by an ending delimiter.

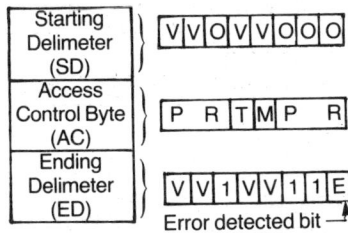

Starting Delimeter (SD)	}	V V O V V O O O
Access Control Byte (AC)	}	P R T M P R
Ending Delimeter (ED)	}	V V 1 V V 1 1 E

Error detected bit →

Figure 5.15   Token format

1 **The access control field**   This byte is made up of groups of bit indicators related to token management in the network.

2 **Priority mode and reservation (PM and PR) bits**   Bits 0 to 2 and 5 to 7 are used for gaining priority access to the ring. They represent a number from 0 to 7 allowing 8 priority modes to be specified. The process involved in priority access to the ring is described below.

3 **The token (T) bit**   This single bit indicator notifies the receiving station whether the arriving packet is in use for the transfer of data or alternatively represents a token. If the bit is a 1, then the packet is in use, if 0 then the receiving station can seize it (i.e. change it to a 1) and begin transmitting a waiting packet.

4 **The monitor count (MC)**   One of the problems inherent in the token-passing access method is that of a continuously circulating packet. This bit is used to eliminate the problem. A monitoring station (one per ring) inspects and sets this bit as the packet passes through it. If the bit is already set, the packet must have gone around the ring more than once. This is an error condition, and the monitor station will remove the packet and reissue the token.

5 **The frame control field**   This byte is made up of groups of indicators that provide information about the content of the frame.

6 **Frame format**   Bits 0 to 1 of the frame control byte describe what type of data is contained in the packet. A bit pattern of 01 denotes user data, while 00 is used to indicate media access control information. This type of packet is used to transfer ring management information between nodes.

   Control bits These bits have a variety of control functions depending on the type of frame specified in the FF bits.

7 **Destination and source addresses**   In the IEEE 802.5 standard, addresses on the ring are either 2 or 6 bytes in length. If multiple rings are involved,

and the number of nodes is potentially very large, the larger type is the most sensible choice. The format of these addresses will be discussed below.

Token access   When a node has data to transmit, it will wait until it receives the next packet or token. It will recognize the starting delimiter, and retransmit it (after a one bit delay) on its output. As the access control byte passes through, it will inspect the token bit. If this is a zero, indicating that a free token is being processed, the station will seize it by transmitting a one bit in this position. The remainder of the access control byte is repeated and then the node will transmit appropriate frame control bytes, addresses and information fields. A frame check sequence that has been calculated while transmitting the above follows. Finally, the sequence is terminated by an ending delimiter and frame status byte.

In order to simplify error control, only one token or packet is allowed on the ring at any given time. If the station has not received the start of its packet back by the time it has finished transmitting it, it will transmit an idle sequence (contiguous 0s) until it arrives. After it has finished transmitting, it releases a new token. In the case where a token is being transmitted, the start of the token must not be received before the station has finished transmitting it. For this reason, there must be at least 24 bits of delay incorporated into the ring. If there are not this number of stations present, the monitor station will use a buffer to provide a suitable delay.

In theory, there is no maximum length specified for the amount of data that may be transferred before releasing a token. In practice, however, each node on the ring is equipped with a *token holding timer*. This is started once a free token has been seized and transmission must be completed before the token holding time elapses. This protects against any node monopolizing the ring.

The above description covers token ring operation at its simplest level. Further complications will be discussed in the sections on priority access, synchronous traffic and error detection/recovery.

Priority access   The access control byte in the packet header contains two groups of three bits that are used to offer nodes an 8 level prioritized access to the ring. This is useful for ensuring that urgent messages will get through at high speed, and is central to the system's ability to handle synchronous traffic.

At any given time, traffic on the network is operating at a particular priority level from 0 to 7. This is indicated by the Priority Mode (PM) bits in the access control byte for the packet or token. Nodes on the network may also be assigned priority levels. This means that a node can seize a token if the station priority is greater than or equal to the current ring traffic priority.

A node wishing priority access may place its level in the priority reservation (PR) fields of a full packet as it passes through. This constitutes a request to raise the ring traffic priority to its own (higher) level.

The packet will, in due course, return to the currently transmitting node, where the reservation request will be noted. This node must then remember the current priority, and issue a token at the higher priority. This newly generated high priority token will travel around the ring, giving each node at that priority and higher an opportunity to transmit, before returning to the issuing node. At this stage, it will be seized, and replaced with a token of the original priority.

An example of this process in action is shown in figure 5.16 (see pages 68–69). The sequence begins with A transmitting to D using a data packet at priority 0. Node C has data to transmit, so it sets the priority reservation bits in the packet to its own station priority of 3. When the packet returns to A, it must release a priority 3 token. This may only be seized by nodes at this or a higher priority i.e. C, E and F. The next node of this set that the token reaches is C. It seizes the token and begins to transmit a packet. At this stage, node E could, if it wanted to, raise the ring priority to 7, thus ensuring that it would get the token next time around. Assuming it does not, C will complete the transmission and the priority 3 token will travel around the ring allowing E and F an opportunity to transmit in turn, before returning to its originating node A. When A sees the priority 3 token, it seizes it and releases a token of the original priority, i.e. 0.

Using this scheme, the number of nodes that are allowed to seize the token can be dynamically changed from every node (priority 0) up to a very small set of crucial nodes (priority 7) on an incremental basis. This is the basis of the ability of token rings to carry synchronous traffic.

Synchronous traffic   The ability to carry synchronous traffic such as digitized voice is an important one. It can be achieved by assigning one of the nodes on the ring to be *synchronous bandwidth manager*. This node is equipped with an independent timing mechanism which causes it to raise the ring priority after a given time interval. The effect is that each node operating at the synchronous priority level will be guaranteed the opportunity to transmit a packet within the specified time limit. The length of the timing interval must be calculated precisely to cope with the number of synchronous nodes connected to the network. If this figure is excessive, the performance for conventional asynchronous traffic will be adversely affected.

Network addressing and routing   The source and destination addresses used are usually 6 bytes in length. This is broken up into a 2 byte ring number, followed by a 4 byte ring element address. This allows nodes to be easily moved from one ring to another in systems consisting of multiple inter-connected rings.

Certain bits in the address give information on the meaning assigned to the remaining bits. As with Ethernet, if the address consists of all 1s, it is a *broadcast address*, to be received by all stations on all rings in the system. The first bit in the address is called the *individual/group bit*. If this indicates an individual, the packet will be routed through the necessary bridges until it reaches the appropriate ring. There, it will be picked up by the node specified

a) A transmitting to D, C requests priority 3

b) A releases a priority 3 token

c) C seizes this and transmits to B

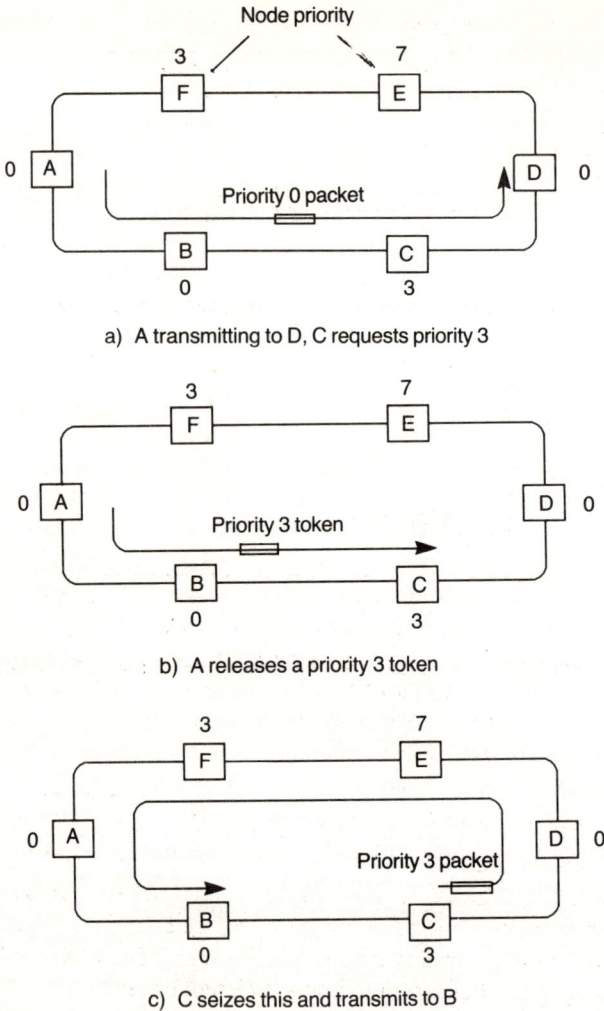

Figure 5.16   Priority access using token passing

by the ring element address. There are special values for the ring number to indicate *this ring* and *all rings*.

If the I/G bit indicates that it is a group address, this means that the packet should be picked up by nodes belonging to the group specified in the ring element address section. There are two ways to specify group addresses and in order to distinguish between these, bit 1 of the ring element address indicates whether the meaning is *bit combination mode* or *bit significant mode*. In the former case, the remaining 31 bits of this field specify the group number involved.

The bit significant mode on the other hand is a little more complicated. Here each of the remaining bits represents a specific group address. If it is set,

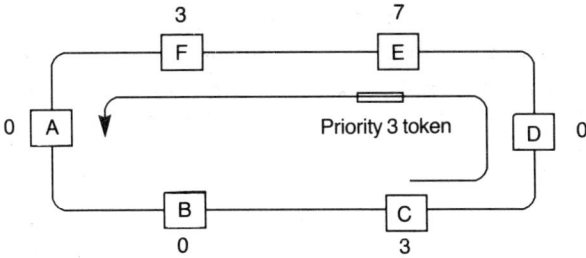

d) C has completed transmission. It releases a priority 3 token.

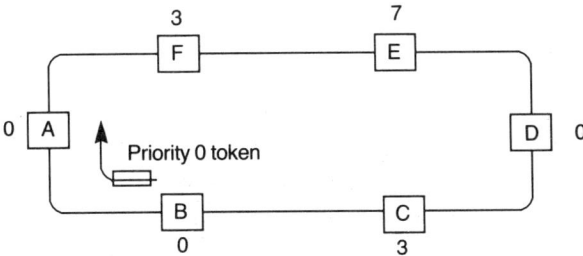

e) A sees priority 3 token. Captures it and releases a token of the original priority (0).

Fig. 5.16—*continued*

then the packet should be picked up by all groups. For example, if the last 4 bits of the address are 1011, then the packet should be received by all nodes belonging to groups numbered 0001, 0010 and 1000, but not 0100, since the bit representing that group is clear. In this way, a packet can be selectively sent to any combination of the 31 groups numbered in this fashion.

The standard-making authorities were aware of the possibility in the future of many rings, belonging to many different organizations, being interconnected. This would involve a need for globally unique addresses. The second bit in the ring number field is called the *universal/local* bit and it indicates if the addresses are locally administered, or conform to some global standard.

Error detection/recovery One of the major strengths of the star-ring token passing system lies in its ability to detect errors and either recover from them or quickly localize the fault so that it can be isolated. This is due in large measure to the presence on the ring of *monitor stations*. These are stations which watch activity on the ring and carry out maintenance functions during normal and abnormal ring operation.

There are two types of monitor station: *active monitors* and *standby monitors*. Only one node will be the active monitor at any given time. All other nodes will be in standby monitor mode, ready to take over in case a failure in the network renders the active monitor inoperable.

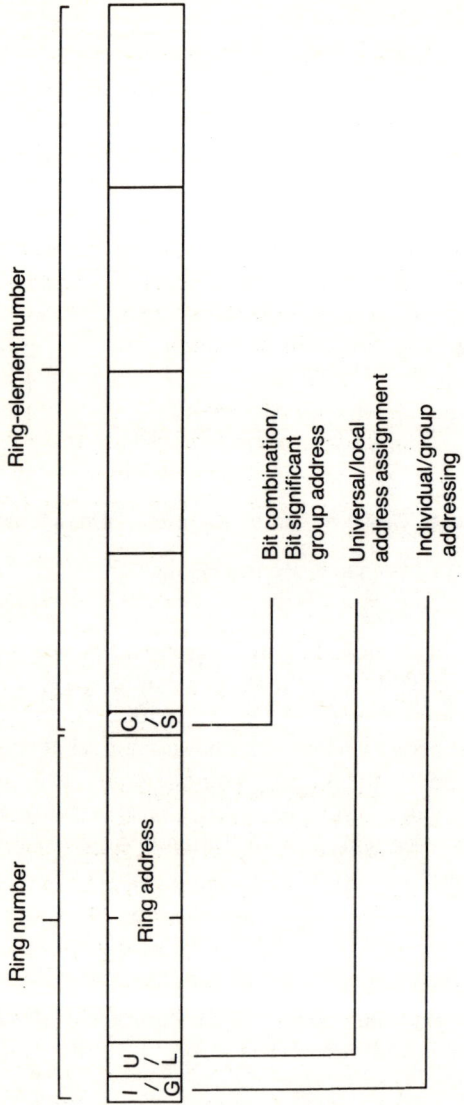

Figure 5.17 Token ring source/destination format

The monitor station is able to cope with common error conditions that may arise on the ring. These include: loss of the token; a persistently circulating packet and multiple tokens on the ring. How these are handled is described below.

1 **Lost token** This condition occurs naturally when power is first applied to stations on the ring. It may also occur due to electrical noise damaging the access control byte. The active monitor is equipped with a timer which is set to a time greater than that taken by the maximum length packet (as determined by the token holding timer) to traverse the ring. If this expires, the ring is purged of all residual signals and a new token issued.

2 **Persistently circulating packet** If a station transmits a packet and some failure causes it not to be removed, the packet will continue around the ring. On its passage around, the monitor bit is set by the active monitor. If a packet is received with the monitor bit already set, it is removed and a new token issued.

3 **Multiple tokens circulating** This can occur when noise creates a token in addition to the one already circulating. In this case, two stations may begin to transmit at the same time. A transmitting station will see this as its packet coming back with the wrong source address, in which case it will not reissue a token. After this, it is handled in the same way as a lost token.

4 **Packet acknowledgement** When a packet sent by a station returns, it can be assumed that it completed its passage around the ring. It cannot be assumed, however, that it was correctly received by the intended station. The frame status byte at the end of the packet contains two bits: the *address recognized indicator* (ARI) and the *frame copied indicator* (FCI). The former informs the station that the destination station exists on the ring and that it recognized its address in the packet. The latter tells if the node decided to receive it or not. Because this byte is not included in the frame checking sequence, these bits are duplicated to provide some means of checking.

5 **Transmission errors** As a packet travels through each station on the ring, the frame checking sequence will be recomputed. If this does not match the FCS in the packet, then a transmission error has occurred in the preceding ring segment. The station which notices this will set the *error detected indicator* in the frame status byte. Stations downstream of this will ignore the error. If a station notices more than a given number of packet errors, it will inform the active monitor of the unreliable network segment.

6 **Network disruption** When the cable used in a ring network is severed, a one way connection path still exists between the nodes. One can take advantage of this fact in finding the location of the fault. If a station, by monitoring its input, detects a serious problem (e.g. broken cable, jabbering station etc.), it will employ a technique called *beaconing*. This involves repeatedly transmitting a network management packet addressed to all stations which contains the address of the node immediately upstream of it

(i.e. the defective node/segment). In this way, the location of the fault can
be determined and isolated.

Notice that for this process to work, each station must know the address
of its immediate upstream neighbor. This is accomplished by a technique
known as a roll call which will be described below.

7 **Roll calling**   At periodic intervals, the active monitor on the ring will
transmit a network management frame addressed to all stations known as
an *active monitor present* (AMP) frame. Its downstream neighbor will
receive this, take note of the source address, set the ARI and FCI bits, and
repeat it. Other stations will take no action. The downstream node will then
issue another special frame called a *standby monitor present* (SMP) frame.
The effect of this is similar to an AMP frame, and serves to give its address
to its neighbor. This process continues, until the active monitor gets an
unreceived SMP frame. At this stage, the cycle is complete. This sequence
of actions is initiated by the active monitor at periodic intervals such that it
does not consume more than 1% of the available bandwidth.

5.4.2.3   Summary of network operation
The IBM star-ring network operates on the principle of token passing to give a
highly reliable system with facilities for detecting and localizing faults that
may occur on the network. The addressing scheme allows for multiple rings to
be interconnected and nodes on them to be addressed individually, or by a
variety of grouping mechanisms. A priority scheme provides eight levels
of access allowing scope for real time and synchronous data transfer.

5.4.2.4   Network components
At the time of writing, IBM's published network connections relate mainly to
their personal computer range of machines. The hardware components of this
set-up consist of an adapter card to fit into each machine, a cabling system and
a wiring concentrator box called the 8288 multistation access unit. This
provides a means of connecting nodes in the star-ring topology.

The network adapter card   The card supplied for personal computer network access is responsible for both the electrical interface to the cable as well
as coping with all the details of the token ring access protocol. Fortunately,
most of the above details have been implemented in hardware. The card
consists of transmitter/receiver circuitry and diagnostic routines and provides
an interface through which it can be accessed from the machine.

The 8288 multistation access unit   The star-ring topology of the network is
implemented by attaching up to eight nodes to a multistation access unit
(MAU). These MAUs consist of a box with ten sockets, eight of which are
used to attach PCs and a ring in and ring out connection. Each of the eight
sockets can be linked into the ring by a relay which is powered by the attaching
node. When the node is powered on, it carries out a self-diagnostic check and
if this completes satisfactorily, it will send a pulse to the relay to include itself

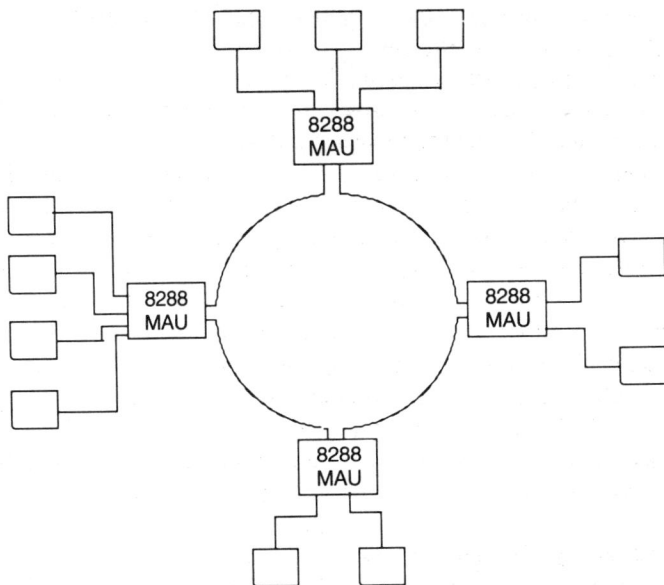

Figure 5.18   A PC-based token ring network

in the ring. In case of fault detection, a node can also detach itself from the ring in the same manner.

The MAU forms the concentration points referred to in previous sections and several of these can be interconnected using the ring in and ring out connection points. Figure 5.18 shows a typical ring configuration. Distance limitations will depend on the type of cable used.

5.5   WANGNET

The previous network examples in this chapter have been covered in some detail. They provide an illustraton of how the various topologies and network access methods can be used. *Wangnet* [17, 18] is mentioned here because it is a good example of how the capabilities of the broadband transmission technique can be effectively used to provide a range of services on a single cable. Accordingly, the discussion that follows will center on the cable used and the range of services that are offered (i.e. the physical layer).

5.5.1   WangNet cabling

In selecting a cabling strategy for its network, Wang borrowed heavily from the technology used in the cable television industry. The basic medium is CATV broadband cable. This is a low cost option with cheap and adaptable connector technology readily available. The topology used is a bus arrangement using two separate cables running in parallel.

The nodes attached to the network transmit on one of these (called the forward cable) and receive on the other. A translator unit repeats the signals from the forward to the reverse cable without doing any frequency shifting. The rationale behind this approach is that a much greater bandwidth is available for use than in the midsplit arrangement used in the IBM PC Network. Wang claim that the incremental cost of the extra cable is very small.

5.5.2 Bandwidth allocation

The massive bandwidth (up to 400 mHz) offered by the dual cable arrangement has been split up into a number of distinct bands each assigned to different purposes. Figure 5.19 shows how these are divided up. The first of these is *Wang band* used for general communication between Wang mainframe computers. *Peripheral band* connects such devices as printers, terminals etc. to the mainframes. Personal computer networks needing to share access to disks and printers will use the *PC service band* while other unusual applications such as point-to-point links and TV channels may use the *utility* and *interconnect* bands.

It can be seen that using a single cabling system, Wang has made provision for most foreseeable communication needs. The facilities offered by each of these bands will be discussed in more detail in the following sections.

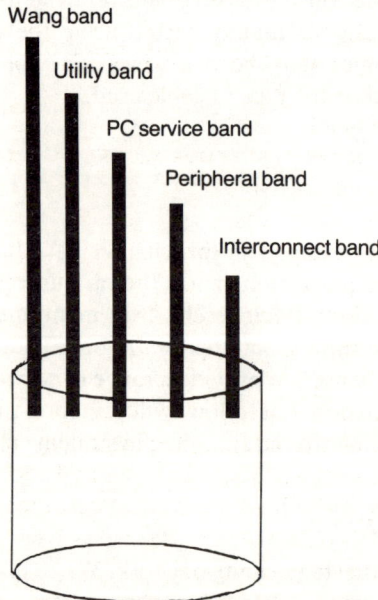

Figure 5.19   WangNet broadband cable usage

5.5.2.1   Wang band

This chunk of bandwidth is occupied by a 10 mbps CSMD/CD link. In many ways it is similar to broadband Ethernet in concept and work is in progress at the time of writing to change this to conform to the standards laid down in the IEEE 802.3 broadband CDMA/CD network standard. The intended use of this channel is for communication between Wang host computers in order to share peripherals and to swap messages and information.

5.5.2.2   Peripheral band

The conventional way of connecting peripherals to host computers made by either IBM or Wang is by using a coaxial cable between either the device and the machine in question, or to an intervening controller. Rather than having an extra cabling system to cater for this, Wang has allocated the peripheral band for this purpose. By using the appropriate interface boxes, this facility allows the connection of any conventional peripheral to its (IBM or Wang) host computer over the WangNet cable.

5.5.2.3   PC Service band

When an organization distributes low cost personal computers throughout its offices, a need arises to share resources such as disks, printers, databases etc. This would normally be achieved using a dedicated personal computer-based LAN. The PC service band consists of 4 distinct 2.5 mbps channels, each of which can accommodate a separate network.

The services available to users of this band can be provided by a separate product called the *local interconnect option*. The idea of providing it on the Wangnet cable is to achieve savings in cable (and cost) for those organizations that intend to use many of the other services offered by Wangnet.

5.5.2.4   Interconnect band

Many of today's intermachine communications needs are catered for by using modems to transmit and receive over telephone lines. This either involves using a switched line, where the user must dial a number to establish a connection, or by using a leased, dedicated line.

WangNet has made provision for this type of connection in its interconnect band. This band provides 48 channels for dedicated connections between devices. 32 of these operate at 9.6 kbps and 16 at the higher speed of 64 kbps. Devices using these channels will interface to the cable using fixed frequency modems set to operate on one of the channels.

In addition to the 48 fixed bands, the interconnect band also offers 256 switched 9.6 kbps connections. These are operated under the supervision of a device called a *data switch*. The devices interface to the cable via a *frequency agile modem*, that is a modem that has the ability to operate on any of the 256 channels, and can switch between them.

If one node wishes to connect to another, it 'dials' its number. The data switch is constantly polling the individual modems for connection requests. If the called modem is not busy, the switch will allocate a channel to the connection and inform both parties. The modems will switch to that channel and communication can then take place. Note that Wangnet imposes no restrictions on the type of communications that take place over the links. Accordingly, both parties must adhere to the same protocol conventions.

Wang is constantly extending the range of services offered to users of the network. The latest service offered, at the time of writing, is a single 6 mHz CSMA/CD channel in the interconnect band that can be used to provide asynchronous connections between CPUs and terminals/printers. This is a useful service for those institutions with computers demanding this type of access for peripherals.

5.5.2.5 Utility band

Since Wangnet is based on CATV cable, it makes sense to provide a facility for transmitting video signals over the network. The utility band provides seven 6 mHz standard TV channels for the connection of cameras, video monitors and television sets. This is useful in situations where security cameras are installed, or where training courses involving video aids are used.

5.5.3 WangNet summary

It can be seen from the above that Wangnet makes good use of the facilities provided by broadband transmission to provide a diverse range of services off the same cable. Conventional LAN objectives are met while at the same time coping with both the older type of point-to-point link and newer applications such as video. Not all of the available bandwidth has been allocated and can be used for new services as the technology becomes available. The more uses that can be found for the cable, the easier it is to justify the high cost of wiring entire buildings. This factor can make a significant impact on purchasing decisions in this area.

5.6 MICRONETS

A number of major LANs have been examined so far. They are typical examples of today's LAN technology. Within the range of LAN developments there is a subtype of network which we will term *micronets*. These differ somewhat from the examples already looked at in this chapter. This section explains what those differences are and examines a sample micronet.

One of the advantages of a LAN is that it allows a means whereby devices can be interconnected cheaply. The term 'cheap' is of course relative. An organization with 10 minicomputers each costing $50,000 would consider a LAN with a connection cost of $5000 per node cheap. The same LAN used to connect 10 microcomputers each costing $1500 would be termed expensive. Accordingly a class of local area networks has appeared specifically designed for the microcomputer area. These LANs are what we call micronets and they occupy the bottom end of the LAN spectrum. Two points in particular distinguish them from normal LANs:

- They are specifically designed for connecting to microcomputers, often only working with machines from the same manufacturer.
- They are very cheap and offer less functionality than the example networks covered earlier in the chapter.

Examples of such systems are QLNet for the Sinclair QL, EcoNet for the BBC micro and 'AppleBus' for Apple computers. The latter is the most sophisticated and we shall use this as an example system.

5.6.1 AppleBus

AppleBus [10] is the name given to Apple's local, or *work area network*.

The transmission medium is shielded twisted pair, with a bus topology. A maximum of *32* nodes can be connected to a single network and the cable must be less than *300 m* in length. The transmission speed is *230.4* kbps.

These figures obviously distinguish AppleBus from the examples previously looked at. In those, the number of nodes per network was measured in 100s, the cable length in kilometers and the transmission speed in megabits. The connection cost per node, in US$, for AppleBus is however measured in 10s as distinct from 100s for the 'full-blown LANs'.

At the data-link layer, the packet format used is similar to the Ethernet packet. There are preamble, address, type, data, frame check sequence and postamble fields. The data field can vary in size up to *600* bytes. Broadcasting is supported, but multicasting is not. (The frame format is actually the same as used in the HDLC/SDLC protocol.)

The basic access method is 'carrier sense multiple access' as described in Chapter 4. The version used on AppleBus is CSMA/CA, where CA stands for *collision avoidance*. In this protocol, collisions are allowed to occur but the access method strives to avoid them happening. As implemented on AppleBus, special control packets are exchanged between a transmitter and the intended destination before the actual data packet is sent. Collisions of these packets can occur but after a successful exchange of control packets the transmitter is guaranteed that all nodes will defer while it transmits its data packet. Obviously 'collision avoidance' does not make the best use of the available bandwidth but it is employed in AppleBus because the physical layer hardware cannot detect collisions.

Individual AppleBus networks can be interconnected and Apple provide a full range of software (AppleTalk) to allow users easy access to resources on the network.

AppleBus is cheap for a number of reasons which also affect its performance. The interface to the network is through the standard serial RS-422 port to a simple 'connector module' (see figure 5.20). This is the same port to which printers are connected. The network 'connector' and the cable are the only additional hardware requirements. The bulk of the data link layer is implemented in software. All this goes a long way to reduce the cost of the network; the price paid, of course, is in terms of performance.

Despite their limited performance capabilities compared with LANs, micronets do offer a good alternative to microcomputer users. The main advantages of connecting machines together are gained at a fraction of the cost of a LAN.

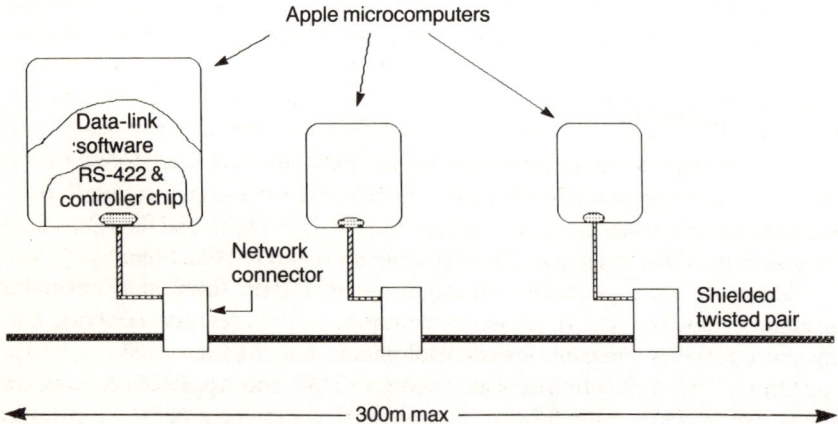

Figure 5.20   AppleBus work area network

5.7   PBX SYSTEMS

The goals of a LAN are to provide a means of interconnecting nodes via a high speed communications channel. Any node connected to the network should have the ability to rapidly establish a low error rate, high speed connection with any other. These criteria are met by the LANs that we have looked at in this chapter. Advances in the technology used in telephone private branch exchanges (PBX) are allowing similar services to be provided to users via the conventional telephone network. Extensions to the signaling and switching techniques involved in conventional telephone systems have allowed high bandwidth connections to be established rapidly between nodes on the network. The dependence of the system on a centralized switch excludes PBXs from our definition of a LAN. Despite this, users requiring LAN-type services may be attracted to the PBX-based solution to their needs.

Practically every office of any size is equipped with a PBX and an extensive cable network connecting it to every desk .This means that the only change necessary is to upgrade the facilities provided by the PBX. Over the years, systems of this nature have proved to be highly reliable, and some are designed with redundancy and fault tolerance in mind. Voice traffic is already fully supported and the capability to carry data efficiently has been evolving slowly over recent years. Coupled with a public telephone network that is also progressing in this direction, the PBX option may prove very attractive to users.

5.7.1 Techniques used

The telephone network is evolving, under the direction of international standardization bodies, towards a standard known as the *integrated services digital network* (ISDN) [19]. In this standard, the interface between a node and the network consists of two types of communication channels: *B channels* and *D channels*. The first of these is used to carry normal user information e.g. voice, data, video etc. Given the historical association with voice traffic, this channel's capacity is 64 kbps – the standard bandwidth used for digitized voice. For applications where this is not sufficient, further B channels may be provided to give extra capacity in increments of 64 kbps. The D channel on the other hand is either 16 kbps or 64 kbps and is used for signaling purposes. It is also able to carry data in the form of packets. In the simplest systems, the D channel may be used for setting up calls, providing directory services etc. It may also serve as a means of transmitting data.

One of the major differences between LANs and the ISDN is that the latter will be implemented as part of the public network, as well as on the user's premises. This means that the same interface is used for transmission of voice and data, regardless of the physical separation of the communicating parties.

5.7.2 PBX summary

The above description of PBX technology has been included here for the sake of completeness. Although the techniques differ from those used in LANs, the services provided by the system significantly overlap. That is, they provide LAN-type connectivity and reliability of transmission at a very low cost. The speed of operation is low if considered on a perstation basis. If, however, the throughput of the central switch is looked at, it is comparable to, or in excess of, those used in LANs.

5.8 REFERENCES

1   *The Ethernet – a local network Version 1.0*, Digital, Intel, Xerox, September 1980.
2   Digital: *Introduction to Local Area Networks*, Digital Equipment Corporation, 1982 (order no. EB-22714-18).
3   Metcalfe, R. and Boggs, D.: 'Ethernet: Distributed packet switching for local computer networks', *Communications of the ACM*, **19**, no. 7, pp. 395–403, 1976.

4   Squibb, N.: 'Broadband versus Baseband – the choice for Ethernet', *DECUser*, pp. 43–45, August 1985.
5   Shoch, J.F., Dalal, D.D., Redell, R.C. and Crane, R.C.: 'The Ethernet' in *Local Area Networks: An Advanced Course*, eds D. Hutchinson, J. Moriani and D. Shepherd, Springer Verlag Lecture Notes in Computer Science, No. 184, Berlin: Springer Verlag, 1985.
6   Needham, R.M. and Herbert, A.J.: *The Cambridge Distributed Computing System*, Addison Wesley International Computer Science Series, London: Addison Wesley, 1982.
7   Banerjee, R. and Shepherd, W.D.: 'The Cambridge Ring' in *Local Area Networks: An Advanced Course*, eds D. Hutchinson, J. Moriani and D. Shepherd, Springer Verlag Lecture Notes in Computer Science, No. 184, Berlin: Springer Verlag, 1985.
8   Wilkes, M.V. and Wheeler, D.J.: 'The Cambridge digital communications ring', *Proceedings of the Local Area Communications Network Symposium*, Mitre Corporation, Boston, May 1979.
9   Blair, G.S.: 'A performance study of the Cambridge Ring', *Computer Networks*, **6**, no. 1, January 1982.
10   *Inside AppleTalk*, Apple Computer Corporation, 1985.
11   Strole, N.C.: 'A local communications network based on interconnected token access rings: a tutorial', *IBM Journal of Research and Development*, **27**, no. 5, pp. 481–496, September 1983.
12   Dixon, R.C., Strole, N.C. and Markov, J.D.: 'A token ring network for local data communications', *IBM Systems Journal*, **22**, nos. 1 and 2, pp. 47–62, 1983.
13   Dixon, R.C.: 'Ring network topology for local data communications', *Proceedings of COMPCON*, Fall, 1982, Washington DC, pp. 591–605, 1982.
14   Markov, J.D. and Strole, N.C.: 'Token ring local area networks – a perspective', *Proceedings of COMPCON*, Fall, 1982, pp. 606–614, 1982.
15   Marsden, B.W.: *Communication Network Protocols*, Bromley: Chartwell-Bratt, 1985.
16   Bacanello, P.: 'Spinning the token ring', *PC Magazine*, **3**, no. 8, pp. 46–48, August 1986.
17   Wang Corporation: *Wang on Networking*, Wang Corporation, 1985 (order no. 711-0514).
18   Cheong, V.E. and Hirscheim, R.A.: *Local Area Networks: Issues, Products and Developments*, Chichester: John Wiley and Sons, 1983.
19   Roca, R.T.: 'ISDN Architecture', *A. T. & T. Technical Journal*, **65**, no. 1, pp. 4–17, January/February 1986.
20   Tanenbaum, A.S.: *Computer Networks*, Englewood Cliffs: Prentice Hall Inc., 1981.
21   Clancy, G.J.: 'A Status report on the IEEE Project 802: Local Network Standard' in *Local Networks and Distributed Office Systems*, pp. 453–489, Northwood: Online Publications, 1981.

CHAPTER SIX

COMMUNICATION PROTOCOLS

The previous chapters have described the essential components of LANs and a number of example systems have been looked at in some detail. These systems vary in the way they operate but all offer the same basic function, i.e. the ability to transfer 'chunks' of data between nodes. A LAN places no 'meaning' or interpretation on the data transferred over it, the network simply provides a means of communication.

The functionality provided by a LAN (or indeed any network) is not an end in itself. The ability to exchange information has to be used in a constructive way. Successfully exploiting this potential is not easy. A lot of additional support has to be offered to the end user to transform a LAN into a useful tool.

As an example of the problems that are encountered in using a LAN, consider the task of transferring a file between two nodes. At first glance this might seem straightforward. A process, or job, on the node at which the file resides, called the *source*, reads the file and transmits it over the LAN. At the receiving node, the *destination*, a process accepts the incoming data and writes it to a local file (see figure 6.1).

On closer inspection a number of difficulties appear which must be overcome to implement a useful file transfer system:

- In the vast majority of cases, a file is too large to fit into a single packet. This means that it will have to be broken up into smaller units to be sent over the network (see figure 6.1). Thus, apart from the actual contents of the file, additional information will have to be transmitted to indicate such things as the start of a file, end of file, size etc. The destination node must be able to distinguish between pure data packets and ones that contain control information.
- Once a packet is received it must be processed. The time taken to do this

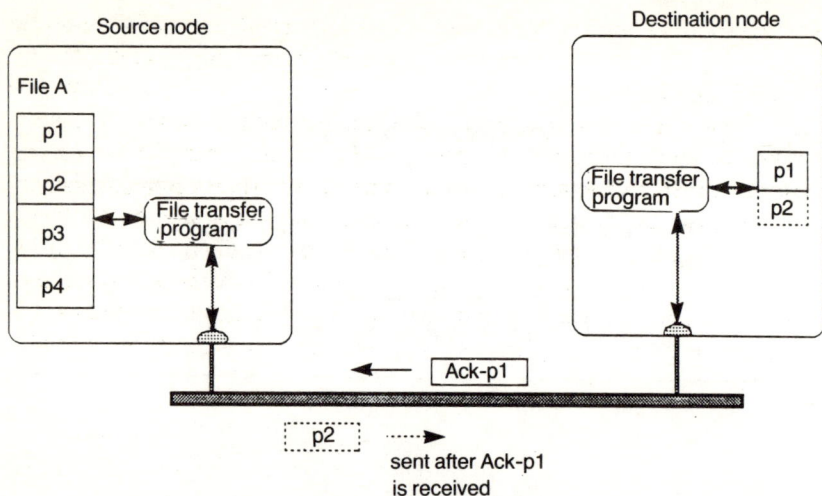

Figure 6.1   File transfer
Note: The file is broken up into a number of blocks. These are transmitted in turn. Each packet is acknowledged before the next one is sent. The file is reassembled from the incoming packets at the destination

can be significant. If the rate of processing received packets is slower than the rate at which they are arriving, the receiver will quickly run out of memory space in which to store them. This can easily happen, if for example, the transmitting node is a faster processor than the receiver or a node is receiving data from a number of sources at the same time.

One solution to this problem of controlling the rate of 'flow' of data is to have the source delay transmission of the next packet until it receives an explicit *acknowledgement packet* (ACK) from the destination. The 'ACK' indicates that the previous packet has been received *and* processed.

- No network is completely reliable, packets may get corrupted or 'lost' during transmission. This can happen if there is 'noise' on the communication medium or a malfunction in some component. Again explicit acknowledgements can be used to inform the source that a packet was received.

If the source receives an acknowledgement to a packet P, that it has sent, it is guaranteed that it was correctly received. If an 'ACK' is not received the situation is ambiguous. There are at least two possible reasons why this can occur:

- The destination is still waiting for the 'packet' from the source, i.e. an error occurred during the transmission of P. The correct action for the source to take is to retransmit P.
- The destination received the source packet but the 'acknowledgement' got lost, in this case the 'correct' action is for the source to send the next packet: $(P + 1)$.

Distinguishing between these cases is very important. Incorrect action by the source can result in a portion of the file being either duplicated or omitted completely.

- On a single LAN there is a direct connection between all nodes, i.e. once a packet is sent, there is only one possible path it can follow to the destination. In a wide area network, to which a LAN is often connected, this is not the case. In figure 6.2, for example, there are a number of *routes* a packet going from node *L* to node *J* can follow. Algorithms have to be developed to pick the *best* route between nodes. Deciding which route is best is not easy, as not all connections may operate at the same speed, nodes can become congested if there is too much traffic through them and links may fail.

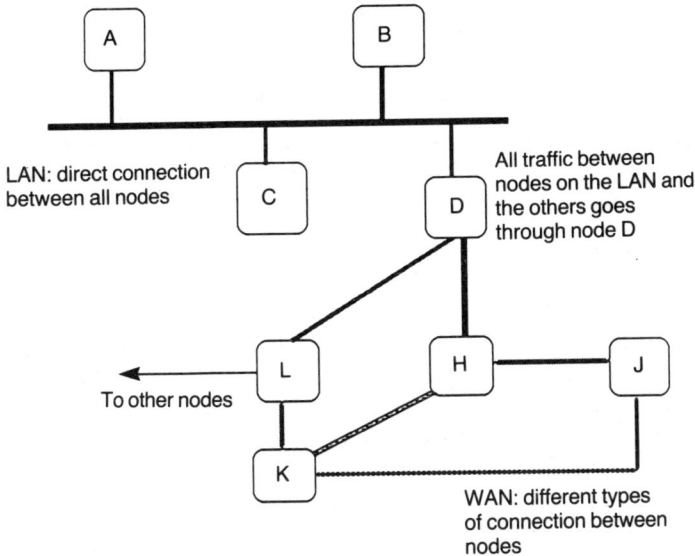

Figure 6.2   Routing
Note: There are three different possible routes between L and J:
L–D–H–J; L–K–H–J; L–K–J

- Other problems to be considered are:
  - transferring files between nodes that use different character codes or word lengths;
  - transferring files between nodes on different networks;
  - the nature of the interface presented to users of the file transfer system;
  - one or both of the nodes involved 'crashing' while the transfer is in progress.

From this very incomplete list it can be seen that communicating successfully over a network is a difficult task. Techniques to overcome these problems have been developed for wide area networks and these can be used as the basis for LAN solutions. There are, however, two important differences between LANs and WANs. LANs transmit data at a much faster rate than WANs and they are also more reliable than their wide area counterparts. These facts should be taken into account when applying wide area solutions to a local area environment.

6.1 LAYERED PROTOCOLS

Successful use of wide area networks has been based around the use of *layered protocols*. This section introduces the topic; a more complete description can be found in any book on WANs.

As seen in the last section, successful exploitation of the potential of a LAN requires that nodes involved in data transfer must agree to adopt the same conventions for exchanging information. In the file transfer example outlined, the transmitter and receiver agree such things as:

- the first packet sent contains the name of the file and its length;
- subsequent packets should not be sent until the previous one has been acknowledged.

This simple convention, or *protocol*, is not intended as a complete solution to the file transfer problem. Instead, it indicates the *manner* in which the problem can be tackled, i.e. the nodes involved exchange information according to some agreed protocol. Information includes not just the actual data but also control information. A different application, e.g. connecting a terminal to a processor over a network, requires a different protocol. This is, in fact, what happened in the area of WANs: different conventions or protocols were devised to suit the various types of application.

Central to the notion of protocols is the concept of *layering*. There are two reasons for this and they are examined in the next section. The first is to do with *functionality* and the second concerns *flexibility*.

6.1.1 Functionality of layers

As an example of a layered protocol, consider the way in which the components of a LAN can be logically broken up (see figure 6.3a).

At the lowest level, a LAN consists of a piece of cable and some circuitry to send electrical signals over it. The physical layer applies a transmission technique to the cable to implement a *bit transmission* function. The data-link layer utilizes this to concentrate on solving the problems associated with packet formats and sharing the available bandwidth. Users of the data-link layer are then presented with a *packet transmission* function.

The important point here is that different problems are tackled at each layer, each in turn making a more useful service available to the one above it.

Higher levels: handle flow control, code conversion, etc

Packets

Interface

Data link layer: handles addressing, access method, etc

Data bits

Interface

Physical layer: Handles transmission techniques, etc

signals

Communication medium

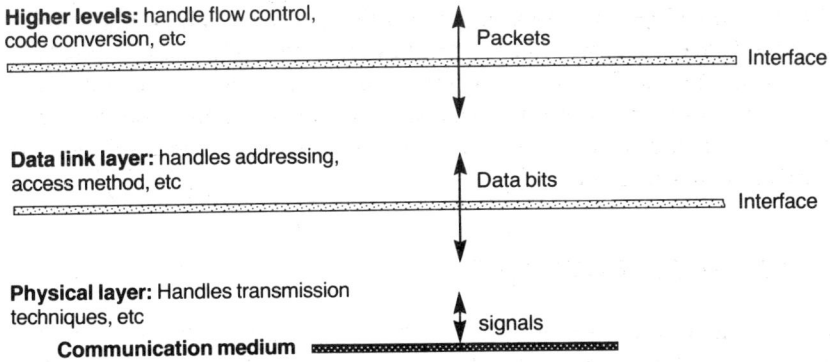

Figure 6.3a   The layered achitecture of a LAN

Note: Each layer is a self-contained unit. The only exchange of information between layers is through well-defined interfaces. The physical layer provides a 'bit' transmission function which is used in turn by the data link layer to implement a 'packet transmission' function

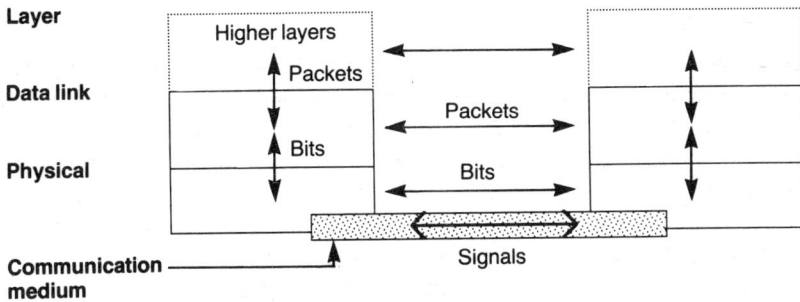

Layer

Higher layers

Packets

Data link

Packets

Bits

Physical

Bits

Signals

Communication medium

Figure 6.3b   Peer-to-peer communication

Note: Each layer logically communicates with its peer on remote nodes. Except for the electrical signals on the communication medium all information exchange is between layers on the same node

This notion of layering protocols can be extended upwards, e.g. there could be separate layers to handle flow control, character code conversion etc.

Figure 6.3b shows how information is actually exchanged in a layered architecture. From the logical viewpoint, corresponding layers on different nodes communicate with each other in what is known as *peer-to-peer* communication, i.e. the data-link layer on one node communicates with its peer, the data-link layer, on the other. In fact, with the exception of the physical layer, information is actually exchanged with adjacent layers on the same node.

6.1.2 Flexibility

Within this type of architecture the internals, or implementation details, on each layer are completely hidden from the others. Information passes between layers through well-defined interfaces, e.g. 'send a packet' or 'receive a bit'. If the interface, i.e. the functions, provided by a layer remain the same then its internal implementation can be changed without affecting the rest of the system. This fact offers designers and implementers of a set of layered protocols great flexibility. The internal algorithms of individual layers can be changed with no knock on effects to other levels.

Assuming that there is only one implementation of each layer on each node, then all nodes must use the same instance of a particular layer. If the data-link layer on one node changes from using CSMA/CD to say token-bus then the data-link layer on all nodes must also be changed, see figure 6.4. As long as the interlayer interface remains the same no other changes are required.

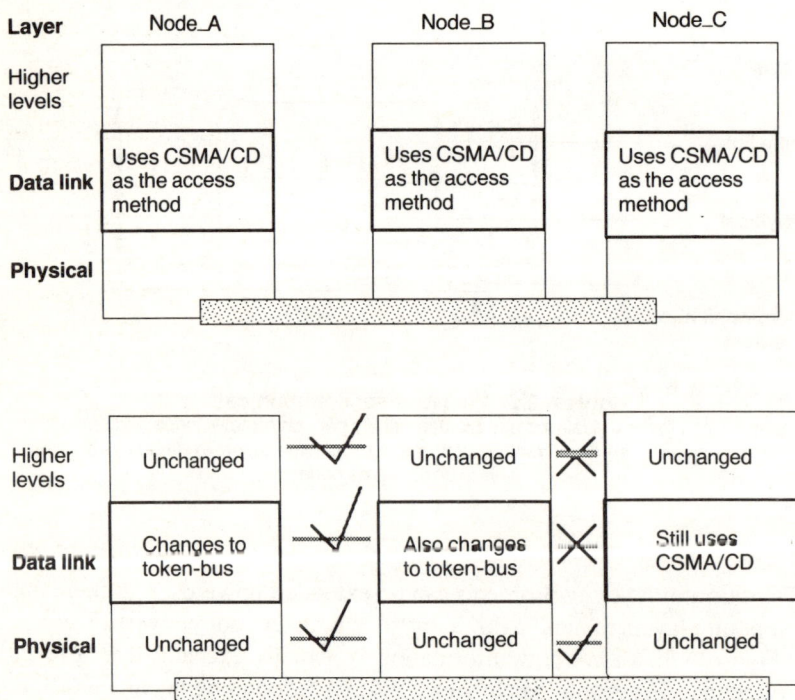

Figure 6.4   Advantages of a layered architecture

Note: Initially all layers on all nodes use the same protocols. The data link layer on nodes A and B is changed. All layers on A and B still communicate after the change. Node C is isolated because its data link layer did not change.
The layered architecture allows flexible changing of peer-to-peer protocols

6.1.3 Virtual circuits and datagrams

Peer-to-peer communication between layers takes two forms. The simplest case is where the layers exchange packets on a once off basis. Packets are not acknowledged and their delivery at the other side is not 100% guaranteed. An example of this type of communication is the data-link layer of Ethernet. It is known as a *datagram* facility.

The other type is known as a *virtual circuit*. In this case, all packets are guaranteed to arrive at their destination in the order they were sent. It is more costly, because both sides must exchange packets to set up the connection, all data packets are sequenced and acknowledged, and retransmissions are performed if necessary.

Virtual circuit type communication is also called 'connection oriented' to distinguish it from datagrams or 'connectionless' communication. There are many examples of each in the remainder of this chapter.

6.1.4 Standards

Once the benefits of using a layered architecture were realized, the main computer manufacturers began to focus their attention on this area. By correctly applying this new technique, they could easily provide a means of transferring information between their individual products. They realized that the adoption of a set of rules and techniques for communication, to which the entire company would adhere, could benefit them in a number of ways. They would be able to provide new services to their customers by combining existing products. The existence of a standardized means of communication would reduce product development costs and allow them to achieve great economies of scale.

From the user's point of view, products from a single vendor could now communicate with each other without too great a cost penalty. New equipment could be interfaced to the machines by adopting the vendor's communication standards and the gate was opened to other manufacturers to produce cheap alternatives to the large company's products.

This trend towards layered architecture culminated with the release in 1974 of IBM's proprietary *Systems Network Architecture* (SNA). The following year, Digital Equipment Corporation responded with the release of *Digital's Network Architecture* (DNA). The details of these two proprietary network standards will be discussed in the following pages.

The establishment by each major computing manufacturer of its own layered network architecture led to a situation where communication was easy between a single vendor's products, but not across multiple manufacturers' machines. The smaller companies were faced with producing products that conformed to the standards of their larger competitors which were subject to change at any time. These obstacles hindered the advancement of communications technology and led to a demand within the industry for a manufacturer-independent standard for layered network architectures.

In 1978, the *International Standards Organization* (ISO) released a document describing a network architecture for connecting dissimilar devices. The document applied to 'open' systems, i.e. systems that are open to each other by virtue of their use of the same communications standards. Accordingly, it was known as the reference model for *Open Systems Inter-connection*. In 1984, a revised version of this document became an international standard: ISO/IS/7498.

In its formative stages, the OSI reference model was heavily influenced by existing layered architecture like SNA and DNA. Since its standardization, however, both companies have expressed a desire to change their systems gradually to conform more closely to the new standard. The detail involved in the OSI model will be covered later in the chapter, but, in essence, it specified a 7-layer architecture for communications between devices, users and processes. The model deliberately does not specify implementation details. In recent years, however, the detail of each of the layers has been progressively filled out in such a way that a variety of network technologies and applications areas can be catered for.

Regarding LANs, the relevant sections of the OSI reference model have been developed further by the Institute of Electrical and Electronic Engineers (IEEE). This organization set up a group of standardization committees collectively known as *Project 802*. The brief of this group was to specify the lower layers of the OSI reference model in the context of local area networks. Their published standards cover the cabling, transmission techniques and topologies required for CSMA/CD, token ring and token bus networks, as well as their relationship to higher layers in the OSI model.

The subject of the OSI and IEEE 802 standards will be discussed after examining the proprietary network architectures in more detail.

6.2 PROPRIETARY NETWORK ARCHITECTURES

6.2.1 Systems Network Architecture

The IBM corporation have been manufacturing computer equipment since the 1950s. Over the years, they found that communication between different machines in their product line was being achieved on an *ad hoc* basis. What was needed was a standardized architecture, for company-wide use, that designers of equipment could conform to. In 1974, they announced such an architecture and called it the Systems Network Architecture (SNA) [5].

The philosophy behind the design of SNA is more easily understood if one considers the computing environment in the mid-1970s. At that time, the expensive resources in a computer system were the processing and storage facilities. This led to a great emphasis on host-based processing. The first networks were simple tree topology systems with a host connected to terminals via controllers. Terminals were low-intelligence, inexpensive devices and needed a direct connection to either a controller, or the host itself. The bulk of the traffic on the network was between the terminals and the host, and all communication was carried out under the supervision of a software system known as the *system services control point* residing in the host.

Over the years, the computing environment changed in emphasis. The relative cost of processing power and storage dropped. This led to many intelligent nodes with considerable resources of their own being attached to the network. It also led to a demand for nodes to communicate directly with each other without involving any centralized supervisor. IBM's response to this trend has been to embark on a policy of distributing the services provided by the SSCP out to the individual nodes on the network. How this is actually implemented will be discussed later in this chapter.

The layered architecture In designing an architecture, IBM recognized that the communication process could be broken down into two subsections. The first of these is concerned with network issues and the mechanism used to transfer the data between nodes. The second section concentrates on issues that are general to any two communicating systems independent of the network used and is covered by a concept called the *logical unit* (LU). Users of the network, i.e. individuals and programs, communicate with a logical unit in their node. This LU will establish communication with another LU at the destination node, and thus information can be transferred between the two. This process is illustrated in figure 6.5 and is the same irrespective of whether a LAN or a WAN is used.

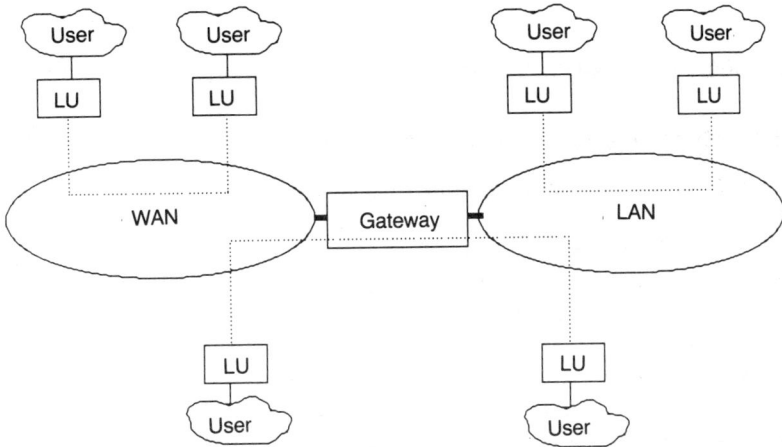

Figure 6.5 LU to LU communication. Details of data transmission etc. are handled by the lower layers

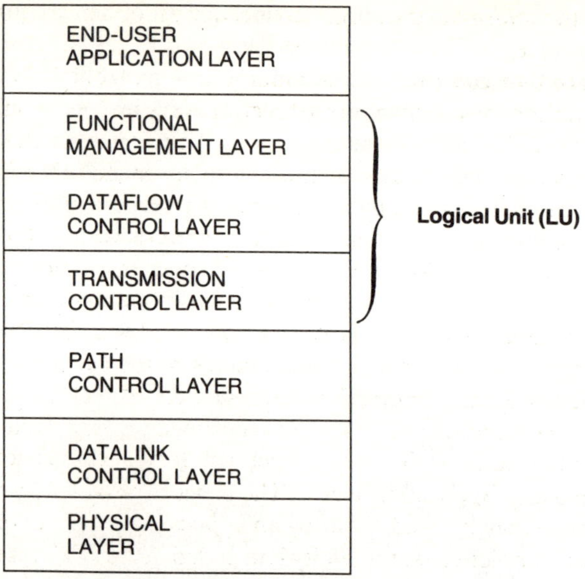

| END-USER APPLICATION LAYER |
| FUNCTIONAL MANAGEMENT LAYER |
| DATAFLOW CONTROL LAYER |
| TRANSMISSION CONTROL LAYER |
| PATH CONTROL LAYER |
| DATALINK CONTROL LAYER |
| PHYSICAL LAYER |

Logical Unit (LU)

Figure 6.6   Layered SNA

The two groups mentioned above are further split into layers (see figure 6.6) to allow the system to cope with different requirements. The functionality provided by each of these layers will be discussed in the following sections.

1 **Physical layer services**   This layer is made up of the physical medium used for transmission. Its specification would include a description of the topology, transmission technique and cabling involved in the underlying network.

2 **Data link control**   The transfer of data between two nodes is the responsibility of the data link control layer. Error detection and recovery facilities provide an almost error-free link facility to higher layers.

3 **Path control**   The two main functions of this layer are: network flow control and message routing. When two nodes are communicating, situations can arise where the sender can produce messages faster than the receiver can handle them. The network flow control functions prevent this situation from becoming a problem.

   The second function, message routing, ensures that packets are routed to the correct logical unit. This can be quite a complex task, as there may be several LUs in the same node, or, in WANs, packets may have to be routed through several intermediate nodes before arriving at their final destination.

4 **Transmission control**   This layer is the first layer that is part of the LU and thus is less concerned with how the data is transported from node to node. The functions of this layer include the setting up of communication sessions between two LUs and matching their data-handling capacity. If encryption

of the information transmitted is required for security purposes, it is done at
this level.

5 **Data flow control**   The communication path between two LUs may allow
simultaneous traffic in both directions (duplex), or in only one direction at a
time (half-duplex). This process is called *interaction management* and is the
responsibility of the data flow control layer. Another function of this layer
is the grouping of data into logical entities. Examples of this would include
grouping lines of a print out into a page or various file update operations
into a transaction, etc. This segmentation of the data is important in
deciding what should be retransmitted in the event of failure.

6 **Functional management data services**   This layer ensures that the character sets used in the communication session are understood by both
parties. Data compression/expansion can also be carried out at this level.
When the information stream is destined for an output device e.g. printer,
screen etc., certain device-dependent format conversions may be done.

7 **End-user application layer**   The services provided by the layers described
above may be used either by an application program or directly by a user.
For completeness, this entity is included in the model as the end-user layer.

SNA Summary   SNA was defined to provide a model for all types of
computer-based communication. It is broadly divided into high level layers
called a logical unit, and low layers which take care of transmission details. In
the LAN context, the lower layers will be filled in by the topologies,
transmission methods, and access methods of the LAN in use.

The logical unit section will be the consumers of these services. In cases
where a LAN is used, this section of the architecture will need to be oriented
more towards the peer-to-peer type of communication than was the case in
older networks. Finally, the transmission speed of a LAN will allow a whole
new range of application services to be contemplated.

6.2.2   Digital's Network Architecture

Digital's Network Architecture [6, 7], fulfills the same role as IBM's SNA. It
is the architecture around which all their communication products have been
designed since 1976. Like SNA it has evolved and grown considerably since it
was first announced. It is a layered architecture, as shown in figure 6.7. This
section briefly describes the various layers and compares their functionality to
their SNA counterparts, where applicable.

1 **The physical layer**   As with SNA, this layer defines the physical characteristics of the transmission medium used.

2 **The data link layer**   Again, as in SNA, this layer defines a link between
nodes.

3 **The routing layer**   The functions of this layer are similar to the 'path
control' layer in SNA; packets are routed through the network and some
flow control is carried out.

```
┌─────────────────────────┬─────┐
│                         │     │
│         User            │ 7a  │ ┐
│                         │     │ │
├·························· ┤     │ │
│ Network                 │     │ │
│ management              │ 7b  │ │
│ (Interacts with all     │     │ ├ These layers provide
│ layers below)           │     │ │  user services
│                         │     │ │
├─────────────────────────┤     │ │
│     Network             │     │ │
│     application         │  6  │ ┘
│                         │     │
├─────────────────────────┼─────┤
│                         │     │
│     Session             │  5  │
│     control             │     │
│                         │     │
├─────────────────────────┼─────┤
│                         │     │
│     End-to-end          │  4  │
│     communication       │     │
│                         │     │
├─────────────────────────┼─────┤
│                         │     │
│     Routing             │  3  │
│                         │     │
├─────────────────────────┼─────┤
│                         │     │
│     Data link           │  2  │
│                         │     │
├─────────────────────────┼─────┤
│                         │     │
│     Physical            │  1  │
│     link                │     │
│                         │     │
└─────────────────────────┴─────┘
```

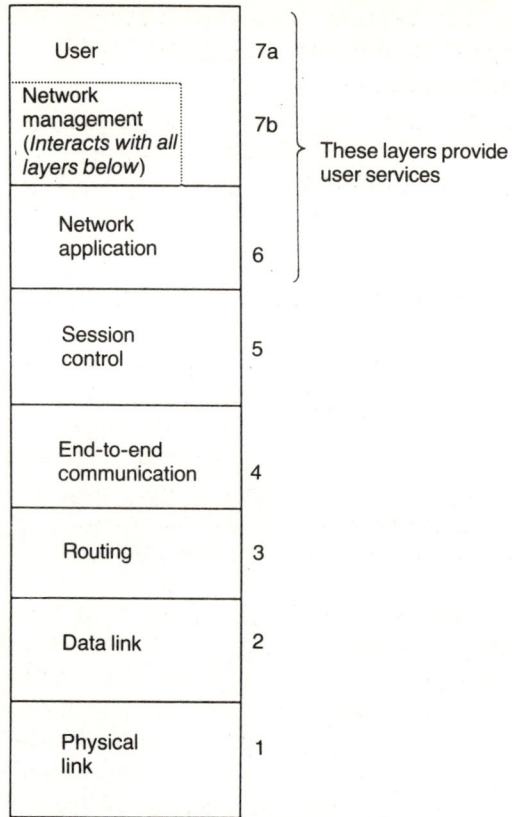

Figure 6.7   Digital's Network Architecture

4 **The end-to-end communication layer** This roughly corresponds to Transmission Control in SNA. It handles the setting up and management of *logical links*. A logical link is a reliable end-to-end error-free connection. Messages sent over a link are guaranteed to reach the corresponding layer on the remote node, in spite of any routing, message fragmentation, flow control problems etc.

5 **The session control layer** This layer is the interface between operating system processes and the logical links provided by the previous layer. It manages logical links on behalf of processes.

6 **The network application layer** This, and the remaining layers, are concerned with applications that use the network. Commonly-used network functions such as file transfer and remote terminal access are implemented here. These are then available to the end users.

7 **The network management and user layers** End users of the network are divided into two groups: ordinary users and those who actually control the operation of the network. Normal users avail themselves of the services provided by application and session control layers.

The network management layer is special in that it controls the operation of the network. To do this it must interface to all of the layers below it.

Note that the correspondence between the functions of the layers in DNA and SNA breaks down after level 4. It should be pointed out that it is possible for users to bypass some layers if the function provided by them is not required.

6.3 NONPROPRIETARY STANDARDS

SNA and DNA were chosen as a representative sample of company-specific standards. Other manufacturers, for example Wang with their *Wang Systems Networking* (WSN), offer their own variations on the theme.

While this approach worked very well for the larger manufacturers, the benefits were not so obvious for users and smaller manufacturers. Company-specific architectures, by their very nature, were subject to change at the whim of their sponsor. Technical information could be difficult to obtain, and users could find themselves 'locked-in' to a particular company's products. Thus, in 1978, when the *International Standards Organization* (ISO) began to work on a manufacturer-independent network architecture, they were well supported.

Initially, the work centered on providing WAN type facilities, but as technology changed, the scope of the ISO standard was widened to accommodate LANs and other devices. The architecture was a 7-layer architecture along the lines of SNA and DNA, and was known as the *Reference Model for Open Systems Interconnection* (RM/OSI, or, simply OSI) [3].

As regards LANs, this international standardization was continued by the IEEE's Project 802. This project will be described in detail later in the chapter.

6.3.1 Open systems interconnection (OSI)

Two types of system are defined for connection to networks conforming to OSI: *open end systems* and *open relay systems*. The majority of stations on the network will be of the first type, and will contain all 7 layers of the architecture. The function of relay stations is to couple dissimilar networks, and accordingly, they only contain the lower 3 layers.

Since OSI is intended to be a standard used by a wide variety of different manufacturers, the layered architecture is specified very precisely. The functionality of a given layer n is defined as that which bridges the gap between the service to be provided to layer $n + 1$, and that provided by layer $n - 1$. A set of primitives known as *service elements* are used to express the service provided by a layer. Its internal functionality is very rigorously defined. In this way, ambiguity is avoided. The standards allow nodes of

Open End system	Open Relay system	Open End system
Application		Application
Presentation		Presentation
Session		Session
Transport		Transport
Network	Network	Network
Datalink	Datalink	Datalink
Physical	Physical	Physical
Medium		

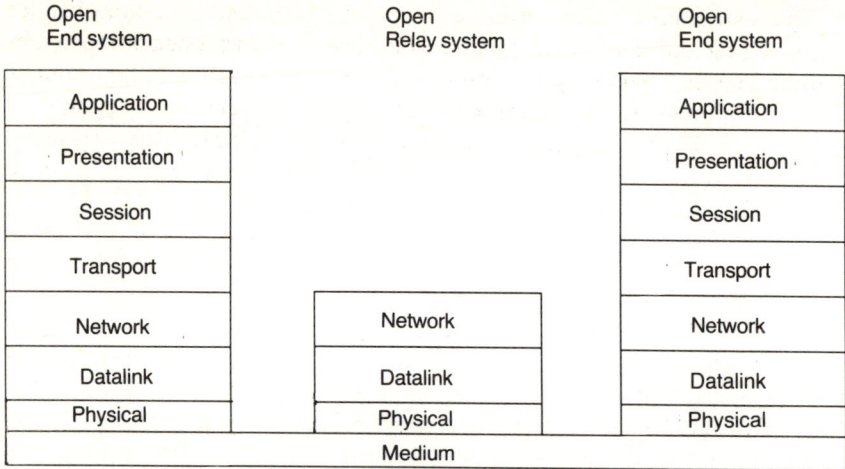

Figure 6.8   Open systems interconnection (OSI)

differing capabilities to be used by specifying different classes of service, all of which need not be available in a specific implementation.

A brief description of the functionality of the layers is given below.

1 **The physical layer**   As with its counterparts in SNA and DNA, this layer is concerned with the electrical and mechanical requirements of communication between systems.

2 **The data-link layer**   This layer frames the data and allows shared access to the services provided by the physical layer. Errors in transmission are detected, and where possible, recovered from. Typically, when the physical connection is a LAN, the link between communicating data-link layers will be connectionless, and thus only error detection will be supported.

3 **The network layer**   The purpose of this layer is to provide the ability to link all open networks together into a single global network. The network layer will be responsible for routing data between networks and, in the process, converting between connectionless and connection-oriented communications. Each of the connected networks may have different constraints on the maximum packet size that can be handled. Thus, this layer must be able to perform segmentation and reassembly of messages.

4 **The transport layer**   The lower three layers of the OSI architecture are, broadly speaking, concerned with details of the underlying network. From the transport layer upwards, the layers are only concerned with end-to-end communication.

The main function of the transport layer is to match the connection requirements of the session layer with those provided by the network layer. In doing this, it seeks to optimize the cost of communication e.g. by multiplexing several transport connections onto a single network connection. Additional error recovery features are also provided.

5 **The session layer** This layer, as its name suggests, is responsible for managing the communication sessions between two open systems. Its functions correspond quite closely with those of SNA's data flow control layer. It manages half-duplex or full-duplex connections by means of passing a token giving permission to transmit. It also provides a means of setting synchronization points in the communication, e.g. for a page boundary in text, or a transaction in a file update.

As with other layers in the OSI model, there are a number of levels of service available giving different combinations of the above, not all of which need be implemented.

6 **The presentation layer** When discussing SNA, we saw that the functional management data services layer did translation between different character codes and limited device-dependent formatting. The OSI presentation layer performs a similar task, but it is expressed in a much more general way.

The manner in which a node stores data types (e.g. characters, integers etc) is called its *concrete syntax*. This may vary considerably between machines from different manufacturers. The way around this is for each node to translate between its concrete syntax and an agreed-upon *concrete transfer syntax* for communication purposes. This translation is carried out at the presentation layer.

7 **The application layer** This layer, as in SNA and DNA, is concerned with the application using the communications service. It may consist of an interface through which a user program accesses the services, or it may be an indivisible part of an application process.

The services available to an application program are divided into subsets of service elements. The most commonly used subset of these is called the *common application service elements* (CASE). For particular applications, these primitives are supplemented by *specific application service elements* (SASE). Examples of these SASEs currently under development are: file transfer, virtual terminal; job transfer/manipulation. As the technology matures, one can expect many of these to be developed to cope with new applications.

The OSI model is now firmly established and will provide a framework in which communications products will work for the foreseeable future. One can expect that the lower layers (data-link and physical) will be subject to constant change, as developing technology (e.g. fiberoptics) allows faster and more reliable data transfer. The application layer should also be quite active, as new applications using LANs/MANs/WANs are developed. The intervening layers deal with generalized communication requirements and should be more stable.

The scope of the OSI model covers communicating nodes of all types, on any kind of network. As this book is concerned with local networks, we will now discuss how those layers relevant to the type of network (i.e. data-link and physical) have been standardized in the LAN area by the IEEE.

6.3.2   IEEE Project 802

In February, 1980, the IEEE created a standards committee, formally known as Project 802, to develop standards for local and metropolitan area networks. This latter type of network refers to systems which cover a reasonably large area such as a city and have transmission speeds and error rates that lie somewhere between those of LANs and WANs.

One of the major objectives of the committee was to work within the scope of the OSI reference model. Accordingly, they identified the lower two layers (data-link and physical) as those relevant to LANs. They then proceeded to develop a set of functions associated with these layers and their interface to the OSI network layer.

One of the first things to be done was to develop a LAN reference model corresponding to these two lower layers of the OSI/RM. This is shown in figure 6.9 and varies from the OSI version only in its division of the data-link layer into two sublayers: *logical link control* (LLC) and *media access control* (MAC). The former is concerned with providing a data-link service to the higher layers while the latter concentrates on providing shared access to the physical layer of the network.

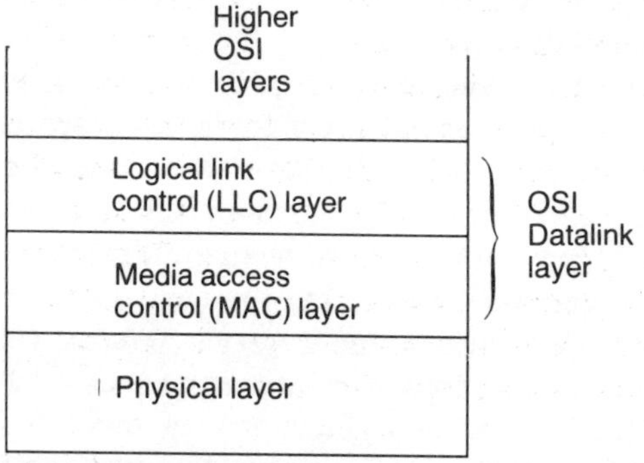

Higher
OSI
layers

Logical link
control (LLC) layer   OSI
                                        Datalink
Media access   layer
control (MAC) layer

Physical layer

Figure 6.9   IEEE LAN reference model

Having segmented the task to be performed, the committee split into 6 working groups, and two associated technical advisory groups (TAG). A series of documents was produced, the most significant of which are described below. The names of these divisions, and their purposes are as follows.

1 **802.1**   This group produced an overview of the work of the project and defined the LAN reference model. They also concern themselves with such issues as addressing formats, network management and interworking.
2 **802.2**   This described the logical link control services and primitives to be used in all IEEE-specified LANs.
3 **802.3**   MAC and physical layers for a CSMA/CD-based bus network.
4 **802.4**   The same as 802.3 but for a token-passing bus.

5 **802.5**   The same as 802.3 but for a baseband token-passing ring.
6 **802.6**   Specifications for a metropolitan area network.
7 **802.7**   This broadband TAG advised the other working groups on issues relating to broadband transmission.
8 **802.8**   The fiberoptics TAG explored ways in which the developing technology of fiber optics could contribute to the work of the other groups.

IEEE 802.2 Logical link control (LLC)   This working group provided a specification of a common interface to be used to communicate between higher level software and a variety of (IEEE-specified) physical layers and access methods. A number of different classes of service, designated 'Type 1 to 3', are provided. The first of these is a basic, connectionless service consisting of two primitives: one to transmit data to a given address, and another that indicates its arrival to higher layers. It is possible to specify the priority of access if this facility is available in the underlying network (e.g. in the token-ring network). This 'datagram' type of service will be that typically used in the LAN context.

The *Type 2* service is connection-oriented, and thus contains primitives for connection set up, termination, reset, flow control and, of course, connection-oriented data transfer. This more sophisticated service is likely to be used where the LAN forms only one segment of the physical connection between the nodes. This may occur if a node on a WAN is communicating with a partner connected to a LAN. Since the error rates on WANs are much higher than on LANs, extra reliability features must be used.

A third type of service – *Type 3*, which was added at a later stage – provides an acknowledged connectionless service. The acknowledgement enhances the reliability without incurring the overhead of the full connection-oriented service. One application area where this service is likely to be used is in factory automation and real-time control systems.

IEEE 802.3 CSMA/CD   The individuals on the IEEE working groups are drawn from industry and academia. Accordingly, the standards produced will reflect developments in the marketplace. In the case of 802.3, the work is largely based on Ethernet, as described in the previous chapter. The same access method is used with extensions to the choice of physical layers and minor changes to the packet format.

The physical layer is now specified by a list of three important parameters: the transmission speed in mbps, whether baseband or broadband transmission is used, and the segment length in hundreds of meters. Thus, standard Ethernet cable is now known as *10 Base 5*, the broadband variant is called *10 Broad 36*, and a low cost version, formerly known as *Cheapernet*, is now referred to as *10 Base 2*. The point-to-point fiberoptic interrepeater link has also been specified in the documents from this working group. At the data-link level, the Ethernet packet format has been updated to conform to IEEE conventions.

IEEE 802.4 Token passing bus   This document describes a network using
the token bus access method, again running on a variety of physical layers.
Broadband or baseband transmission can be used on coaxial cable, and a
number of different transmission speeds are allowed (1, 5, 10 and 20 mbps).
The packet format is closest to that used in the token-passing ring system
described in the previous chapter, except that a preamble is used for station
synchronization.

The access method specification is complex, and contains procedures to
initialize the logical ring, add or delete stations etc. The specifications from
this working group have been adopted in the factory automation standard
MAP which is described in detail in Chapter 11.

IEEE 802.5 Token-passing ring   The working group producing the 802.5
specification has a large IBM representation, and the IBM token ring network
is compatible with the documents produced. For a detailed description, the
reader is referred to the previous chapter.

IEEE 802.6 Metropolitan area network   At the time of writing, this working
group is defining the requirements for a metropolitan area network. Initially,
the work has concentrated on using existing CATV-based technology, but is
now examining the option of a 50 or 12 mbps-fiberoptic slotted ring with the
ability to carry voice and data.

Summary of IEEE Project 802   This project set out to develop standards to
cover the LAN/MAN area, under the umbrella of the OSI reference model.
The end result was a series of documents describing systems closely aligned
with products already on the market. All of these diverse LAN systems can
now be used through a single LLC layer, ridding higher level software of
concerns relating to the transport of data over the medium.

The results of the project have gained widespread acceptance, with
Ethernet moving towards 802.3 compatibility, the IBM token ring network
using 802.5 guidelines, and the acceptance of 802.4 as the basis for the
Manufacturing Automation Protocol. The way has also been paved for semi-
conductor manufacturers to develop chipsets to implement these low level
functions in hardware.

6.3.3   Cambridge Ring-related standards

Of the main example networks covered in the previous chapter the
Cambridge Ring is the one that has failed to gain widespread acceptance. The
'empty slot' approach has not been adopted by any of the major manufacturers and it has not been included in the 802 standard. Thus it is unlikely to
become a much-used technology on a worldwide basis.

Within the UK, the Cambridge Ring has been more successful, several
products have been developed around it and it has been standardized by the

'Joint Network Team', a UK networks standard body. This standard is known as the *Cambridge Ring 82* (CR-82), or Orange Book, and it differs somewhat from the original Cambridge design. As well as describing the operation of the ring, it covers higher level protocols. In all, four layers and the interface primitive operations between them are defined. These are termed the *R, P, V* and *N* layers.

- The *R*, or ring, layer defines the minipacket format etc., and is effectively the data-link layer.
  The minipacket format differs slightly from the original Cambridge one. Broadcasting is not supported and a destination address of 0 is illegal. There is an additional 2 bit type field included after the data field. Its purpose is similar to the type field in an Ethernet packet, in that it is for the use of higher level protocols. This extra field brings the entire minipacket length up to 40 bits.
- The *P*, or packet, layer is a network layer protocol that is similar to the 'packet protocol' used in Cambridge described earlier.
- The *V*, or virtual circuit, layer defines a reliable virtual circuit service between nodes. The Cambridge system defined two protocols at this level: the 'byte stream' and the 'single shot'. The former is a virtual circuit protocol and the latter a 'datagram' one. *CR-82* does not cater for datagrams.
- The *N*, or network layer. In the UK academic community the 'Coloured Book' standards are a set of high level network protocols that cater for such things as network mail, file transfer etc. The lowest layer of the set is the 'network independent transport service' layer. The N layer is an implementation of this on top of the V layer.

Within the protocol, allowances are made for different implementations that include or omit some services (e.g. some implementations allow broadcasting).

6.4 LAYERED ARCHITECTURE IMPLEMENTATIONS

In the above sections, we have described two company-specific layered architectures: SNA and DNA, and also the effort going on to establish non-proprietary standards in this area. A description of a layered architecture only gives the framework that software/hardware developers work within. In this section, we will examine some specific implementations of elements of these architectures in software and hardware products that are currently on the market. Firstly we will take a look at the higher level software involved in the two IBM LANs described in Chapter 5, and then go on to look at the DECnet implementation of DNA. Throughout the discussion, reference will be made to specific applications e.g. file servers etc. For a detailed explanation of these concepts, the reader is referred to the second part of this book.

6.4.1   IBM LAN software

The networking situation in IBM's product line is complex. Firstly, they are supporting a large installed base of products that communicate using SNA over WAN-type networks or isolated point-to-point links. In the personal computer area, the IBM PC has been touted as having an 'open' architecture, and thus should have the ability to communicate with a wide variety of machines. Because of this, IBM is committed to supporting two layered architectures, i.e. OSI and SNA. This is further complicated in that they currently have two LAN products: the PC Network and the Token Ring Network.

The main purpose of the PC Network is for communication between their personal computers only, while the Token Ring is designed to be used by their complete product line. The former was the first product to be released, and the main interface for applications programs was known as the *network basic input output subsystem* (NETBIOS). This provides support for the OSI-like layers up to and including the transport layer. Running on top of this interface are a number of applications providing the remainder of the layered architecture.

When the token ring network was released, the user was given the option of choosing the NETBIOS interface or an alternative conforming to SNA. In the former case, use could be made of existing NETBIOS-conforming applications, while in the latter, the machine would become part of an SNA network using applications already available on the mainframe and mini-computer families.

6.4.1.1   The PC Network

The lower level details of the IBM PC Network are covered in the previous chapter. The adapter card implements broadband transmission of the physical layer, and the CSMA/CD of the data-link layer. This card also contains a substantial amount of software in ROM which implements higher level functions and is called the NETBIOS. The functions implemented roughly correspond to those of the OSI network, transport and session layers.

Communication is established with another node on the network by specifying its *name*. The software in the adapter can have up to 16 of these names (e.g. SERVER1, BILL, GATEWAY5 etc.) associated with itself, each of which has been added to the table by an application program running in that node.

NETBIOS offers both datagram (connectionless) and virtual circuit (connection-oriented) communication between nodes. When using the datagram facility, messages of up to 512 bytes in length can be sent to a named user; a group name, where it will be received by all nodes with that group name; or a broadcast datagram that will be picked up by all nodes. No acknowledgement is given, and successful message transfer cannot be relied upon.

The virtual circuit facility (called session services) allows the setting-up of up to 32 simultaneous, full-duplex sessions with other nodes. Reliable data transfer of messages of up to 64K bytes in length can be achieved. More than one session can be established between the same two names.

The PC Network program   The session level interface provided by NETBIOS is available for use by user-written programs. In most cases, however, an IBM-supplied program called the *PC Network program* will provide further layered architecture support. The combination of this program and the machine's operating system provides the presentation and (part of) the application layer.

The functions provided are mainly based on resource sharing. Any machine on the network equipped with a large disk can become a file server machine. Access to the file server is transparent to the users of the service. The directories on the server appear as extra disk drives attached locally to the machine. Because the operating system on the IBM PC was designed for the single user, the protection modes that could be used with files have been extended. For example, files may be opened in shared or exclusive modes. The ability to lock records in a file was another necessary extension.

The PC Network program also allows printer sharing. In this case, a machine with a locally attached printer sets itself up as a print server. This gives it the capability to store a print queue of up to 100 files. As with the file server, this capability is transparent to the client nodes. They use the same print commands as normal, and the redirection is managed by the local copy of the PC Network program.

All interaction between the file/printer servers and their clients is carried out using the *server/redirector protocol*. The basic construct of this protocol is called the server message block (SMB) and it gives the nodes a predefined format in which to send commands (e.g. send file, receive file), control information and data.

The final service provided by the PC Network is electronic mail. Messages can be composed at any node on the network, and addressed to any named node. If that node is active on the network, the message will be received by it for subsequent display, filing etc.

6.4.1.2   The token ring network
In the case of the token ring, the adapter card provides less functionality and greater flexibility. The ROM and hardware on the card provide physical and data-link layers conforming to the IEEE 802.5 standard for token ring systems. In the PC itself, the user has the option of running either the *Token-Ring Network NETBIOS Program* or the *APPC Program Product*. The former gives a NETBIOS-type interface on top of the token-ring based

data-link and physical layers. This allows one to use any program that had been developed for the PC Network. The APPC program gives an SNA-type interface, described below.

Advanced program-to-program communications When describing the SNA layered architecture, we saw that communication across the network(s) could be modeled as application layers communicating with a logical unit (LU). This LU can establish sessions with LUs in other nodes using the facilities provided by the path control, data-link control and physical layers of SNA.

When two LUs are communicating, they must follow an agreed protocol. This protocol will cover such things as establishing a session, transferring data etc. The type of protocol used is specified as the 'type' of the LU. For example, *LU type 2* is used to communicate between a host machine or controller and a 3270 terminal. The type that we are concerned with here is *LU type 6*. This provides a generalized program-to-program communication facility and forms the basis for IBM's distributed computing efforts. At the time of writing, it has gone into release 2 and is known as *LU 6.2* or *Advanced Program-to-Program Communication* (APPC).

In order to see how LU 6 can be used as a tool to implement distributed operating systems, consider figure 6.10. In this example, program 1 running on node A uses certain resources, e.g. files, printers, disks etc. All resource requests are channeled through the LU local to that node. If the resources are local to the node A, the LU will schedule access to them. If program 1 wishes to use resources local to node B, it requests this from its LU in the normal way. The LU sets up a session with the controlling LU in node B, and the resource access is carried on over an SNA session. This remote access is transparent to the application program. Further details of how this is achieved are given in [10].

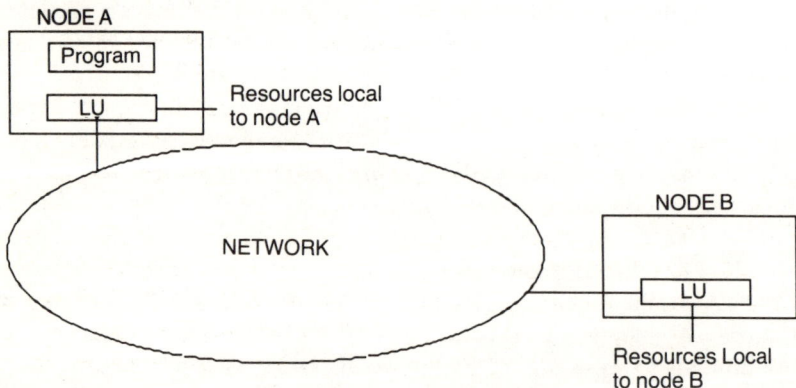

**Figure 6.10   Logical units as a mechanism for implementing distributed
operating systems**

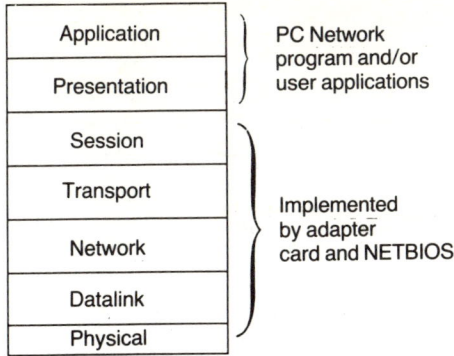

Layered architecture implementation in PC Network

Figure 6.11a   Layered architecture implementation in the PC Network

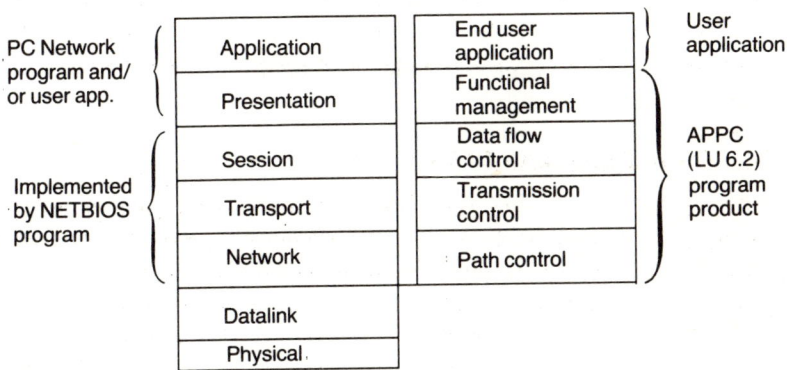

IEEE 802.5 Token Ring implemented by Adapter Card

Figure 6.11b   Layered architecture on the Token Ring

The APPC token-ring program provides the functionality of LU 6.2 built on top of the data-link and physical layers that are provided by the adapter card. This means that it implements the functional management, data flow control and transmission control layers of SNA. Figure 6.11 shows how the two layered architectures are implemented on the token-ring network.

It can be seen from the above that the use of a LAN to provide the capability to communicate between nodes does not restrict the choice of layered architecture that will be used at the higher levels. By implementing both SNA and OSI-like architectures, IBM has ensured that its existing base of network applications can be used with LANs, and that new OSI-based applications can be used in conjunction with their personal computers.

L.A.N.—H

6.4.2 DECnet

This is the name given to Digital's family of communication protocols and products. DECnet [7] is an implementation of DNA described earlier. Since it was announced in the mid-70s DNA has gone through a number of development phases. The original DECnet software ran only on PDP-11 machines and nodes had to be directly connected to one and other to be able to communicate. The facilities offered were limited, e.g. file transfer or direct program-to-program communication. Improvements in machine hardware, operating system software and communication technology have allowed DECnet to be expanded in a number of ways. This section examines some of the implementation details and facilities provided by DECnet.

6.4.2.1 The physical and data-link layers

Within any layered architecture specification there can be several different implementations of the same layer. The 'physical' and 'data-link' layers of DNA define the actual communication sub-system and DECnet offers 3 possible implementations of these layers.

- Digital data communications message protocol (DDCMP) which is for point-to-point or multidrop lines.
- A packet-switched data network based on the international X.25 standard.
- Ethernet is the latest addition to the DECnet range, and both baseband and broadband versions are available. The introduction of local area network technology makes DECnet suitable for office environments etc. This is reflected in some of the facilities available at the user level.

A large wide area DECnet configuration can consist of a number of Ethernets along with the more traditional point-to-point and X.25 links between nodes.

6.4.2.2 The routing layer

The 'routing layer' is responsible for routing messages between nodes. DECnet uses what is known as *adaptive routing*. As well as finding the 'shortest' path between two nodes, this layer responds to changes in the network topology by picking a new route between nodes. Topology changes can be due to the addition of new nodes or the failure, or removal, of existing links.

When an Ethernet is part of a wide area network, one node on the LAN is designated the *router server*. It is connected to both the Ethernet and the WAN. All messages from nodes on the LAN bound for ones outside it, and all messages from nodes outside bound for ones on the LAN, go through the router server. In redirects the message as appropriate.

The 'routing layer' uses a 16 bit address giving a maximum of 65536 nodes per network. Some flow control is also performed at this level and packets that have been in circulation for too long are discarded.

6.4.2.3 The end-to-end and session layers

As previously stated, the end-to-end communication layer provides reliable logical links. Corresponding layers on both of the nodes involved exchange messages to set up a link, and there can be many logical links over the same physical connection. Messages are fragmented into segments before being passed to the routing layer. It is the responsibility of the end-to-end layer to distinguish between segments arriving for different links. Reliability is achieved by assigning sequence numbers to all segments transmitted. The receiver acknowledges each segment in turn. When the transmitter receives the ACK to segment 'm' it knows that all segments with numbers less or equal to 'm' have been received. Flow control is achieved by the receiver specifying the number of segments it can buffer (B). The transmitter should never have more than B unacknowledged segments outstanding. The receiver can also send messages to stop or start the transmitter.

A link actually consists of two separate channels, both of which are full-duplex. One is used for normal data and the second for special messages which bypass the normal flow control, i.e. a message sent over the second channel can be received and acted upon before ones sent earlier on the normal channel. Stop/start and interrupt messages from higher layers are sent over the second channel.

The session layer manages logical links on behalf of operating system process. It creates and destroys links on behalf of local processes and requests from remote nodes to set up connections are passed on to it by the end-to-end layer.

When a process wishes to set up a link with a remote node it is not required to know its actual physical address. Instead, it uses a symbolic name, e.g. BIGVAX. The session layer maintains a data base of names and network addresses and accesses it to determine the actual address. The request to set up a link is then forwarded to the appropriate node. On receiving an incoming request from a remote node to set up a link with a local process, the session layer checks to see if the required process actually exists. In some cases it will create a new process to handle the request.

Validation is also performed at this level. Access to resources local to a node, e.g. a file, requires a valid 'user name' and 'password'. The session layer first validates the access information provided by the caller before passing the connection request to a higher level. The higher level is one of those covered in the next section.

6.4.2.4 Application and user layers

The top three layers of DNA implement end-user facilities and all rely heavily on the functions provided by the lower layers. The following is a brief overview of some of those functions.

One of the most obvious uses of a network is for file transfer. At the network application layer DECnet implements a *data access protocol* (DAP). This allows users access to files on remote nodes. Entire files may be transferred or *record level* access can be performed. Where possible, DAP works across different operating systems, which allow, for example, a user on a node running the VMS operating system to access files on a node running ULTRIX. As well as file access, remote file execution is supported, allowing a user on one node to execute a command file on another. Access to printers on remote nodes is also supported.

Various types of terminal-oriented communication are also possible. Probably the most useful of these functions is the ability to set up a logical connection between a terminal and a remote node. Once the connection has been made the user is then, in effect, logged into the remote node just as if the terminal was directly connected.

Finally it is possible to connect different types of network together. DECnet implements both DECnet/SNA and DECnet/X.25 gateways to achieve this. This allows user-written programs on DECnet to communicate with programs running on different networks. The gateway nodes implement both DECnet protocols and the protocols of the foreign network.

6.4.3   TCP/IP

The previous sections have discussed two important proprietary network architectures, SNA and DNA. This section focuses on one widely-used non-proprietary high level protocol *TCP/IP* [12]. These are actually two distinct but closely related protocols that were originally designed for arpanet, one of the first and most influential wide area networks. They have gained wide-spread popularity on LANs, in particular with the UNIX community. A brief overview of these protocols is given in the following sections. A more complete description is given in Appendix C.

6.4.3.1   IP

IP stands for *internet protocol* and is a network layer or level 3 protocol in ISO terms. Briefly, IP provides for the *unreliable* transmission of variable size datagrams between hosts on a network or on interconnected networks. Thus IP provides two primitive operations to higher levels: *send* and *receive* a datagram. IP is implemented on top of whatever facilities are provided by the underlying data-link layer.

The specification of IP is reasonably complex, the header alone consists of 14 fields, and a complete description will not be given here.

IP addresses are 32 bits, some of which are used to specify the network and the rest to address an individual host within a network. Datagrams can vary in size up to a maximum of 65535 bytes, thus a size field must be included in the header. An integral part of IP is the fragmenting of datagrams. This is required because the maximum size of a packet that can actually be transmitted will vary from network to network. IP handles the breaking up of datagrams into *fragments*, which are transmitted separately and reassembled at the destination.

No guarantees are made about the reliability of transmission of IP datagrams. Reliability must be provided at a higher level.

6.4.3.2 TCP
Transmission Control Protocol is an Arpanet, transport level (in ISO terms) protocol. It is usually used in conjunction with IP but it can be implemented on top of any network layer that provides a basic datagram facility.

TCP provides a reliable end-to-end duplex communication path between any two processes on an internetwork, i.e. a virtual circuit. Virtual circuits in TCP are known as *connections*. Reliability is achieved by sending acknowledgements for all data that is received. (TCP actually uses 'sequence numbers' that are piggybacked along with the data.)

TCP provides its users with the following primitive operations.

- Open or close a connection. (A process may be involved in a number of connections at the same time.)
- Send and Receive data over a connection. (The basic unit of data transfer is a *segment* which contains a variable number of data bytes. Segments are encapsulated in IP datagrams for transmission.)
- Return the status of a connection.
- Abort a connection. (Any data currently being sent is discarded.)

Closely associated with TCP/IP are three high level services: Mail; FTP for file transfer; and Telnet for terminal traffic.

6.5 LIGHTWEIGHT PROTOCOLS

Layered architecture and their protocols are very much a product of wide area network technology, where the data transmission rate is low and the error rate is high. On a local area network, much simpler, *lightweight protocols* can be used. In particular, many of the protocols developed for the LAN-based systems described in the second part of this book follow what is known as the *end-to-end argument* [11].

If a program on one node issues a request to read data from a remote file, the acknowledgement that it requires is the actual data. Low level acknowledgements sent by intermediary layers of software are of no concern to the program that issued the read request. If the actual data requested is not returned then the program will have to take some error handling action. The complexity of the layered communication protocols does not free the 'requester' from having to perform error handling, it merely decreases the frequency that errors occur – which should be low in a LAN environment.

The 'end to end argument' states that high level error checking is always required, but low level checking is needed only for efficiency. In a long haul network, the cost of implementing low level acknowledgements is justified because of the high error rates. The same argument does not hold for a LAN environment.

Errors do of course occur on LANs, e.g., the read request could get lost on its way to the remote node or the data could get lost on the way back. The user will deduce that an error has occurred if a reply has not arrived in a reasonable amount of time. The simplest action for the user to take is to repeat the original request. This requires that all 'operations' are *idempotent*.

An idempotent operation is one that has the same effect whether it was done once or many times. For example the operation

- { set P to 6 } can be repeated many times and the final value of P will be the same,
- but { add 1 to P } cannot be repeated without changing the final value of P.

In the case of file access, *absolute* rather than relative block numbers should be used. For example an idempotent 'read' operation is of the form *read block P*, while a nonidempotent version is *read the next block*.

When using lightweight protocols, all operations should be idempotent so that they can be repeated in the event of an error. It is possible that in the course of retransmitting a read request that the same data might actually be sent out a number of times.

Thus the philosophy behind implementing a reliable end-to-end protocol can be summarized as follows:

- Keep the protocol simple and lightweight. Avoid doing work at a low level that will functionally have to be repeated at a higher level anyway.
- Keep all operations idempotent so that they can be repeated as often as required.

6.6 COMMUNICATION PROTOCOLS SUMMARY

In this chapter, we have seen how the complex process of internode communication can be made manageable by the imposition of a layered communication architecture. A brief overview was given of the company-specific SNA and DNA, followed by a look at the non-proprietary standards of OSI, IEEE and CR-82.

In examining IBM local network software and Decnet, we saw how these two companies had implemented products in the framework provided by the different architectures. Examples of full-blown OSI applications are beginning to make an appearance at the time of writing, and will, no doubt, be equally influential.

SNA, DNA and OSI provide support for communications between a wide variety of nodes, over many different forms of network. In cases where only LANs are involved, the 'end-to-end' argument makes a case for the adoption of much simpler protocols. The remaining chapters will concentrate on how to use the facilities provided by LANs. Most of the examples do not involve the use of complex architectures. This situation is changing, and one could expect the next generation of LAN software to have a heavier OSI involvement.

6.7 REFERENCES

1 Peatfield, A.C.: 'Standards open markets to multivendors', *Communications/ Communications International*, pp. 30–34, October 1985.

2 Kearsey, B.N. and Jones, W.T.: 'International standardization in tele-communications and information processing', *IEE Electronics and Power*, pp. 643–655, September 1984.

3 Jenkins, P.A. and Knighton, K.G.: 'Open Systems International – the reference model', *British Telecom Technology Journal*, **2**, no. 4, pp. 18–25, September 1984.

4 Rusnak, J.G.: 'Local Area networking and higher level protocols: an SNA example', contribution to *Working Papers of IEEE Project 802 on Local Area Networks*, IBM CPD Publication, March 8, 1982.

5 IBM Corporation: *Systems Network Architecture Introduction*, IBM Corporation, 1976 (order no. GA27-3116-0).

6 'DNA: The Digital Network Architecture', *IEEE Transactions in Communications*, **Com28**, no. 4, April 1980.

7 Digital: *Digital's Networks: an architecture with a future*, Digital Equipment Corporation, 1984 (order no. ES-26013-43).

8 Marsden, B.W.: *Communications Networks Protocols*, Bromley: Chartwell-Bratt, 1985.

9 *Worldwide Standardization Activities on Open Systems Intercommunications*, Institution of Electrical Engineers, 4. March 1986.

10 Gray, J.P. *et al.*: 'Advanced program-to-program communications in SNA', *IBM Systems Journal*, **22**, no. 4, pp. 298–318, 1983.

11 Saltzer, J.H., Reed, D.P. and Clark, D.D.: 'The end-to-end argument in systems design', *ACM Transactions in Computer Systems*, **2**, no. 4, November 1984.

12 'DOD transmission control protocol', *ACM Computer Communications Review*, **10**, no. 4, October 1980.

PART TWO

DISTRIBUTED SYSTEMS

CHAPTER SEVEN

UTILIZING A LAN

The essentials of LAN technology have been covered in the previous section. This chapter looks in a little more detail at what LANs are used for in practice. It begins with a recap of the motivation behind developing LANs. It then lists both the advantages that are to be gained by their use and the problems faced in actually achieving those advantages.

7.1 MOTIVATION

The main motivations behind the development of LANs, and, more importantly, their increasingly widespread use, are as follows:

- the decreasing cost, and consequent increased use, of computers;
- rapid improvements in communication technology;
- the marriage of these two distinct disciplines, computing and communication, together.

Other considerations which make this area even more fruitful are to do with the nature or type of computing that is being performed. Two strong trends are emerging [2]. Firstly there is one towards personal, user friendly, interactive computing. Examples are full screen editing, wordprocessing with graphics etc. The emphasis here is very much on fast, and friendly, I/O (input/output). Secondly there is a trend towards using dedicated processors to perform specific tasks, for example, real time control of devices in factory automation.

Neither of these two cases is suited to large mainframe systems but more towards using personal or dedicated workstations. Thus over the past few years there has been a large increase in the use of workstations to cater for these situations. There are however a number of desirable properties of centralized systems which are not present when there is widespread use of small workstations. A LAN provides a mechanism whereby nodes can be interconnected thus combining the flexibility of small machines with the advantages of large mainframes.

The following section examines the supposed advantages of a LAN-based system, it is followed by a discussion of the nicer properties of traditional systems and finally a look is taken at how these much quoted advantages of LANs can be actually attained in practice and at what cost. The chapter concludes with a section on sharing and a brief look at some of the different types of facilities that can be provided using a LAN.

7.2   ADVANTAGES OF LANS

There are two ways of viewing machines connected to a LAN. They can be treated as distinct computer systems which occasionally exchange information across the network; this is very much the way WANs are regarded. A second approach is to treat the resulting configuration as a *single* computer system, which is made up of a number of nodes (see figure 7.1).

The following is a list of some of the potential advantages of a *LAN-based system*.

- **Sharing**   This is the key to the attractiveness of LANs, i.e. the ability to share resources between users of the network. Ideally, if a user is connected to the network all the resources on it, hardware or software, are available to him. This topic is returned in detail later in the chapter.
- **Incremental growth**   A computing system based around a LAN has the ability to expand easily, and to contract. New resources can be added on to the network as they are needed or become available, or, as is often the case, the finance to purchase them becomes available.
- **Placing power where it is needed and used**   Computing power, be it processors or peripherals, can be physically placed where it is needed and used.
- **Autonomy**   By placing resources where they are used, it is possible to give responsibility for the control and administration of that resource to the people who use it directly. These are the people with the greatest awareness of its needs. This differs from centralized systems where decisions on availability, division of resources etc., are made in a broader context.

  This point, while not being technical in nature, is a very strong motivation towards a LAN-based system. Centralized computing centers are quite often kingdoms in themselves. Users are rarely allowed access even to see the computer on which they are working. Services are provided by the 'computing center' as best they can, often to the inconvenience of a particular section of users. In a LAN-based system, where each node can retain as much local autonomy as it pleases, these issues do not arise.
- **Redundancy**   This can be easily built into the system, e.g. two copies of the

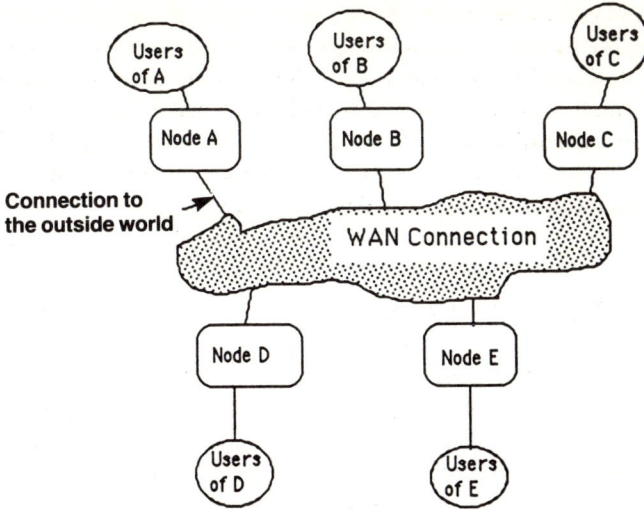

Figure 7.1a   The user's view of a WAN
Note: Users regard the node to which they are directly connected as their computer
system. The rest of the world is contacted over the WAN

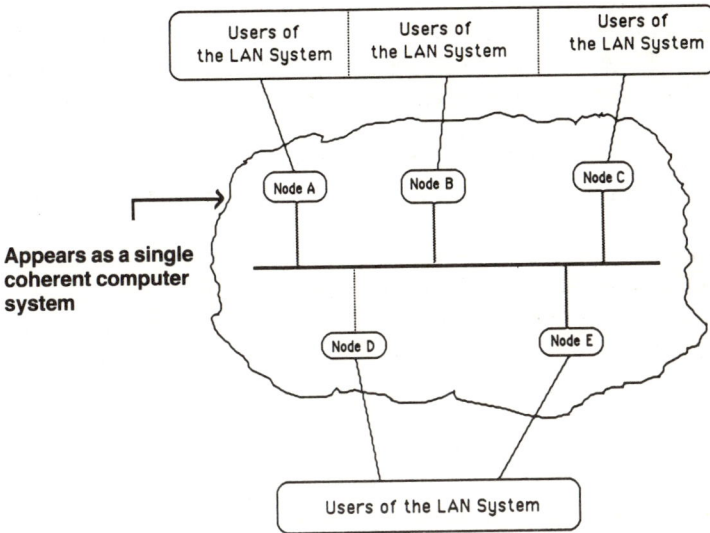

Figure 7.1b   The user's view of a LAN-based system
Note: The system can be regarded as a single unit with all the nodes acting in
cooperation

same file can be stored at different nodes. Thus if one node is temporarily unavailable or overused the information can be obtained from the second copy. Similarly, if there are a number of printers connected to the LAN one can be taken out for maintenance, and printouts redirected to another printer. Any desired level of redundancy can be built in, depending on the operating environment.

There are two distinct advantages to this. The first is in increased availability of resources which should lead to improved performance. Secondly redundancy can be used to give better resilience in the face of failure by any of its components. Errors may be recoverable if sufficient redundancy is built in, but if not, the effect should be localized to the users or nodes directly involved. Thus any individual node may fail and the system should continue to operate or at least degrade gracefully.

7.3 PROPERTIES OF CENTRALIZED SYSTEMS

Centralized systems have a number of properties which should be preserved in LAN-based ones.

- **Sharing information**   This is provided on a centralized system via access to shared files or a common data base.
- **Communication**   Human users may communicate with each other via electronic mailing and, at a lower level, operating system processes communicate using some type of 'interprocess communication' facility.
- **Expensive peripherals are easily shared**   All the users have access to any of the peripherals connected to the system.
- **Powerful number crunching**   For CPU-intensive applications, access to a powerful 'number cruncher' is essential. This is typically not available on personal workstations.

7.4 PROBLEMS WITH LANS

None of the potential advantages of centralized systems outlined above comes free of charge. A large amount of software must be developed to achieve even some of the possible advantages. The following is a list of some of the problems encountered and it is towards overcoming them that the remainder of the book is devoted.

- **Backup**   As there is no centralized control in a LAN-based system, automatic taking of backups cannot easily be carried out.
- **Security**   Centralized systems have their own security problems, but using a LAN introduces additional ones. Firstly, if key resources are not located in the same place, supervision becomes a problem. Secondly, there is a new window of vulnerability to confidential data. This occurs while it is

being transmitted over the network. It is all too easy for a malicious user to listen to the network traffic and eavesdrop on sensitive data. The normal solution [1] is to *encrypt* the data before transmitting and *decrypt* it on reception.

- **Creation of standards** Standards have to be imposed, not only *within* a network but also *across* networks. This has been discussed in detail in Chapter 6.
- **System failure** Failure is a problem in any system but particularly so in a network-based one. This was previously seen when introducing communication protocols and it is a problem returned to in the remaining chapters. Failure covers not only hardware faults but also errors in software and problems arising from local autonomy. An extreme example of the latter might be the administrator of a node withdrawing it from the network while a user is doing a file transfer!

7.5 SHARING

To exploit fully the potential advantages of LANs it is necessary to provide an easy and flexible means of sharing. There are three distinct types of sharing, and they are looked at in order of increasing complexity. All are provided, in some form, by centralized systems and must be catered for in a network environment.

1 **Peripherals** These are often expensive. It is impractical for each processor to have both its own letter quality and high-speed printer. A mainframe may have one of each connected to it allowing all users controlled access in a cost effective manner. There is a detailed discussion of how peripherals can be shared on a LAN in the following chapter.
2 **Information** Users of a multiuser system can share and exchange information in a number of ways. Examples are sending electronic mail or having controlled access to the same files or data base.
3 **Control** In a traditional time sharing system, all control is performed centrally, if the processor fails then the entire system fails. In a network system this need not (and should not) be the case. To support incremental growth, graceful degradation and flexible service, it is essential that control is not centralized in one particular location. The failure of one node should not have a 'domino' effect on the rest. This is called *distributed control* and is a very lively area of research at present.

7.6 EXAMPLES

The remainder of this chapter gives a brief overview of what LANs are being used for in practice. The areas outlined are returned to in more detail in the following chapters.

7.6.1 File transfer

A LAN provides a means whereby files can be transferred between any machines on the network. It involves running some file transfer utility on both of the nodes, and typically requires setting up some sort of virtual circuit between the two ends. File transfer has been dealt with in Chapter 6. LANs however can be used for much more than file transfer and this is the reason for their increasing popularity.

7.6.2 Office automation

This is another area where LANs can have an impact. Computers can play a much larger role in an office than just word processing or spread-sheet calculations. The processing and retrieving of all sorts of information are being automated. This includes not just standard text, like most documents, but unstructured documents, hand-written letters, photographs, voice and video. As the use of computers in offices increases, LANs will play an important role in enabling information to be exchanged and shared. The protocols being developed to cater for this are covered in Chapter 11.

7.6.3 Industrial control

A LAN can also be a very useful tool in a factory environment. A typical working organization might consist of a number of small or dedicated processors performing real-time monitoring functions. These would periodically communicate with a central node to perform status updates etc., or with each other to exchange information. A LAN is ideal for such an arrangement because of its flexibility and speed. The protocols to cover this area are also covered in Chapter 11.

7.6.4 Distributed systems

As previously stated, a LAN-based system can be regarded as a single computing facility rather than a collection of individual ones. How this can be implemented is the subject of Chapters 8 to 10. Chapter 8 introduces the *server concept*, Chapter 9 focuses on one very important type of server, namely *file servers* and Chapter 10 looks at *distributed operating systems.*

A distributed operating system, or *DOS* is an attempt to provide support for applications that are network based. It does so by imposing a large degree of order on the components connected to the network. Ideally, the user of a distributed operating system should not be able to tell the difference between a centralized system and a distributed one. Networking and all other underlying issues are taken care of by the DOS.

7.7 SUMMARY

This chapter has outlined the advantages and disadvantages of using LANs. The type of uses they can be put to have been covered and the structure of the rest of the book has been given.

7.8 REFERENCES

1 Tanenbaum, A.S.: *Computer Networks*, Englewood Cliffs: Prentice Hall Inc., 1981.
2 Yalamanchilli, S. *et al.*: 'Workstations in a LAN environment'. *IEEE Computer*, **17**, no. 11, pp 75–86, November 1984.
3 Le Lann, G.: 'Motivations, objectives and characterization of distributed systems' in *Lecture Notes in Computer Science No. 105*, eds B.W. Lampson, M. Paul and H.J. Seigert, Berlin: Springer Verlag, 1981.

CHAPTER EIGHT

NETWORK SERVERS

8.1 INTRODUCTION

The goal of this chapter is to examine how a LAN can be used as a tool for sharing resources on a network. We begin by introducing the idea of a network server and explain how peripherals, e.g. printers, terminals and disks, can be shared. The discussion on disks leads us into the topic of how stored information, in this case files, can be shared, which is taken up in the following chapter.

8.2 RESOURCE SHARING

LANs can be used to provide a mechanism whereby potentially expensive peripherals can be shared between a number of users. Thus it may not be necessary to equip each processor with a full set of peripherals: terminals, printers and disks. This applies especially to microcomputers, where the peripherals and, in particular, disks, can cost more than the processor unit.

The rationale behind this is that it is not necessary for machines joined together in a LAN to have their own private set of peripherals; instead it is sufficient that they are provided on the LAN, and that each processor has access to them.

Regrettably, one rarely gets anything for nothing and to share resources, new software must be written to allow for access over the network. The complexity and cost of this additional software introduces overheads of its own, so a new trade-off is introduced. The advantages of a network system must be greater than the cost of attaining them. This is an old problem in computing, but one that occurs again and again. It is now the problem facing people implementing network-based systems.

The remaining chapters in this book are devoted to studying how this additional software changes a number of loosely connected machines into a useful working system.

8.3 THE CLIENT/SERVER MODEL

A common strategy used in many systems, e.g. the Cambridge Distributed System [3], is to designate a particular node, which is at a 'well-known' and fixed address, to provide a service to the network as a whole. The node providing the service is known as the *server* and nodes which use that service are known as *clients* of that server. There may be any number of servers on a network, some of which may provide the same service. A node which provides a particular service may itself be a client of a different server.

The following sample servers are looked at:

1 **A print server**   One node has a printer connected to it and the other nodes on the network communicate with it in order to print files (see figure 8.1).
2 **A terminal server**   (Better known as a *terminal concentrator.*) Terminals are connected directly to the concentrator, which is in turn connected to the network. To access a processor from a terminal all communication traffic is directed through the concentrator.
3 **A disk server**   A node which provides a large amount of secondary storage to users of the network. Figure 8.2 shows a possible network configuration with a number of servers attached to the network.

These three servers are now examined in closer detail.

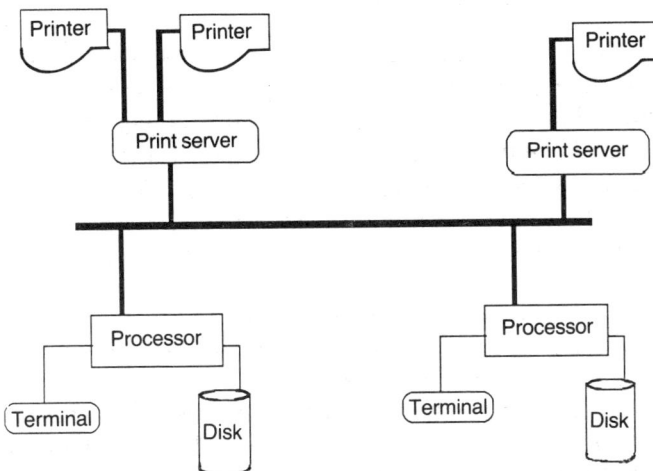

Figure 8.1   A network with two print servers attached to it

Processor
Pool

Diskless
processor

Diskless
processor

Diskless
processor

Printer

Print server

Disk
server

Disk

Disk

Processor
Own peripherals

Terminal
concentrator

Terminal

Disk

Terminal

Terminal

Terminal

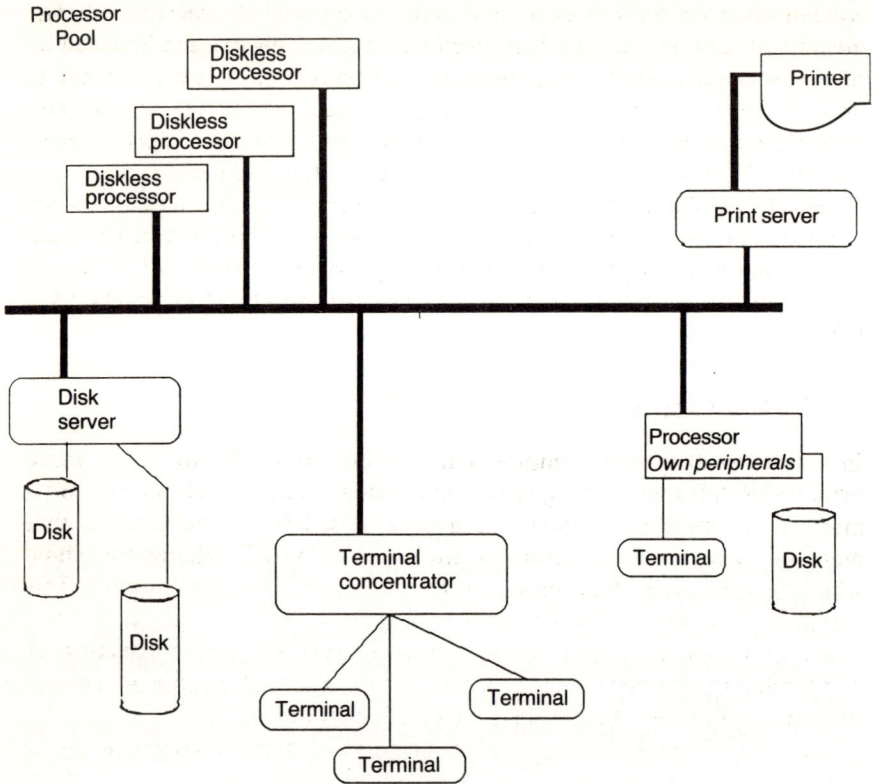

Figure 8.2   Various servers on a network

8.4   COMMUNICATION ASPECTS

Network communication is achieved by adding a network driver to the
operating system running on each node. It handles the transmission and
reception of packets and all the other details of interfacing to the network.
Suitable high level protocols are developed to suit the various applications.

There are two approaches to designing these protocols. The first is to write
them as part of a complete layered architecture, e.g. application level
protocols in the OSI model. This gives all the advantages of standardization
but at the cost of having to implement all of the layers. Because of the low
error rates on LANs, a full OSI-type implementation is not actually required
to achieve reliability. The second approach, therefore, is to use lightweight,
problem-specific protocols. These are based on the 'end-to-end' argument
covered in Chapter 6 and are designed to meet the requirements of one
specialized task, e.g. client-to-file server communication. Problem-specific
protocols are, by definition, very efficient, but not standardized. An example
of this approach is DIGITAL's LAT terminal server. It acts as a terminal

concentrator on an Ethernet, and rather than use Decnet to exchange message it uses its own problem-specific protocol. This trend is followed by most systems described in the remainder of the book. It can be expected that, as final agreement is reached on the higher layers of the OSI model and hardware and firmware implementations become available, many of these systems will review their decisions not to use standardized protocols.

Finally it should be noted that the servers and LAN-based systems described in subsequent chapters are independent of the actual LAN used. The emphasis will be placed on the facilities provided rather than on details of the network. For a detailed example of a protocol used by a typical server see [3].

8.4.1 Print server

In a traditional system, computers are directly connected to one or more printers of different printing speeds and quality. This is cost effective on a mainframe where the printer(s) can be accessed by all the users of that machine. The cost considerations are different on a single-user machine where it is necessary for a processor to have direct access to a printer. This usually results in each processor having its own local low-quality printer. Sharing is possible only in the most primitive of ways, i.e. by disconnecting the printer and then connecting it to another processor. High-quality or very fast printers are not cost effective in this type of environment.

A LAN provides a means by which printer(s) can be shared practically. If a printer is connected to the network via a print server, any processor on the network can have access to it. It is the responsibility of a print server to control this access. In addition to the cost considerations, there are also the added advantages of ease of maintenance and administration, in that a shared printer can be located in a suitable room which is supervised and noise can be cut down.

A print server (PS) can be implemented as an application program running on a general purpose processor or, for performance reasons, it can be implemented on a dedicated system. In either case, the functionality is the same.

- The PS resides at a known location, and users communicate with it via an agreed protocol.
- Packets addressed to the PS are of two types:
  - commands,
  - data.

Possible commands are *print a file* and *cancel print request*. On receiving a request to print a file the PS can:

- refuse the request;
- queue it up to be serviced later;

– accept the request, informing the requesting node which then, and only then, begins to transmit the file.

- A *cancel* request deletes a file from the print queue or stops the current file being output.
- Data blocks are treated as part of the current file being transmitted and are either stored or printed immediately.
- Invalid or erroneous packets from the client are rejected with or without an error response being returned to the sender, depending on the protocol.
- A protocol-dependent error code can be returned to the user if the server malfunctions.
- A number of printers may be connected to the same server and a number of servers may reside on the network, see figure 8.1.

In a conventional system, when a user requests that a file be printed the operating system does so by sending the data to a printer driver within the operating system, the driver actually controling the printer. To access a printer over the network all that needs to be changed is the body of this driver. It is modified so that the data is sent to the remote print server, using the agreed protocol.

8.4.2 Terminal server

The usual way of connecting a terminal to a host is over a direct line. A terminal can also be connected to a host via a LAN. To transmit data over the network the data must be encapsulated in a network packet. This is done by using a *terminal concentrator* (TC) or *terminal server*. A TC is the device to which the terminal is directly connected. It takes the normal terminal input, encapsulates it in a network packet and transmits it to the host. On the host side, the data is decapsulated by the terminal driver within the host OS. Again some protocol has to be agreed upon by both sides.

This is a good example of where a virtual circuit type connection is desirable. The action of the TC might proceed as follows.

1 The terminal signals it wants attention from the TC, e.g. by pressing the break key.
2 The TC responds, and its first task is to communicate with the host's network interface, be it special hardware or the OS terminal driver. The two sides then set up a virtual circuit (VC).
3 The TC responds to the user by saying that a connection has been set up.
4 All data typed in by the user is then taken by the TC, encapsulated in the appropriate packet and addressed to the host on the newly created VC.
5 As far as the user is concerned the connection to the host behaves just like a direct one.
6 To terminate the connection the user can interrupt the TC.

A LAN and TC offer an alternative to the traditional wiring system for connecting terminals to a mainframe. Traditionally, when laying terminal cables, additional ones are put in place to cater for later growth. When all these have been used, adding new terminals in involves laying more wires.

When using a LAN to carry terminal traffic, a single cable can be wired around the building and all terminal traffic goes over it. To connect a new terminal or move an old one, the only wiring that has to be done is from the terminal to its nearest concentrator. Additional concentrators can be added as desired.

An additional advantage of the TC/LAN scheme is that, if there are a number of hosts on the network, it is possible to have the TC act as a switch connecting a given terminal to different hosts at different times. If the TC is sophisticated enough, it could cater for a number of terminals and allow a user to open a number of connections at the same time. This allows a user simultaneous access to a number of hosts.

8.4.3 Disk server

Disks are expensive and obvious advantages are to be gained from sharing them. An important consideration is that the cost per byte of disk storage decreases as the capacity of the disk increases. Thus a 10 Mb disk offers the same storage as 10 individual 1 Mb disks but at a much lower cost per byte. The larger the disk, the greater the saving.

In the same way that a print server is used to control a printer and a terminal concentrator to control terminals on a LAN, a disk server can be developed to share a disk in a network environment. In the simplest case, one machine on the network has a large amount of mass storage, the disk server. Each of the client machines has its own local storage plus access to some space on the disk server.

The remainder of this section examines in some detail the changes that have to be made to allow a process to access blocks on a remote disk rather than a local one. But before that it is advisable to define exactly what is meant by the terms *file server* and *disk server*.

8.4.3.1 Disk and file servers

File server is a much used, and abused, term. A good definition of each is given in [2]. It distinguishes between a *backing store server* or *disk server* which places no meaning or structure on its data other than it consists of blocks that users can read and write, and a *file server* which provides users with some of the functionality of file system component in an operating system, e.g. creating and deleting *files*. Quite often the latter will be built upon the former, but they remain distinct services.

8.5 DISK SERVER IMPLEMENTATION

This section deals with the actual implementation of a disk server; file servers are covered in the following chapter.

8.5.1   Client machine implementation – local disk

Before looking at the software needed to access a remote disk, it is necessary to understand the steps involved when a user program reads data from a local disk. See [1] for a description of file systems etc.

- The user program issues a read request to the operating system (OS).
- The OS is presented with a request to read data from a particular file at a given offset. Using information held in its internal tables it works out its address, or block number, on disk. A command is then issued to the appropriate disk driver. The parameters to the driver call are

   – the drive number, in case the driver is controlling more than one drive,
   – a start address to read from,
   – the number of blocks to be read,
   – an address in memory specifying where the data is to be read into.

- The disk responds with the appropriate data which is passed back to the user. Note that disk I/O is done in blocks so even if the original read was for only a few bytes an entire block will be brought in from disk. The OS may perform some internal buffering of blocks, so that a read request may be satisfied without accessing the disk if the data is already in memory.
- The details of the write operation are similar.

8.5.2   Client machine implementation – remote disk

In the case where the block is on a remote disk server, the read operation differs from the above description in the following ways. The driver realizes the disk is not local and proceeds to make up a network request. This is done by forming a protocol-dependent packet addressed to the disk server station. The packet contains a command to the disk server, read block, and the parameters:

   { start address, amount of data to read }

This packet is then transmitted across the network. The disk server in turn responds with a packet, or packets, containing the requested data. The client driver unpacks the data and returns it to the OS as it would data from a local disk. Thus the only difference between a local and remote disk access is within the implementation of the driver.

   It is possible to configure most systems with a number of different disks, there being a different driver for each disk type. It is a function of the operating system to call the appropriate driver depending on where the file is stored. To access a disk over the network, all that has to be done is to write a new driver and link it to the operating system. Read and write calls to this driver are then transmitted over the network to the remote disk.

   It is the driver's responsibility to handle the communication aspects of the remote access. It does so on top of the facilities provided by the system. These will include at least a 'data-link'-type service from the actual network driver.

If a layered architecture is used then all layers below the 'application layer' will be available and the disk driver will implement an 'application'-level protocol. If a problem-oriented protocol is used, the disk driver will implement it on top of the data-link layer.

8.5.3 Disk server implementation

Having seen how the client side can be implemented we now turn our attention to the server.

On the server, storage is partitioned between all the users. The disk server software consists of the following components, as shown in figure 8.3.

- A network module which handles the network interface and any layered protocols.

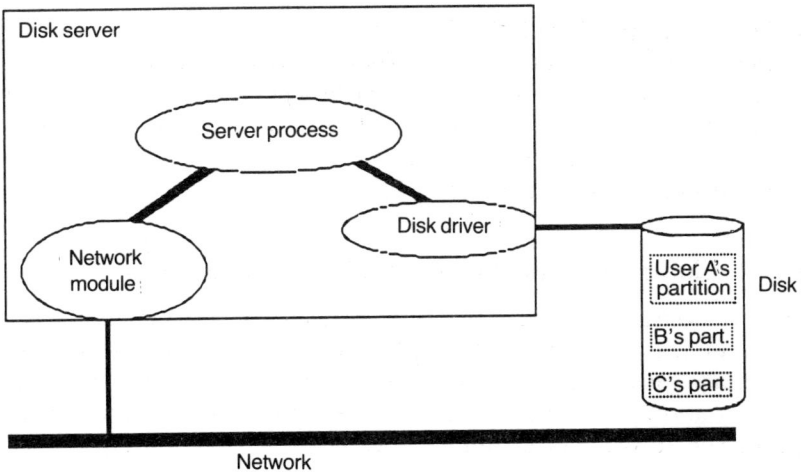

Figure 8.3a   Disk server implementation

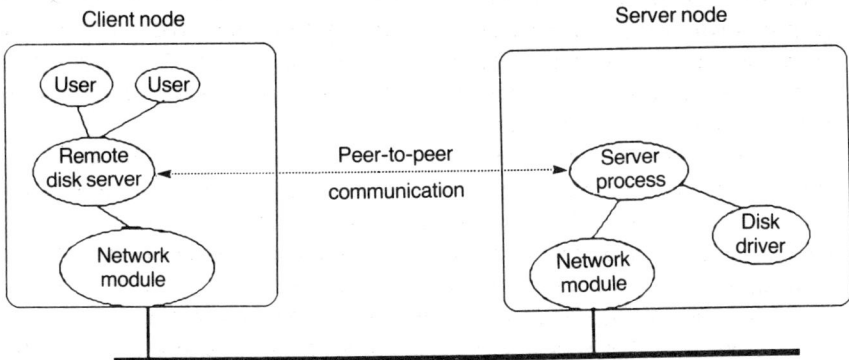

Figure 8.3b   Interaction between client-server components

- A server process which handles all client requests. The clients are the modified 'disk drivers' described above, and the server process implements the actual 'client-disk server' protocol.
- A conventional disk driver which actually accesses the disk.

Commands from the client to the server include the following.

- **Open a circuit**   This is to establish communication with the server and may involve a password or some other security check.
- **Close a circuit**
- **Read a block**
- **Write a block**   In both these cases, the parameters include a disk address and size indicator. This is the address of the data as if it had been on a local disk. The disk server maps the address onto the corresponding physical location within that user's partition on its disk. For example, if the user wants to read block 3 and its partition starts at physical block 232 then the actual block read from disk is $232 + 3 = 235$. More complicated mappings are possible, but the point is that it is the server's responsibility to convert the address the client supplied to the real physical location on its disk.

    It is also the server's responsibility to protect users' data and ensure that one user does not access another's partition. This can be done using a combination of password control to identify users and applying the mapping function to ensure that valid users do not access blocks outside their partitions.

Note that opening and closing files and all other filing system functions are performed by the local operating system in the client node. This may involve reading and writing a block on the remote disk (e.g. to update a directory) but the operation proceeds as if to a local disk. The actual read/write request is transmitted over the network.

8.5.4   Shared areas

Each client machine on the network has its own local storage plus optional access to some space on the shared disk. This shared space is partitioned between users and the disk server ensures that users do not read/write other users' space. Within this system, a limited amount of sharing of data can be catered for. The disk server can allow a certain area of its storage to be a common shared area between all users. This must be a read only area which users are not allowed to modify. Such an area would be suitable for storing a single copy of files that many users would wish to have access to, e.g. system utilities such as compilers, editors etc. New releases of these could be distributed by updating the single version in the common area.

    A read/write locking mechanism is very difficult to implement without a major modification to the client OS. This topic is dealt with in some detail in the section of file servers.

8.5.4.1 Diskless systems

A conventional system, with its own local disks, can gain access to additional storage as previously explained. It must, however, have some local disk capacity to hold a copy of the operating system so that the processor can be booted.

It is also possible to have a system with no local storage of its own. All disk I/O is performed over the network. A further modification has to be made to the client system in that the bootstrap program has to be modified to access the network server rather than a local disk to load in the OS.

When a processor is powered up, control is passed to a bootstrap program in ROM whose function is to read in the OS from disk. In a diskless system, this bootstrap program has to be modified to read from a remote disk.

If there are a number of diskless systems on the network then the operating system could reside in the shared area on the disk server. The option of performing remote booting can also be offered to systems with their own local storage, the user being asked to specify what device to boot from.

8.5.4.2 Use

The use of such a system is similar to disks on a larger, centralized system. The disk server requires an administrator to partition the disk, give quotas, passwords etc. Some limited file system functions can be offered, in that backups can be taken on a regular basis, and a utility can be offered to users for loading and storing data to and from tapes. The server can have multiple disks and clients can have multiple partitions within the same server. A network can be configured with more than one server, in which case users can be assigned to specific servers or can have partitions on different servers.

8.5.4.3 Advantages

A shared disk system has a number of attractions:

1 It offers online storage to users in addition to their local capacity.
2 It makes more efficient and cost-effective use of expensive disks.
3 It is possible to share read only data between all users on the network. This saves each of them space and facilitates distributing new copies of software.
4 It allows for some centralized control of data with the advantages of mainframe systems, backups etc., while at the same time allowing individual machines control of their own local storage.
5 Systems may be configured without any disks which decreases cost. This has particular advantages when the processor is running a dedicated application, e.g. controlling or monitoring an automatic device.

8.5.4.4 Efficiency

The efficiency of a disk server depends on a number of factors:

1 The data transmission speed of the network, and the rate at which the interface between the network and the host operates.

2 The hardware the server is implemented on.

3 The level of disk activity generated by each client.

The danger is that a bottleneck can develop at the disk server if the number of requests it receives is too large to handle. In this case, the use of multiple servers is a good solution. This problem is returned to in more detail in the chapter on file servers.

8.6 TRANSPARENCY

It is worth emphasizing that the only changes that must be made to the local operating system are at the *driver* level. No modification is required to user programs or to the operating system on the client machines. Adding new I/O drivers is a very common occurrence and most operating systems provide a mechanism to cater for it. If utilizing the features of the network requires a major change to the OS/user interface, it will be very difficult to change application software to utilize those new features.

By modifying the OS at driver level, the network is 'transparent' to the user program. At application level, device names may have to be changed but the format of read and write calls remains the same.

This has two advantages to the user: firstly he does not have to learn a new method of accessing remote files. Secondly, because local and remote access differ in only the disk name, it is trivial to move that file from a local to a remote disk and back without a major alteration to any program that accesses the file.

In the case of the print server and terminal server, the transparency issue is handled the same way, i.e. by modifying the I/O drivers. The user of a terminal concentrator will of course have to interact with the TC to select which host he wishes to connect to but once the connection is made all terminal I/O and any software that ran on a directly connected terminal will behave the same on the TC connected one.

8.7 SUMMARY

Three important points have been made in this chapter:

Firstly, the server model has been introduced as a tool for providing services on a LAN.

Secondly, details of how a system has to be modified to use a resource over a network have been outlined.

Finally, the notion of *transparency* has been introduced. This is very important in network systems and is one of the issues addressed in more detail in the following chapter.

8.8 REFERENCES

1   Lister, A.M.: *Fundamentals of Operating Systems*, London: Macmillan, 1979.
2   Birrel, A.D. and Needham, R.M.: 'A universal file server', *IEEE Transactions on Software Engineering*, **SE-6**, no. 5, pp. 450–453, September 1980.
3   Needham, R.M. and Herbert, A.J.: *The Cambridge Distributed Computing System*, Addison-Wesley International Computer Science Series, London: Addison-Wesley, 1982.

CHAPTER NINE

FILE SERVERS

9.1   INTRODUCTION

The previous chapter dealt with sharing and in particular how peripherals may be shared. The notion of the server model as a tool for structuring network systems was introduced. This chapter is devoted to examining one particular and very important type of server, namely a *file server* (FS). The 'file handling component' is a very important part of any system, so it is only to be expected that file servers play a crucial role in network and distributed systems.

Many of the problems encountered in file server design are neither new nor specifically related to LANs. Such issues as protection, concurrency and transactions are well explored in the area of operating system and data base design. What is new is the *environment* in which these problems must be tackled, i.e. a collection of loosely coupled systems which can be a mixture of microcomputers, personal workstations, minicomputers and mainframes, connected together over a fast, but not 100% reliable, network. This chapter discusses some of these issues. The treatment is not meant to be exhaustive and readers are referred to the references for further reading.

9.2   FILE SERVER INTERFACE

An FS, unlike a disk server, supports the concept of a *file* and the standard operations *create*, *delete*, *open*, *close*, *read* and *write*. (In addition, an FS which supports transactions, described later, will implement the operations *begin*, *end* and *abort*.) Unlike a disk server, an FS can allow access to data in varying sizes ranging from bytes through blocks to entire files. This fact, combined with the ability to share files, makes an FS a much more powerful tool than a disk server.

The interface to an FS is a rudimentary one. Files do not have symbolic names but rather *file identification numbers* (FIDs). It is the responsibility of the client to map symbolic names, e.g. test.dat recognized by a user, to FIDs, 2089346, recognized by the server. This and other file system functions, e.g. directory trees, must be implemented by the client. Thus an FS is best regarded as a building block on top of which more useful functions can be built, rather than a service with which end-users directly interact (see figure 9.1).

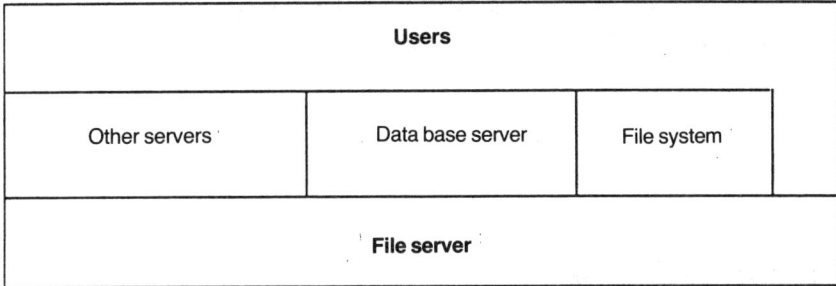

Users		
Other servers	Data base server	File system
File server		

Figure 9.1   Interfacing to a file server

Note: Users interface to the file server via other servers or directly to the file server if desired. The data base server is acting both as a server to the users and as a client with respect to the file server

The clients of an FS can be broken down into three broad application types. Each places slightly different demands on the functionality of the FS.

- **File systems**   As a File Server does not usually provide the full functionality of a file system, the first class of application built on top of a file server is usually that of a full file system. Typically this will involve providing a directory structure, file protection mechanism etc., on top of the facilities already provided by the FS. Any number of distinct File Systems can be built on top of the same File Server and end users interface to the file system, not to the File Server, figure 9.2.

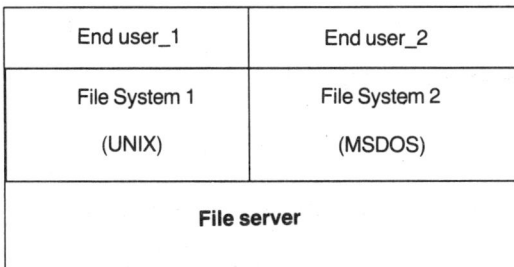

End user_1	End user_2
File System 1 (UNIX)	File System 2 (MSDOS)
File server	

Figure 9.2   File systems and file servers

Note: Different groups of end users interface to the same file server via two different file systems

- **Database server** (DBS)   This is a server providing a 'data base system' to its users. In a data base system, user data is usually accessed in terms of records. This differs from a file system where the most common unit of data is a disk block.

- **Virtual memory system**   Within the operating system of a conventional processor a *page faulting* [1] technique is often used to make use of secondary storage as an extension of main memory. The same effect can be achieved on a diskless system where the local operating system uses the FS to provide its secondary storage.

    Again the requirements are different from the previous two cases – page faulting involves reading and writing fixed sized data blocks and does not require the concept of a file. Virtual memory support can therefore be offered by a disk server just as well as a full FS.

Figure 9.3 shows a possible configuration of servers on a network. The database server resides on the same node as the file server. The other processors on the network run one of two file systems. These file systems in turn use the services provided by the file server Node_C which has no local disks and page faults across the network.

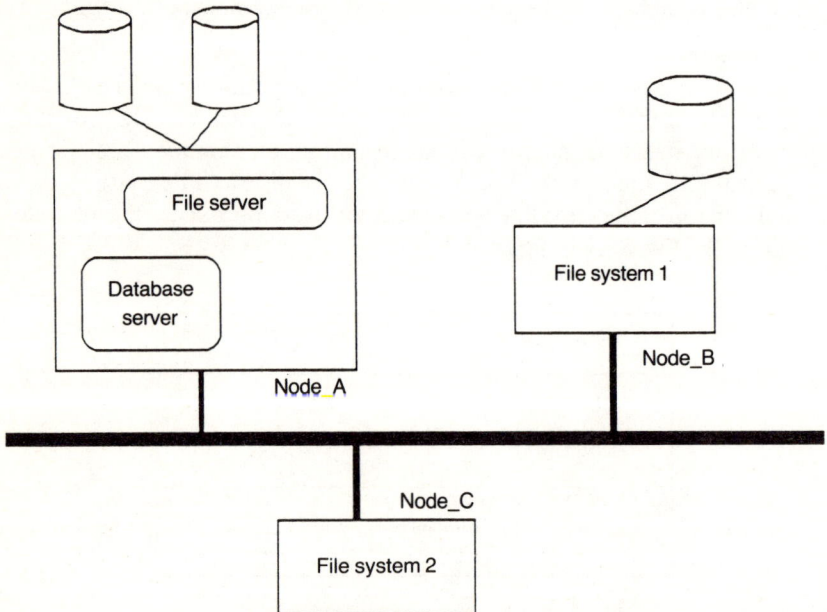

Figure 9.3   A possible network configuration

9.3 ISSUES

Having described the motivation for using an FS, the next task is to address some of the more important issues involved in its design [14].

9.3.1 Independent failure modes

As previously stated, many of the issues in FS design are not unique to network systems. What is new is the environment in which these problems have to be solved. In particular, a network-based system is one made up of many different components. These components include the different processors connected to the network as well as the network itself. The components interact and cooperate with each other to provide a service to users of the system.

Any one of these components may fail, e.g. a processor can crash or the transmission medium can be cut. In a stand-alone environment failure is complete, e.g. a processor crash results in total system shutdown. This is not the case on a network where failure can be *partial*, i.e., a subset of the system is affected.

This is the case because the components that make up the system exhibit what is known as *independent failure modes*, i.e. failure of one component should not automatically mean the entire network fails. This is one of the main differences between stand-alone and network environments, and it greatly affects the way in which servers and any network applications are designed.

This is a very important point and one which will be returned to again in this chapter.

9.3.2 Protection

In any multiuser system, there are two standard ways of providing protection, *access lists* and *capabilities*.

An access list [1] is a table which is looked up each time a user accesses a file. It contains an entry for every user that has permission to use the file and there is one access list per file. An entry is held in the list for each user that has access to the file and it shows the access modes allowed for that user. Figure 9.4a shows two access lists associated with the files A and B. User 'Mary' for instance has read access to file A and no access to file B.

Another form of protection is capabilities [3]. An analogy can be drawn between holding a capability and a *key* which fits a *lock*. A capability contains a unique field to identify it and a second one which contains the access rights associated with it. The system keeps a per user list of capabilities and a single capability for each file. A user, on wishing to access a file, presents his capability to the file system. If it matches the capability for a file, the user is allowed access as given in the access field.

File A Access List

User	Access Rights
Fred	Read Write Execute
Mary	Read
System	Read Write Execute Delete

File B Access List

User	Access Rights
Fred	Read Write
System	Read

Figure 9.4a   Access lists for two files, A and B

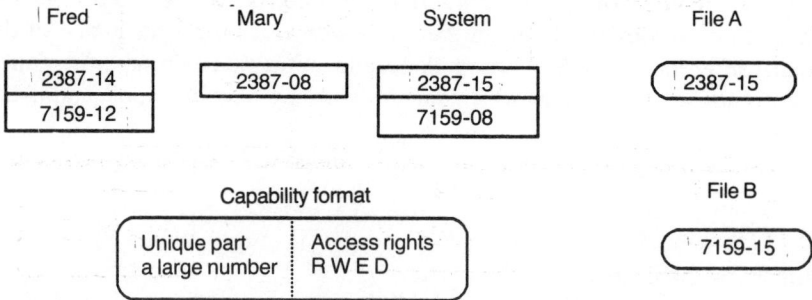

Fred	Mary	System	File A
2387-14	2387-08	2387-15	2387-15
7159-12		7159-08	

Capability format

Unique part a large number	Access rights R W E D

File B

7159-15

Figure 9.4b   The same system as 9.4a, but using capabilities to protect the two files

Uniqueness of a capability can be achieved by representing it as a very large integer, which it is impossible to guess. Figure 9.4b shows a capability implementation of the access lists in figure 9.4a. Mary has a single capability 2387–08 which is for file A. The rights associated with it are 08 i.e. read access only.

Access lists suffer from the disadvantage that there must be one associated with each file. They are usually stored in the directory entry for the file. As most file servers do not have a built-in directory structure, it must be provided at a higher level if access lists are to be used for protection. Capabilities do not suffer from that problem and are used in many file servers.

9.3.3 Robustness

Once a file is written to disk, a number of things can happen to corrupt it. A file is said to be *robust*, if, once it has been written, it can survive crashes or errors on its storage medium. There are two ways of achieving this.

The first and simplest is to take regular backups or archives of all files. This is what is usually done in a centralized system. If a file is destroyed or lost it can always be restored to its latest backed-up version.

A network provides an additional and interesting way of providing robustness. If there are a number of file servers on the network they will have independent failure modes, e.g. a disk error on one server does not mean that any other servers are affected. It is therefore possible to store a number of copies of the same file on different servers (see figure 9.5). Nodes can choose which of the two file servers, FS1 or FS2, to use when accessing File A. If one copy becomes corrupted, another, up-to-date one, is available. This technique is known as *replication* because copies of the same file are replicated on the network.

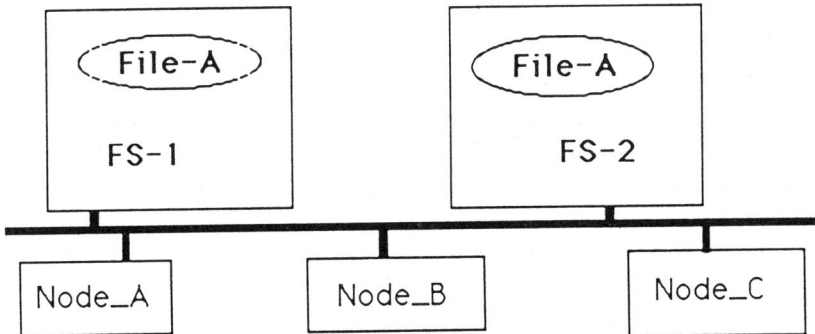

Figure 9.5   Replication
Note: Nodes can access file-A on either of the two servers on the network

9.3.4 Replication

Replication is an area of ongoing research and offers much more than just robust files. Access to any replicated resource can be more efficient than access to a resource of which there is only one instance. This was seen in the previous chapter where a number of print servers could be connected to a network to provide a better overall service.

Frequently accessed files can be replicated so that different copies can be used in parallel, giving greater throughput and increased system performance. In an office environment for example a file containing frequently used telephone numbers and addresses might be replicated.

9.3.4.1   Accessing a replicated file

Access to a replicated resource is, however, more complicated than accessing a nonreplicated one. When a file is replicated *each* of the servers storing copies of it must cooperate in controlling access.

Reading a replicated file is relatively easy as a read operation does not change the contents of the file. Writing is more complicated. The servers must ensure that updates made to one copy are carried out on all the replicated copies. This can be difficult if there are simultaneous writers to different instances of the same file. In figure 9.5, for example, a user on Node-A can update the copy of File A on FS1 while a user on Node-B is writing to the copy on FS2.

Difficulties also arise if one of the servers is *offline*, i.e. temporarily disconnected from the network for maintenance or some other reason, or in the extreme case if the network is *partitioned*. Depending on the underlying network, a break in the communication medium may result in two independent partitions, with communication being possible *within* partitions but not *between* them. In figure 9.6 there is a copy of the replicated file in each partition. Any updates made can only be done on the copy within the partition. If updates are made to the copies in both partitions then the files will be inconsistent with each other when the network is repaired.

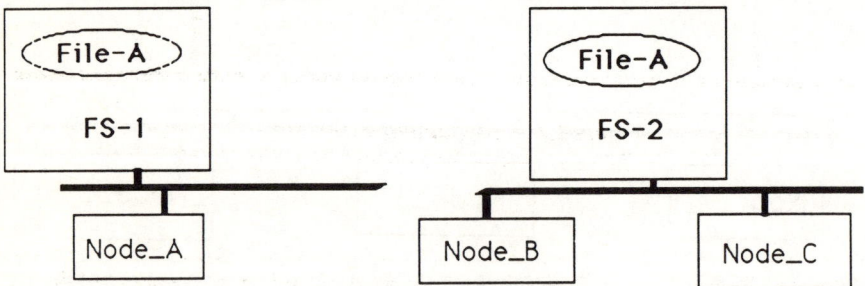

Figure 9.6   Network partition
Note: Partitioned network nodes C and B cannot access file server FS1

9.3.4.2   Updating a replicated file

There are two basic techniques for managing the update of a replicated file. In both cases the most recent copy is identified by inspecting the *version number* of the file. When a file is created it is assigned a version number (VN) of 1 and on each subsequent update the VN is incremented by 1. Thus the current copies of the replicated file have the highest VN.

Primary copy   This strategy adopts a centralized approach [13]. Any copy can be opened for read access, but to write to a file, one copy is designated the *primary copy* (PC) and all updates are made to it. When the write is completed the VN of the PC is incremented. The PC is the master version of the file and the server on which it resides takes responsibility for propagating the updates made to all the other storage sites. This goes on in the background so that different versions of the file will exist at the same time (see figure 9.7).

- Old versions of the file can be read while the update is going on or the user may choose, when issuing the read request, to wait on the PC to read the current version.
- Offline copies are updated when they are brought back into the system if their version number is out of date.
- Updates cannot be made in a partition that does not contain the PC.

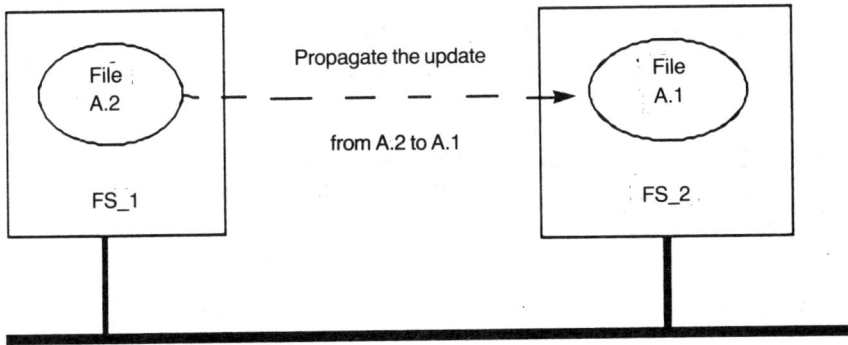

Figure 9.7   Propagating an update
Note: File server1 propagates the update of file A to file server2

Voting   In the primary copy method, control of updating a replicated file is centralized, i.e. one storage site takes responsibility for the update. Voting on the other hand is an attempt at more distributed control of accessing the file.

In the basic scheme [4] an update can only be made if it can be done to *a majority of the copies*. Before writing to a file the server must contact a majority of the other storage sites. This majority is known as a *write quorum*, and each storage site in the quorum locks its copy. The write quorum is then treated as a single unit and none of the locks is released until each copy within the quorum, and version number, has been updated. When all these copies have been updated the locks are released and the update is propagated to the remaining copies, as for the primary copy algorithm.

The file can be read by accessing any of the replicated copies but to avoid reading an out of date version a so called *read quorum* must be obtained. Locks are set and released as for the write operation.

Note that not all the copies in a quorum need have the same VN. What is required, and is guaranteed by voting, is that at least *one* copy in the quorum is current. This is the one to which reads and writes are directed.

Example 9.1 shows how voting is used to update a replicated file F of which there are five copies a, b, c, d, e.

Fa.1 Fb.1 Fc.1 Fd.1 Fe.1	Initial configuration of the 5 copies.
(Fa.1 Fb.1 Fc.1)Fd.1 Fe.1	Lock a write quorum
Fa.2 Fb.2 Fc.2 Fd.1 Fe.1	Update as a unit
Fa.2 Fb.2 (Fc.2 Fd.1 Fe.1)	Lock a second quorum before the updates are propagated.
Fa.2 Fb.2 Fc.3 Fd.3 Fe.3	Update as a unit
Fa.2 Fb.3 Fc.3 Fd.3 Fe.3	Propagate update
Fa.3 Fb.3 Fc.3 Fd.3 Fe.3	All files have the same version number

Example 9.1   Voting

Initially all copies of the file will all have version number 1, Fa.1 Fb.1 Fc.1 Fd.1 Fe.1. A write is carried out on the quorum 'Fa Fb Fc' giving, Fa.2 Fb.2 Fc.2 Fd.1 Fe.1. Before the update is propagated to versions 'Fd Fe' another write is done to the valid quorum 'Fc.2 Fd.1 Fe.1'. Because updates are made to a majority of the files, any quorum must contain *at least* one instance of the most recent version. In the worst case of the quorum, Fc.2 Fd.1 Fe.1 the only current version of F is Fc.2 and it is used for the update. Copies Fd Fe are also updated *before* the locks are released giving, Fa.2 Fb.2 Fc.3 Fd.3 Fe.3.

• Offline copies of a file are updated when brought back online as for primary copy update.

- Updates cannot be made in a partition if it does not contain a majority.

9.3.4.3 Summary of replication

As can be seen from the above discussion, replication is a powerful technique which is available only in a network environment. This is because nodes have independent failure modes.

Two different algorithms have been outlined for updating a replicated file. The strategies are radically different and variations of both schemes exist. Voting is an attempt to provide more generality and availability, while primary copy update is easier to implement but restrictive in that no updates can be made if the PC is unavailable.

Because updating a replicated file is complicated, a simple solution that is often adopted is to confine the use of replication to 'read only' files.

9.3.5 Transactions

Transactions are very common in the field of data bases and they play an important role in most file servers. In this section, *transactions* are explained. An outline is sketched of how they are implemented for a traditional system before going on to describe how the implementation has to be extended to work in a network environment. So-called atomic *transactions* provide two things and they are examined in turn. The first is *atomicity* and the second *concurrency* control.

9.3.5.1 Atomicity

This is also known as the *all or nothing* property of a transaction and is best illustrated with an example. Consider the piece of pseudocode in example 9.2 which transfers money from one bank account to another. This code reflects the steps needed to perform the required update and will function correctly 'most of the time'. If, however, the program crashes *after* updating account A but *before* updating B then A will have been debited but the money will not have been credited to anyone, it will be lost.

What is required is that the updates, to A and B, be done atomically, i.e. they are both done correctly *together* or neither is done.

Atomicity should also ensure that the data is not corrupted *while* it is being written to disk, i.e. if the disk crashes during the write operation then the data should be either:

- not written at all;
- or written correctly as if no error occurred.

9.3.5.2 Concurrency

This is the second aspect of transactions and is concerned with controling access to data by more than one user at the same time.

```
* Transaction Number 1
* Transfer £100 from bank account A to account B


      Read(BalanceA)                    * Read the 2 balances
      Read(BalanceB)

      IF BalanceA > 100 THEN            * Transfer the money

                  BalanceA := BalanceA-100
                  Write(BalanceA)       * Update A
danger
area              BalanceB := BalanceB+100
                  Write(BalanceB)       * Update B

      ELSE                              * Insufficient funds

                  Write("A does not have £100")

      END
```

**Example 9.2   Transaction 1 – transfer funds between two bank accounts
(A and B)**

In a single user system or systems where there is no shared data, concurrency is not an issue. When users are sharing data, some control is needed
to prevent inconsistencies arising in the data if more than one user tries to
update it concurrently.

Example 9.3a describes the steps needed to withdraw money from account
B. Example 9.3b shows what could happen when transaction T2 accesses
account B at the same time as transaction T1, from example 9.2, is also
updating the account. At the end of these two concurrent transactions B's
account has been incorrectly updated to 400. The debit made by T2 was
overwritten. This is known as the *lost update* problem.

A mechanism is required that ensures the integrity of data while at the
same time allowing as much concurrency as possible to improve performance.

```
* Transaction  Number 2
* Debit £100 from account B


    Read(BalanceB)                    * Read the balance

    IF BalanceB > 100 THEN            * Debit the account

            BalanceB := BalanceB-100
            Write(BalanceB)           * Update the account

    ELSE

            Write("B does not have £100")

    END
```

Example 9.3a   Transaction 2 – Debit bank account B
Note: This program is correct as long as it has exclusive access to account B while it is
running

9.3.5.3   Types of transaction

Transactions are a method of providing both atomicity and concurrency control. They are usually bracketed by the operations *begin transaction* and *end transaction*. Any updates made within the transaction are *tentative*, in that they are not actually made visible outside the scope of the transaction until it completes or passes the so-called *commit* stage. When a transaction commits then *all* the updates are made visible in a single indivisible atomic operation – how this is implemented will be explained later.

- A crash before the *commit* is the same as if the transaction never took place.
- A crash after the *commit* has been completed has no effect as the changes have actually been made.
- A crash after the *commit* has been issued but before all the updates have been made is the most serious case. Once the *commit* point is passed, there is a window of vulnerability where the user regards the updates as completed but the server is still carrying them out. The server must ensure that the changes are correctly made even if there is a crash while it is writing the data. This is of course the most difficult part of the implementation.

Transaction 1	Transaction 2	Operation
T1.BalanceA := 200		T1 reads A
T1.BalanceB := 300		T1 reads B
	T2.BalanceB := 300	T2 reads B
T1.BalanceA := BalanceA - 100		T1 calculates new balance for A
Write(T1.BalanceA)		and updates it to 100
	T2.BalanceB := T2.BalanceB - 100 Write(T2.BalanceB)	T2 calculates new balance for B and updates it to 200
T1.BalanceB := T1.BalanceB + 100		**T1 calculates the incorrect balance for B (300+100)**
Write(T1.BalanceB)		**and overwrites the update made by T2.**

Example 9.3b   Lost update
Note: This diagram shows what could happen if the transactions to debit funds and
transfer funds (i.e. examples 9.2 and 9.3a) run at the same time. Assume that account A
has an initial balance of 200 and account B has an initial balance of 300. By the time T1
uses the value it read for BalanceB it is out of date.

- A user can decide to discard the transaction at any stage before the *commit*
  by issuing an *abort* command to the server.

Thus a file server which supports transactions must provide or export to its
users these fundamental operations:

    BeginTransaction
    End/CommitTransaction
    AbortTransaction

along with the traditional file operations to open and close file etc.

Transactions are also the unit of concurrency control, in that updates done
by a transaction are not visible to other concurrent transactions until the
commit.

There are three different types of transactions:

- Transactions involving a single file only, which is the simplest case.
- Those involving multiple files which reside on the same server. These two types occur in conventional data base management systems.
- Finally there are transactions in a network environment involving multiple files on multiple servers, or so-called *distributed transactions*.

The following are examples of each of the different types of transaction:

- Transaction T2 (example 9.3a) is a single file transaction, the file in question being the one containing B's bank account.
- Transaction T1 (in example 9.2) is an example of a multiple file transaction, if the two accounts A and B are stored on different files.
- If the accounts A and B are on different servers, T1 is a distributed transaction.

9.3.5.4 Implementing transactions

There are different requirements for implementing the atomicity and concurrency aspects of transactions. An additional protocol is required to commit distributed transactions. These are described below.

Atomicity   To achieve the 'all or nothing' property of transactions it is necessary that existing *user data* is not discarded until after the transaction has completed, i.e. it is *recoverable*. While the transaction is running there is some *state information* that must be maintained reliably even in the event of a crash; an example of this is given later.

In the next two sections, techniques are described for writing user data in a *recoverable* fashion and writing state information *reliably*. Finally it is shown how these can be combined to implement the crucial *commit phase* of the various types of transactions.

Recoverability   It is necessary that user data is written in a recoverable fashion. The way to ensure recoverability is to introduce a certain amount of redundancy, i.e. both the old and new values of the data are kept until the end of the transaction.

Take the sample transaction, T1, from example 9.2. After it writes the new balance to account A it may decide to *abort*. If this happens, the old value of bank account A should be restored. For this reason when writing the new balance to A the old balance must not be destroyed.

Shadow pages is a widely used technique to ensure recoverability. Data is never written in place, i.e. the old data is never overwritten when updating. Figure 9.8 shows a simple file containing 2 pages, P1 and P2, and an index, I, which points to those pages. Page P1 for example may contain A's bank account in the sample transaction T1. To update the data on P1 it is first read into memory then updated and finally written back out to disk – but to a different disk page, e.g. page P3. At this point both the old and new versions of the data are available. To commit the update, the pointer in I is simply changed from P1 to P3.

In the previous example, page P3 is known as a *shadow page*, for the obvious reason that its contents shadow the contents of the original page, P1. Recoverability is ensured because the old data is never overwritten and the update remains uncommitted until the page pointer is updated. This later update must be done atomically and is an example of state information which must be written reliably. A technique to do this is described in the next section.

Shadow pages can be very wasteful of space, especially if the granularity of the update is small. For example, the record describing A's bank account may occupy only a few bytes but an entire page is being shadowed during the update. An alternative scheme is to use some form of *logging*, which is a widely used technique in the data base world.

A log is an additional data structure in which a record of all updates is kept. In the simplest case, a checkpoint, or backup, is taken of the system on a regular basis. Any updates are recorded in the log in nonvolatile storage. If a crash occurs, it is possible to reconstruct the correct data from the most recent backup and the contents of the log.

Typically the log will contain an *old value*, *new value* pair for each update. If the actual user data is updated in place it is necessary to write to the log *before* writing the data. This is called a *write ahead log* (WAL). Logs can get quite large so they are usually written to some cheap, long-term storage device such as tape.

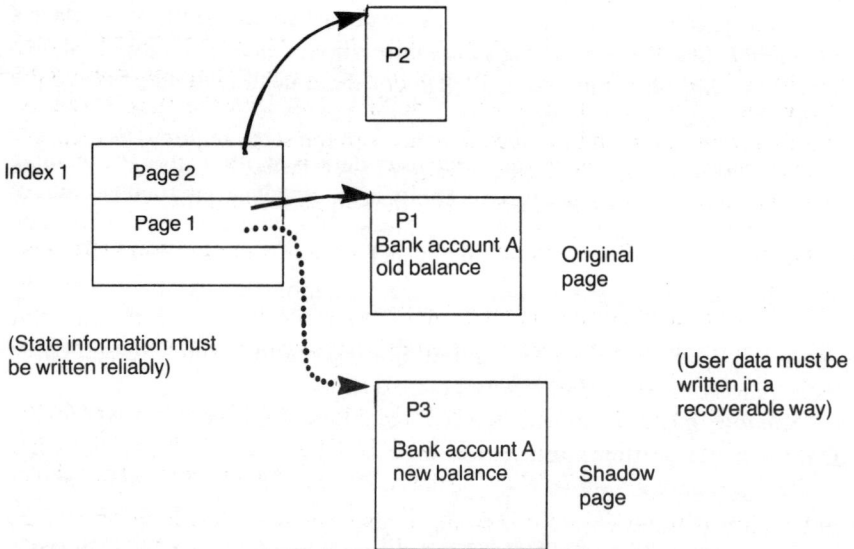

Figure 9.8   Shadow pages
Note: Updating data in recoverable fashion using the shadow page technique

These two methods of achieving recoverability, shadow pages and logging, are not mutually exclusive and are sometimes used in conjunction with each other.

Reliability There is some state information associated with a transaction which must be maintained reliably for its lifetime, e.g. the index in figure 9.8. This state information includes any information needed to complete correctly the transaction if there is a crash during the commit. It must therefore be stored in nonvolatile memory to ensure it survives power failures etc. Writing it to disk is not sufficient to ensure reliability, as an error could occur while the write was actually taking place.

A widely used strategy to store data reliably is that of *stable storage* [12]. The concept is simple in that it assumes that the storage medium used is 100% reliable. It can be implemented or, more correctly, approximated by using two ordinary disk pages for every one *stable page*. These pages should not be contiguous on disk and ideally should be on different disk packs to insure that they fail independently.

Figure 9.9 shows how such a stable page is updated. The contents of the page are the index from figure 9.8. Both physical pages are written in turn. If a crash occurs while writing to one, the other will contain valid data. A stable page is successfully updated when *both* pages have been updated. Note this differs from simple shadow pages where only one page contains valid data.

Obviously this is expensive in terms of resources. Two disk pages are used for every one required, and it is also slower to write to stable storage than to normal storage. For these reasons, stable storage is only used for holding state information and not user data.

Committing transactions Having described the underlying techniques, the next task is to show how these are used to provide a typical implementation of transactions. There are two aspects. The first deals with the steps taken to commit a transaction and the second deals with the steps required to recover correctly from a crash. The basic technique is as follows:

Associated with each transaction is some state information.

- The transaction ID – a unique number generated when the transaction is begun.
- The FID of the file or files involved in the transaction.
- Transaction status – the current state of the transaction. Possible states are *begun*, *committed* or *completed*.
- A list of the changes that need to be made to complete the transaction successfully. These are not the updates to user data but rather such items as the file pointers that have to be changed, as in the file index in figure 9.8.

This list of transaction information is also called an *intentions list* and is needed to complete the transaction in the face of server crashes. It must, therefore, be stored reliably. User data, on the other hand, must be stored in a recoverable fashion.

Index I on stable storage

a	b
P2	P2
P1	P1
–	–

Stable page
made up of
2 normal pages a,b

Update 'a' first

a	b
P2	P2
P3	P1
–	–

Stable page

Update 'b'

a	b
P2	P2
P3	**P3**
–	–

Stable page

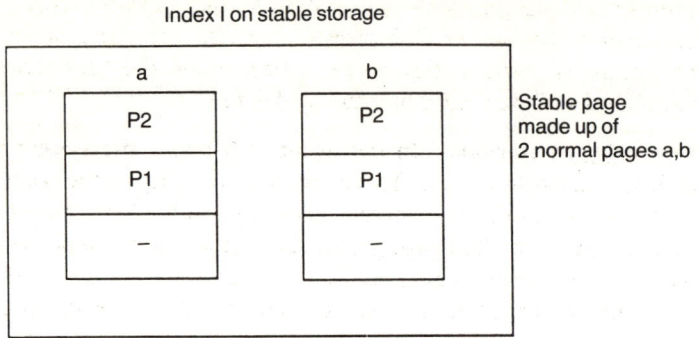

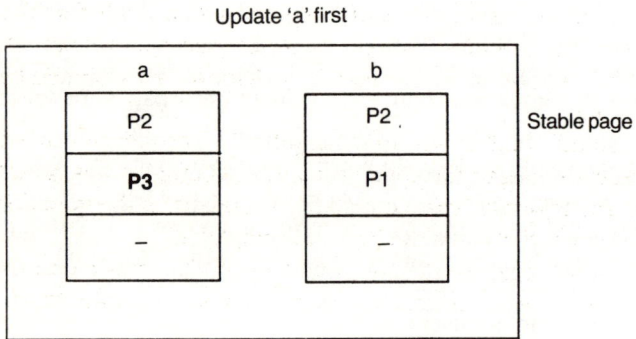

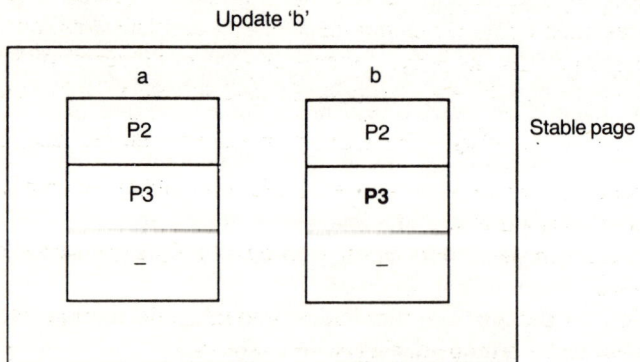

Stable page is now updated.

Figure 9.9 Updating a stable page

To commit a transaction, the status field is set to commit. The entire intentions list is then written to stable storage. This effectively commits the transaction. The server then proceeds to carry out the changes listed in the intentions list. When they have all been done the transaction is marked completed and the record of it can be deleted.

Recovering transactions In the event of a crash, the system must restore itself to a consistent state. This is the responsibility of the *recovery manager* (RM) module of the File Server. Recovery can be done on system restart or the RM can be invoked during normal operation when the server detects a file involved in an uncompleted transaction. Remember that enough information is stored in the intentions list to complete the transaction and that the intentions list is itself immune to failure, as it is stored reliably.

To recover a transaction, three cases arise – they are identified by inspecting the status field of the intentions list.

1 The status field is set to 'begun'. The crash occurred before the commit, the transaction is aborted and the intentions list can be deleted. Any resources held by an aborted transaction, e.g. shadow pages, should be returned to the system.
2 The status field is set to 'committed'. The crash occurred after the transaction passed the commit point, but before it was completed. In this case, the RM must carry out all of the updates in the intentions list. When this is done, the status can be set to completed.
3 The status field is set to 'completed'. The crash occurred after the transaction was successfully completed so the intentions list may be deleted.

The server may crash again during crash recovery, at a stage where some of the updates have been made and others have not. This requires that the list of updates must be either idempotent, in that carrying them out several times has the same effect as carrying them out once, or the server must be able to tell from the state of the file what updates have and have not been made.

Summary of atomicity The above points can be summarized as follows:

- User data is written in a recoverable fashion so that old data is not lost when new data is written.
- Transaction state information is stored reliably to ensure it survives a server crash.
- The transaction state includes enough information to complete a transaction correctly during crash recovery.

Distributed transactions/two phase commit The above scheme will work equally well for a transaction involving one file or many files, as long as they all reside on the same server. For distributed transactions, the commit protocol becomes more complicated. A widely used protocol for committing distributed transactions is *two phase commit* [7].

For a transaction involving more than one server, a coordinator server must be chosen. This is often the server to which the initial 'begin transaction' request was directed. The other servers involved act as slaves or cohorts, so-called because they must obey the coordinator.

When the commit is issued by the user, the coordinator must ensure that either all the slaves commit together or they all abort together. It should never arise that some cohorts commit and others abort.

To complete a distributed transaction, the coordinator server takes the following steps.

1 It marks the status of the transaction '*tentative commit*'.
2 It sends an 'are you ready to commit?' message to all the cohorts.
3 If a cohort has aborted or wishes to abort, it responds with a negative reply.
4 Otherwise, the cohort prepares itself to commit by writing its intentions list to stable storage. The status of the local transaction is marked 'tentative commit' and not committed. The cohort server then replies favorably to the coordinator.
5 If the coordinator receives any negative replies then it aborts the entire transaction and sends out abort messages to each of the cohorts. They in turn abort their local transactions.
6 On receiving positive replies from *all* the cohorts, the coordinator updates the state of the transaction to committed and sends a '*go ahead and commit*' message to each cohort.
7 Each cohort, on receiving a 'go ahead and commit' message from the coordinator, marks its transactions committed and completes as for the single server case.

There are a few points worth noting here:

- Any cohort is free to abort or tentatively commit independently until it replies to the coordinator. From that stage on it must obey the coordinator.
- There are a number of weak points in the protocol. In steps 5 and 6, the coordinator has to wait for *every* cohort to respond. There is no fixed bound on how long this will take, as there can be communication errors between the coordinator and the cohort. Timeouts must be used to ensure that the transaction does complete. A nonreply within the specified timeout period must be treated as a negative reply and cause the transaction to be aborted.
- If a server crashes after setting its state to 'tentative commit' but before it gets the final commit/abort message from the coordinator, it must still be able to complete the transaction properly on recovery. This is more complicated than recovering a conventional transaction because the coordinator had not decided whether to commit or abort when the cohort crashed. To complete successfully, the cohort must be able, on recovery, to discover the fate of the transaction. This can be done by interrogating the coordinator but demands that the coordinator does not delete its record of the transaction until *all* the cohorts reply that they have completed.

- If the coordinator crashes, it will be detected by the cohorts that choose a new coordinator.
- This protocol can be quite expensive in terms of the number of messages required and the total execution time. Optimizations of this basic protocol do exist and they are described in the references.
- Two phase commit is actually a very old and widely used protocol. Gray [7] points out that, in the usual Christian marriage ceremony, the Man and the Woman are the cohorts and celebrant/official acts as the coordinator:

> *Coordinator:* Do you Cohort1 (Man) take . . .?
> *Cohort1:* Replies
> *Coordinator:* Do you Cohort2 (Woman) take . . .?
> *Cohort2:* Replies
> *Coordinator:* Then I pronounce this transaction committed!

Up to the point where each partner replies, they are free to choose whether to marry or not. After giving a favorable reply, each partner must abide by the final decision of the coordinator.

9.3.5.5 Concurrency

This is the second important aspect of transactions. The problem is to ensure the correctness of data even if a number of transactions access it concurrently. Example 9.2 earlier in the chapter showed how an update was lost when two transactions accessed the data at the same time. The simplest solution is not to allow any concurrency i.e. transactions run one after each other in a *serial order*. The transactions A B C D E F can be run in any serial order, e.g. C D F A B E or D F C B A E. Both of these orders will produce 'correct results', because only one transaction is accessing the data at any one time. The final state of the data will of course be different, depending on the actual order, but it will always be correct in that there will be no lost updates.

Eliminating concurrency ensures correctness but it does not give optimal performance. The vast majority of transactions will not share data and it is impractical to require that only one transaction runs at the time. Much better performance can be obtained if some amount of concurrency is allowed. The problem is to maximize the amount of concurrency while still being able to guarantee the correctness of the results.

Serializability This is a widely used technique [7] to ensure the correctness of concurrent transactions. If executing a number of transactions concurrently has the same effect on the initial data as 'some' nonconcurrent serial order, that order is said to be *serializable* and to produce correct results.

The rationale behind that is as follows: *all serial orders are correct, so if a concurrent ordering gives the same results as any serial order, it too must be correct.*

Serializability gives correctness and one way to obtain it is to use *locking*.

---

* Transaction 1 - with locks
* Transfer £100 from bank account A to account B

    Read(BalanceA)   *** Read the 2 balances**
    Lock (BalanceB)   *** Lock B before accessing it**
    Read(BalanceB)

    IF BalanceA > 100 THEN * Transfer the money

                  BalanceA := BalanceA-100
                  Write(BalanceA)   * Update A

                  BalanceB := BalanceB+100
                  Write(BalanceB)   * Update B

    ELSE   * Insufficient funds

                  Write("A does not have £100")

    END

    UnLock (BalanceB)   *** Unlock B**

Example 9.4a   T1 with locks

Locking Before updating shared data, a transaction first *locks* it. When an item is locked by a transaction, no other transaction can access it until the lock is released.

Transaction T1, to transfer funds from A to B, and T2, to withdraw funds from B, used in examples 9.2 and 9.3 can be rewritten using locks. This is shown in example 9.4.

Example 9.5 shows how the lock on BalanceB ensures that T1 and T2 update it in a serial order. It does not matter which transaction locks BalanceB first. What is important is that while one transaction is updating the balance, reading it, calculating the new balance and writing it back, the other transaction is kept waiting. Note that only shared resources have to be locked.

```
* Transaction 2 - with locks
* Debit £100 from account B


Lock (BalanceB)              * Lock it
Read(BalanceB)               * Read the balance

IF BalanceB > 100 THEN  * Debit the account

              BalanceB := BalanceB-100
              Write(BalanceB)          * Update the account

ELSE

              Write("B does not have £100")

END

UnLock (B)                   * Unlock it
```

Example 9.4b   T2 with locks

For more complicated examples than this, the *order* in which locks are set and released becomes important. Different protocols exist to ensure that using locks gives the correct results. The next section describes one such protocol.

Two-phase locking   Serializability can be guaranteed if all transactions obey a *two Phase Locking Protocol*[7]. In this protocol, all locks are acquired in the locking phase, and are released in the releasing phase. Once a transaction releases any lock, it enters the releasing phase and no new locks can be acquired within that transaction, see figure 9.10a.

The most common implementation of this protocol is *contracted two-phase locking* (see figure 9.10b). All locks are held until the end of the transaction, i.e. there is no releasing phase, or rather, all locks are released together.

This account of serializability may be summarized as follows. If concurrent transactions run in an order which produces the same results as some serial order, the results are consistent. This is known as a serializable order and can be achieved by all transactions obeying the two-phase locking

Transaction1	Transaction2	Operation
T1.BalanceA := 200		T1 reads A
Lock(BalanceB)		**T1 locks BalanceB**
T1.BalanceB := 300		T1 reads BalanceB
	Lock(BalanceB)	**T2 cannot lock BalanceB as it is already locked**
T1.BalanceA := T1.BalanceA - 100		T1 debits A
Write(T1.BalanceA)		and updates it
T1.BalanceB := T1.BalanceB + 100		T1 credits B
Write(T1.BalanceB)		Updates it to 400
UnLock(BalanceB)	Unlock it	
	Lock(BalanceB)	**Lock granted NOW**
	T2.BalanceB := 400	**Read the value set by T1**
	T2.BalanceB := T2.BalanceB - 10	calculate correct value (300)
	Write(T2.BalanceB)	update it
	UnLock(BalanceB)	

Example 9.5   Concurrent execution of transaction T1 and T2 using locks

protocol. This does not produce the maximum amount of concurrency but gives acceptable performance. Other types of locking do exist.

Timestamping   An alternative method to locking for ensuring serializability is that of *time stamps* [9].

Associated with each transaction in the system is a globally unique timestamp. This is a number assigned to each transaction when it begins. The smaller the number, the 'older' the transaction. A timestamp can be

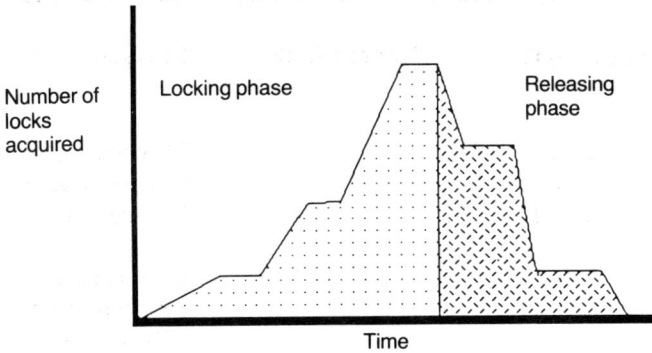

Figure 9.10a   Two-phase locking

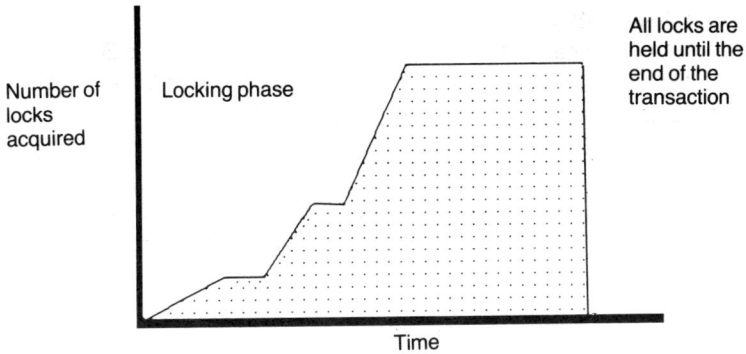

Figure 9.10b   Contracted two-phase locking

generated by concatenating a local clock reading to give the time, and the processor ID number to ensure uniqueness.

Timestamps reflect the passage of time and thus can be used to give an ordering of transactions. If updates are only allowed in the order dictated by the timestamps, that order must be serializable and therefore correct. The ordering of updates is ensured as follows.

Each item to be updated, a file or record, keeps two time stamps (TS). One stamp is that of the last transaction to read it (RTS) and the other for the last one to write it (WTS). Reads and writes are only allowed to go ahead if they do not affect the *time order*, as described below.

Reading data   A transaction T1 with timestamp TS cannot read an item if it has already been written by a younger transaction T2, i.e. $TS < WTS$. This is because in a serial order the older reading transaction (T1) would have completed before the younger one (T2) began, and performed the write. Thus the transaction is not allowed to read data which according to its own timestamp value has not yet been written. The transaction is aborted and restarted with a new and younger timestamp.

This argument can be rephrased as follows: if all reads and writes were done strictly according to the timestamp order then the data read by T1 would not have been written to by T2.

T1 is permitted to read data that has already been read by a younger transaction, T2, because reading in no way affects the value that was read by T2.

Writing data   A transaction cannot write an item if it has already been read or written by an older transaction, i.e. $TS < RTS | WTS$. Again the offending transaction is aborted and restarted.

Obeying these rules and aborting offending transactions and restarting them ensures that the order is serializable (see example 9.6).

Both timestamping and locking are widely used in practice with locking being more common.

9.3.5.6 Transaction summary
Support for transactions is a very important function of a file server. This discussion has focused in on two important aspects of transactions, namely *atomicity* and *concurrency*. More detailed descriptions of these and other aspects of transactions can be found in the references.

9.3.6 Protocol and performance issues
The design of protocols used by a file server to communicate with its clients and other servers usually follows the principles outlined in the previous chapter. Most file servers implemented to date use lightweight problem-oriented protocols with idempotent operations. Unlike a disk server, a file server may have a built-in file transfer protocol.

An important performance consideration in implementing a file server is the relationship between the following items:

- the packet size used in the communication protocol by the file server;
- the size of the servers' buffers for storing data;
- the number of those buffers on the server; this will be determined by the amount of available main memory;
- the block size on disk;
- the rate at which data arrives at the server, i.e. is the load evenly distributed over time or is the traffic uneven?

When a single server is handling a number of clients, it becomes a potential

Record R

	Read timestamp	Write Timestamp
Initial values	0	0
A writes to R	0	1
B reads R	2	1
A reads R	2	1
B writes to R	2	2

A tries to write to R but is
not allowed because the write
timestamp is younger than its
own value.

**Example 9.6   Controlling concurrent access to a record
using time stamps**
Note: Transaction A with timestamp 1 and transaction B with timestamp 2 concurrently
access a record R

bottleneck in the performance of the system. The following steps can be taken
to improve performance.

- **Better hardware** More powerful hardware can be used to implement the
server. In particular, the data handling speed of the network adapter card,
or interface, and the amount of buffer space available have a significant
effect on throughput.
- **Multiple servers** More servers can be added to the network.
- **Front-end to the file server** This is the solution adopted in the Cambridge
Distributed System [8]. The network consisted of a single file server (CFS)
and a number of processes running different operating systems. In
particular the TRIPOS [8] operating system was run by a large number of
the workstations on the network. The initial configuration had each
machine running TRIPOS communicating directly with CFS (see figure
9.11).

This was modified so that the file system function from TRIPOS was
provided by a dedicated server, called the front end. All Tripos systems
interfaced to the front end which in turn interfaced to CFS.

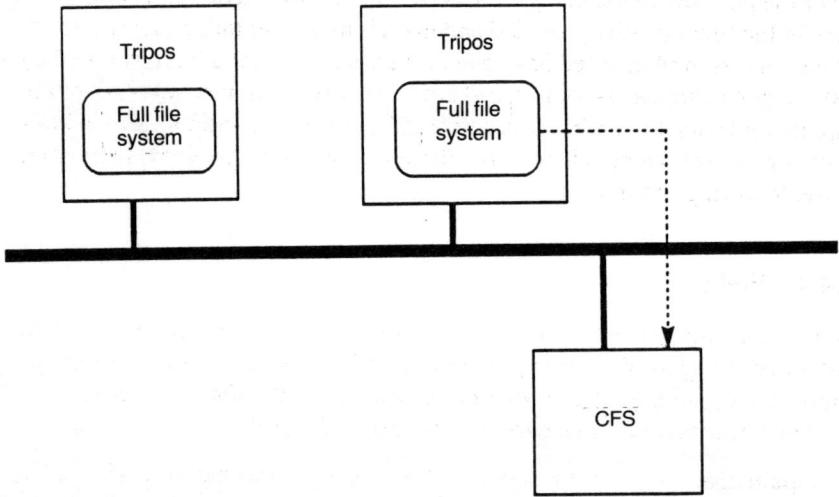

Figure 9.11a   TRIPOS using CFS

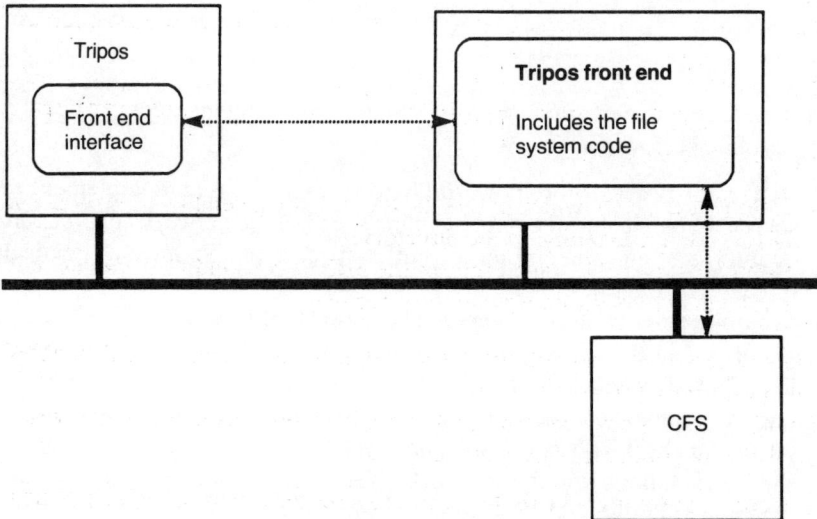

Figure 9.11b   TRIPOS interfacing via the front end

9.4 EXAMPLE SYSTEMS

Over the past few years, many file servers have been designed and built. They vary in the functionality provided and in their implementation. The majority of file servers implemented have been for research projects but recently they have begun to appear as commercial products. These commercial versions are rapidly replacing the earlier disk servers. This chapter concludes with a brief overview of two sample file servers. Further examples of file servers are given in the following chapter.

9.4.1 Felix

Felix is the name given to a file server developed at Bell Northern Research [10] in 1980 as part of a larger project in distributed systems. Its aims were to support *page faulting*, the *secure storage of data* and the *sharing of files*.

The key features of Felix are summarized as follows.

- **Capabilities** These were chosen as the protection mechanism. When a file is created the server returns a unique capability to be used in all further references to that file.
- **Block I/O** All file I/O is done in terms of disk blocks. Disk blocks are the same size as virtual memory pages. This greatly simplifies the handling of page faults.
- **Atomic update** This is supported for single files and collections of files (known as a set). In the case of sets all the files must reside on the same server, as Felix is not a distributed server.
- **Directories** A very limited amount of support is given for directories. The server maintains a single directory file to be used by all users. Two operations are exported

    - Enter(Name,FID), which enters the file with the given File Identification (FID), i.e. a capability, in the directory.
    - Search(Name,FID), which returns the FID corresponding to 'Name' if it has been previously entered in the directory.

    These operations, and optional password protection, can be used to build up any desired directory structure.
- **Sharing** This is provided for by allowing files to be locked for read or write access in any of the following modes.

    - **Copy** A user is given a copy of the most recent version of the file. When locked in this mode, for reading or writing, the version given to the user will not change but updates can be made to the original version. These updates will not be seen by the user.
    - **Original** This is the usual locking mode used when the file is being updated. The most recent version of the file is locked and no other

'original locks' are granted. Copy type locks are allowed. Any updates
made cause a new version of the file to be created with a higher version
number.

– **Exclusive** The file is locked and no other locks of any type copy or
original, are allowed.

Felix uses standard techniques in its implementation. A hierarchical tree of
disk blocks is maintained. This includes both free and allocated blocks. Data
is not written in place and all blocks are shadowed while being updated. The
root of the tree is held in stable storage, at two well-known blocks.

9.4.2   NetWare

NetWare is the name of a layer of network software developed by Novelle
[11]. It runs on a PC Network (IBM PCs) and enhances the functionality
provided by the PC Network environment. Its application is very different
from that of Felix. NetWare is a commercial product running on small
personal computers connected over a medium speed network. The applications that use its services are the usual office ones, spreadsheets, data bases
etc. It allows a number of file servers to be connected to the LAN. Each file
server also acts as a print server capable of handling a number of printers.
Access to a file server is transparent to users and directories on the server
appear as if they were on local disks. The server offers a transaction facility for
updating files. A powerful protection mechanism is available. The access
rights on files include *open*, *read*, *write*, *create* and *delete*. A *modify right* is also
associated with each file which is required if the existing rights are to be
changed. Users can be categorized into groups and access rights can be
associated with groups.

Locking is catered for both at record level where a lock is placed on an
individual record within a file and at file level where a number of files can be
locked in the same set. It is also possible to archive and restore entire files.

9.4.3   ISO file transfer and access management (FTAM) protocol

This chapter has introduced two example file servers that are currently in use
in industry and academia. For completeness, we will now discuss the evolving
international standard in this area. In Chapter 6, when studying the OSI
reference model, we saw that the software to provide and use network
services resides in the application layer (layer 7). This is made up of a
commonly used set of primitives called CASE, and *specific application service
elements (SASE)* to cope with particular applications. The name given to the
SASE that deal with remote file access is known as the *file transfer and access
management* (FTAM) set.

At the time of writing, this ISO standard is still very much in its infancy.
The main service offered is that of file transfer from one node on the network

to another. The definition of FTAM is, however, very open-ended, and it is expected that it will evolve in the direction of a fully fledged file server.

Figure 9.12 shows a *file service provider* (responder) and a *file service user* (FSU) in session. The FSU carries out operations on files contained in a *virtual filestore*. This is an idealized filestore with operations expressed in a generalized form. It is up to the responder to map this virtual system onto the one used to store files locally before the operations are carried out.

The set of primitives provided by FTAM cover initiating/terminating a session and selecting/deselecting a file. Once selected, a file's attributes (e.g. access, size etc.) can be examined or changed, or its contents can be read/ written.

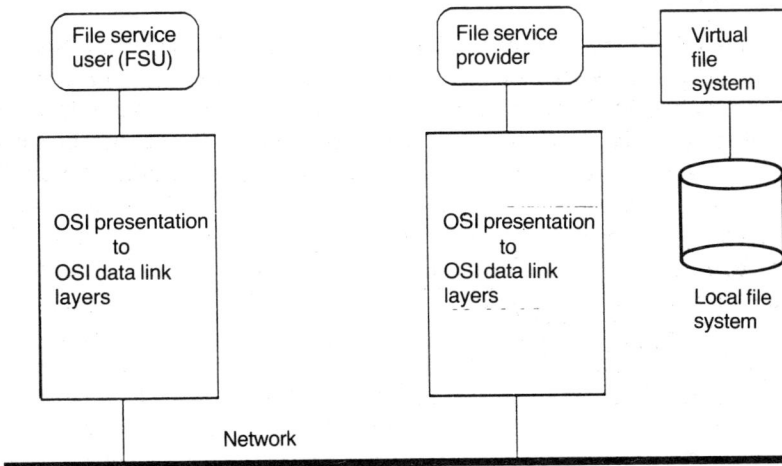

Figure 9.12   ISO FTAM

The internal format of the file is specified when it is opened, and can be either variable length records of up to 80 characters, terminated by a carriage return/line feed combination, or it is taken as a nonstructured bitstring. In future versions of FTAM, this aspect of file access will be dealt with by a process of negotiation between the two presentation layers involved in the transfer.

Transactions are not supported in phase 1 of FTAM, but primitives are available in CASE to support this at a later date. Similarly, in the event of failure, FTAM leaves the file in an indeterminate state (called *no rollback*). This is also likely to change in the future.

As it stands, the services provided by FTAM are incomplete. However, by the time it becomes a mature international standard, one would expect it to provide the full range of file server functions across all types of network and between dissimilar systems.

9.5 SUMMARY

This chapter has introduced file servers. The aims and motivations have been covered as have key parts of the implementation. Two sample servers aimed at very different uses have been described and standardization efforts in this area have been outlined. More detailed descriptions of file server implementations are found in the next chapter, where they are described as an integral part of distributed systems. The references contain a list of further reading on the topic.

9.6 REFERENCES

1   Lister, A.M.: *Fundamentals of Operating Systems*, London: Macmillan, 1979.
2   Date, C.J.: *An Introduction to Database Systems, Vols 1 and 2*, London: Addison-Wesley, 1986.
3   'The CAP filing system', *Proceedings of the Sixth Symposium on Operating Systems Principles*, Purdure University, 1978.
4   Thomas, R.H.: 'A majority consensus approach to concurrency control', *ACM Transactions on Database systems*, **4**, no. 2, June 1979.
5   Gifford, D.K.: 'Weighted voting for replicated data', *Proceedings of the Seventh Symposium on Operating Systems Principles*, 1979.
6   Lampson, B.W. and Sturgis, H.E.: *Crash recovery in a distributed data storage system*, Research report, XEROX, Palo Alto Research Center, 1979.
7   Gray, J.N.: 'Notes on database operating systems' in *Lecture Notes in Computer Science No. 60*, eds X. Goos and X. Hartman, Berlin, Springer Verlag, 1978.
8   Needham, R.M. and Herbert, A.J.: *The Cambridge Distributed Operating System*, Addison Wesley International Computer Science Series, London: Addison Wesley, 1982.
9   Lamport, L.: 'Time clocks and the ordering of events in a distributed system', *Communications of the ACM*, **21**, no. 7, pp. 558–565, July 1978.
10 Fridrich, M. and Older, W.: 'The Felix file server', *Proceedings of the Eighth Symposium on Operating Systems Principles*, Pacific Grove, California, 1981.
11 Krumrey, K.: 'Netware in control', *PC Technical Journal*, **3**, no. 11, pp. 103–119, November, 1985.
12 Sturgis, H.E., Mitchell, J.G. and Israel, J.E.: 'Issues in the design and use of a distributed file system', *ACM Sigops Operating Systems Review*, **14**, no. 3, pp. 55–59, July, 1980.
13 Alsberg, P.A. and Day, J.D.: 'A principle for resilient sharing of distributed resources', *Second International Conference on Software Engineering*, 1976.
14 Svobodov, L.: 'File servers for network based distributed systems', *ACM Computing Survey*, **16**, no. 4, pp. 353–399, December 1984.

CHAPTER TEN

DISTRIBUTED SYSTEMS

A *distributed computing system* is one in which the components of the system, printers, processors etc., are connected together via a network but which offers to its users a single coherent computing environment. Two important aspects of such a system have been examined in previous chapters, namely servers; and file servers in particular. This chapter continues this discussion and begins by listing some of the main difficulties encountered in achieving this goal.

- **Failure** Nodes on a network exhibit independent failure modes, as explained in the previous chapter.
- **Naming** Resources have to be uniquely named and located on the network.
- **Distributing control** Algorithms which favor one particular node over all others should be avoided to improve reliability.
- **Heterogeneity** Nodes on the network may be heterogeneous, with different word sizes and byte ordering. Heterogeneity can also extend to the software level, with nodes running different operating systems.

When users write application programs on a single processor, they are not required to know the underlying details of the hardware. Everything from naming to interfacing to disks is taken care of by an intermediate layer of software, i.e. the operating system. Similarly the user of a distributed computing system should not be required to know the details of the system that he/she is working on.

This chapter focuses on the layer of software which performs that task, i.e. hides the network, in a distributed computing system. We will refer to it as a *distributed operating system* (DOS) or just *distributed system*.

10.1 APPROACHES TO BUILDING A DISTRIBUTED SYSTEM

There are three different starting points that can be taken when writing a distributed operating system, see figure 10.1.

- **From scratch** Because the type of system envisaged is different from any existing ones, there are strong arguments in favor of designing a distributed system from scratch. This gives complete freedom to the designer but means that all system and application software also has to be written.
- **Modify an existing system** This is the second possible starting point. By maintaining compatibility with some existing system, the amount of new software to be written is minimized, there is a working version to compare

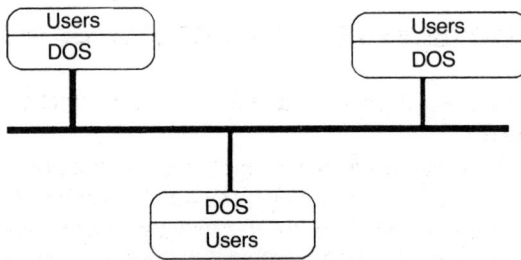

Approach 1: DOS is built from scratch

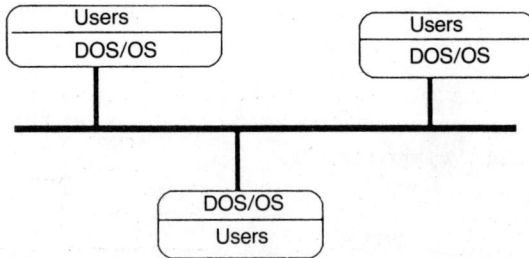

Approach 2: DOS is based on modifying an existing operating system

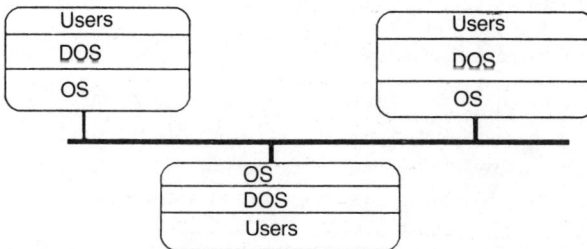

Approach 3: DOS is built on top of an existing operating system

Figure 10.1   Three approaches to building a distributed operating system (DOS)

with during development and there is a base of users to test the system. A disadvantage is that some design decisions will be compromised by a need to remain compatible with the original.

- **The layered approach** It is not always possible or desirable to modify existing system software. The final approach is to take an existing operating system and add an additional layer of software between it and the user, to provide the distribution. This type of system is also known as a *network operating system* and has the same attractions as the previous method, but does not require changing the existing operating system. The disadvantage is that performance will be compromised because all calls to the operating system go through the intermediate network layer.

10.2 THE SERVER VERSUS THE INTEGRATED MODEL

No matter what starting point is used, there are two distinct architectures for a distributed system.

The first is the *server model* which has been covered previously. Standard operating system functions are not implemented on each node but on specific server nodes. Client nodes contain just enough software to access the server (see figure 10.2a). A disadvantage of this architecture is that machine boundaries have to be crossed with associated performance penalties when remote services are invoked.

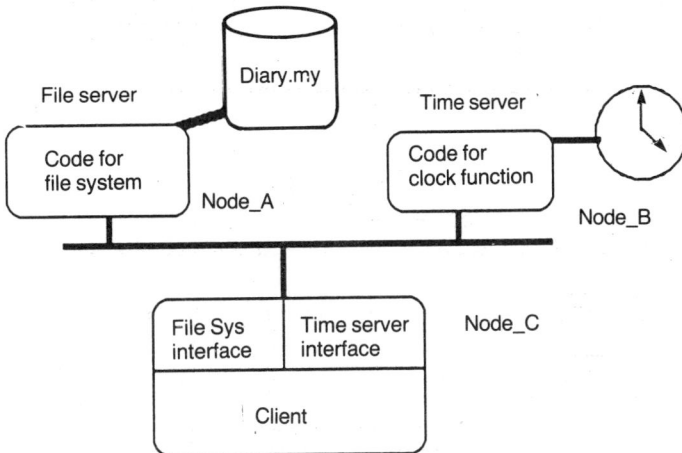

Figure 10.2a Server model

Note: The client node does not have a code to implement all operating system functions. Instead they are implemented on server nodes. Clients run enough software to interface to the servers. The advantage is that the servers offload much of the work from client nodes. The disadvantage is that machine boundaries have to be crossed to invoke the services

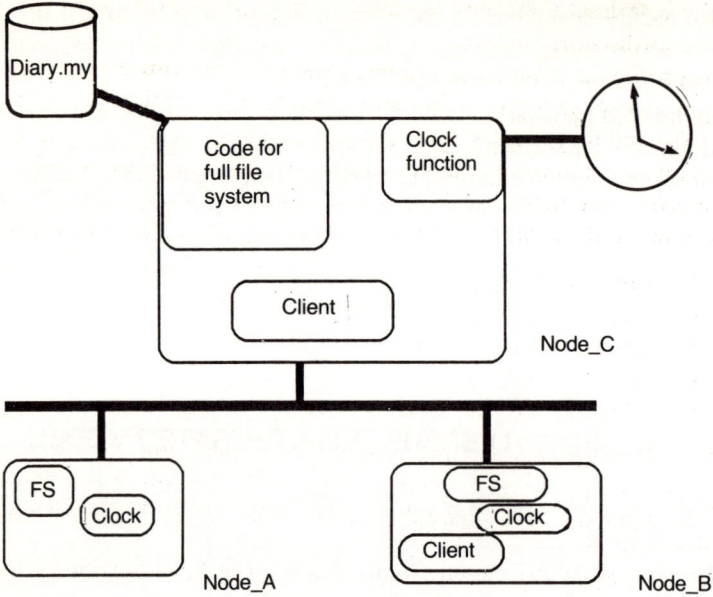

Figure 10.2b   The integrated model
Note: Each node runs a full copy of the operating system. As much work as possible is
done locally. Remote resources can still be accessed

An alternative architecture is the *integrated model*. Each node is configured with a 'complete' (integrated) version of the operating system, i.e., the code used to implement standard operating system functions runs on every node (see figure 10.2b). Locus [2] is a good example of such a system and it is examined in more detail later. There is nothing in the integrated model to stop a node accessing files or resources on remote nodes. If there was, it could hardly be called a distributed system. The point is that each node has a full copy of the operating system which means that much of the work can be done locally and machine boundaries are only crossed when necessary. In the server model, servers perform much of the work whereas in the integrated one the emphasis is on each node doing as much as it can for itself.

10.3   THE IMPORTANCE OF THE FILE SYSTEM

Just as the filing system is at the heart of any conventional operating system, it also plays a crucial role in the design of a distributed one. It is at this level that such issues as transaction support, replication, naming etc. must be tackled. The importance of the file system is brought out in each of the examples looked at towards the end of the chapter.

10.4 ISSUES

The following is an incomplete list of some of the main issues and problems that are faced in developing a DOS. Some have been dealt with in previous chapters and will not be discussed in detail again here.

- **Protection** Access lists or capabilities can be used, as discussed in the previous chapter.
- **Replication/availability** Replication can improve the performance of a system by increasing the availability of critical resources. Any resource can be replicated, e.g. files, printers, etc. It is the responsibility of the DOS to control the amount of replication, concurrent access to replicated resources and redirection of access in the event of failure.
- **Transactions** The file system of a DOS should provide as general and as flexible a transaction mechanism as possible.

The following sections discuss some of these issues in more detail.

10.4.1 Naming

All objects, e.g. files, devices or processes, in a system must be named. Each object will have at least two names. A symbolic name recognized by the user, e.g. the file called test.dat, and an internal name used by the system, e.g. 42595. The internal name may be the actual location of the object, i.e. its address, or it may provide a means to find the address of the object.

Names can be used for many things apart from locating objects, e.g. sharing, scheduling etc. [18]. There can be many names for the same object and the same name can be used to refer to different objects. User names are converted into internal names via some sort of *mapping*, e.g. looking up a table or directory.

Figure 10.3a shows a simple file directory structure. User *Fred* has three files. Fred's directory contains an entry for each and a *pointer* to the corresponding file on disk. User *Mary* also has three files. The same name can be used to refer to different files, e.g. both directories contain the name s.pas but they point to different files. Different names can be used to refer to the same file, e.g., test.dat in Fred's directory and old.dat in Mary's both point to file 1.

Because a system may have a number of users, directories are often organized into a hierarchical structure, as shown in figure 10.3b. A *root* or master directory contains an entry for each user. File names must therefore include not just the name itself but also the names of all directories between it and the root.

The full file *pathname* for Fred's file *test.dat* is ROOT:FRED:TEST.DAT. Most systems allow a user to set a default or *current* directory. Users do not have to supply a full path name when accessing a file, as the system prefixes the name given by the user with the name of the current directory. For example Fred

L.A.N.—L

2 Directories   Files on disk

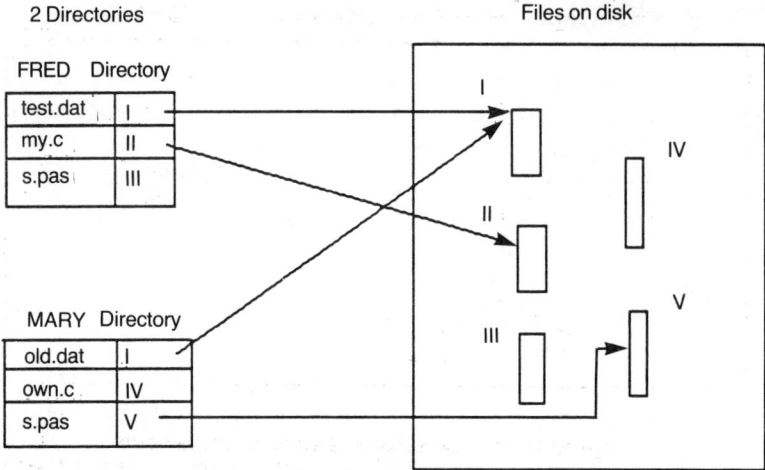

Figure 10.3a   Two directories

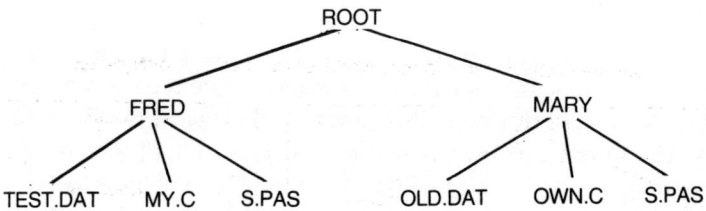

Figure 10.3b   Hierarchical structure

could set his default directory to be ROOT:FRED, and on using the name, MY.C the system would automatically prefix it with the default directory name to give the full path name ROOT:FRED:MY.C.

This is an example of associating *context information* with a name. The name MY.C is interpreted not on its own, but as a part of some wider context. This is how Fred, with default directory ROOT:FRED, and Mary, with default directory ROOT:MARY, can use the same name to refer to different files. Similarly the name S.PAS is interpreted to mean file III when used in Fred's context and file V when used in Mary's.

10.4.1.1   Naming in a distributed environment

A distributed system must also provide a naming mechanism. The mapping becomes more complicated because names are used to refer to resources on different nodes. A simple solution to the problem is that adopted in DECnet [6]. DECnet nodes run standard Digital operating systems, like *VMS*, *RSX* and *ULTRIX* and one of the facilities offered is for files to be accessed from any node on the network.

VMS File Name Format: Device: [directories.dir1 . . . . dirN]file.ext

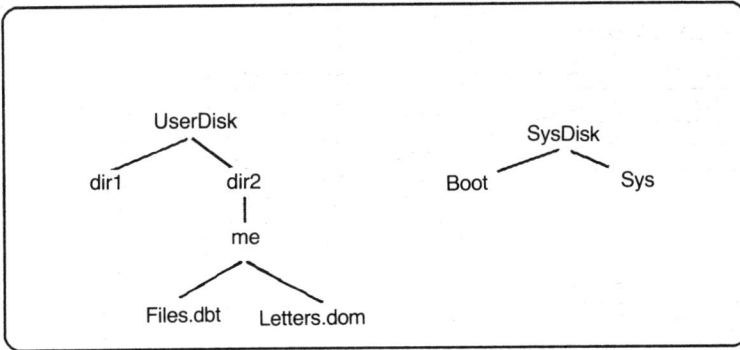

Figure 10.4a   VMS directories on a single node

Note: The diagram shows the VMS-style directory structure on two devices, UserDisk and SysDisk. There are two directories on the device UserDisk. The directory 'Dir2' has a single subdirectory 'me'. It contains two files Files.dbt and Letters.dom
The full pathname of the file Letters.dom is UserDisk: [dir2.me]Letters.dom

Decnet VMS file name format: Node::device:[dir1 . . . . dirN]file.ext

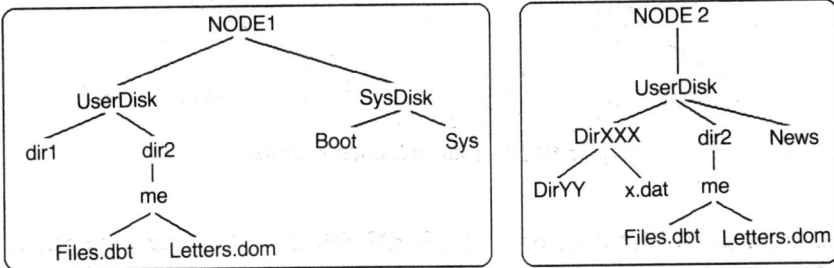

The directories on two VMS nodes.

Figure 10.4b   DECnet naming

Note: The naming hierarchy is extended up one level to include the node name. The full pathname of the file Letters.dom on node1 is now:
Node1::UserDisk:[dir2.me]Letters.dom
Users can access files from anywhere on the network by preceding the local pathname with the node name

Most naming systems are hierarchical and VMS [9] names are no exception. A full VMS path name consists of a *device* name followed by any number of *directory* names followed by the *file* name and extension (see figure 10.4a).

Network-wide naming is achieved by extending the hierarchy up one level to include the *node name* (see figure 10.4b). Files on remote nodes are accessed by putting the node name in front of the path name of the file.

For this scheme to work, node names must be unique and each node must know the name of all the other nodes on the network. (In Decnet and the Newcastle Connection, described later, the system looks after all details of converting from node names to physical addresses.) This scheme is relatively easy to implement and simple for users to grasp, as the interface to remote files is a minor extension to the local naming convention.

Simple as the technique is, it suffers from a number of drawbacks. Because the location of the file is an integral part of the file name, moving the file from one node to another means that the file name must be changed. Thus all references to the file will also have to be changed. Nor is access to replicated files supported. If two copies of the file exist then they will have different names and have to be updated individually.

The problem with this naming mechanism is that some of the underlying details of the network are visible to the user. In this case, the location of a file, in the form of its node name, is embedded in the file name. This notion of hiding the network from the user has been previously referred to. It is known as *network transparency*.

10.4.2 Transparency

Network transparency requires that the details of the network are hidden from the end user. Thus a user of a truly transparent distributed system should be under the impression that he is using a single large mainframe and it should be possible to move a file without changing its name. If this can be achieved, writing programs for a distributed system should be no more difficult than writing for conventional ones. There are a number of different aspects to transparency [2].

- For reasons outlined above, the *location* of a resource should not be embedded in its name.
- Names should be globally unique and have the same *meaning* no matter at what site they are used.
- The same name should have the same *effect* no matter at what site it is used.

To illustrate the last two points, take the following command line EDIT C::myfile.pas, and the network configuration as shown in figure 10.5 – for convenience Decnet VMS style network names are used, but the device and directory name have been omitted for simplicity. The command is a request from the user to invoke an editor on the file C::myfile.pas.

The name C::myfile.pas used on NodeA or on NodeB refers to the same physical file, which happens to reside on NodeC, i.e. the network-wide name C::myfile.pas *means* the same thing on all nodes.

The command EDIT invokes an editor. To achieve transparency the same command should invoke exactly the same editor on any node. It is unacceptable that the *effect* of EDIT should be to invoke a line editor on Node1, and to invoke a full screen editor on Node3.

Thus it can be seen that transparency is more than simply hiding the

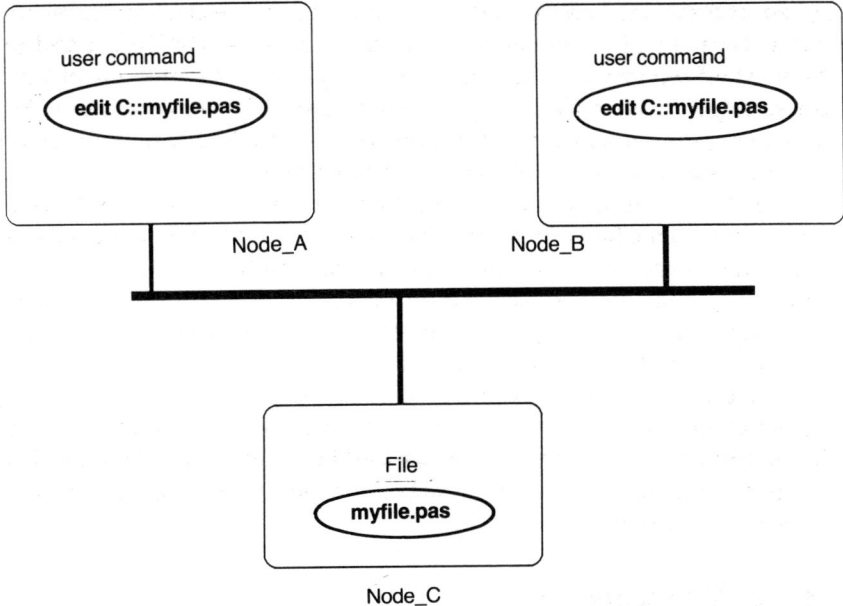

Figure 10.5   Transparency

Note: The name 'myfile.pas' should mean the same thing when used from both nodes A and B. The command 'edit' should invoke a copy of the same editor when used on nodes A or B

location from the user. How various systems tackle, or do not tackle, the transparency problem is investigated later in this chapter.

10.4.2.1   Problems with transparency

Providing full transparency is not always possible or indeed desirable. Transparency conflicts with the following requirements of distributed systems in particular.

- **Local autonomy**   It is natural for the administrator/owner of a node in a distributed system to want to retain as much local control over his own resources as is possible. This can sometimes conflict with network-wide transparency. Take the 'edit' example from the previous section. As the same command must have the same effect on all nodes, the system manager of NodeA cannot change the default editor used locally. Such decisions must be taken at a network level. Thus the manager loses authority over his node: autonomy is sacrificed for transparency.
- **Optimization**   In some cases the user may wish to have explicit knowledge and control of the location of resources. This may be required to optimize the system performance, by locating frequently used resources where they can be accessed quickly. What is required is a mechanism whereby transparency can be bypassed, or side stepped, if desired.

- **Heterogeneity**   Full transparency is difficult to achieve. The problem arises at two levels. The first is if the underlying hardware varies from node to node, e.g. a program compiled to run on a 32 bit processor cannot be expected to execute on a 16 bit one. Locus, described later, goes some way towards getting around this. A more severe problem arises if the nodes run different operating systems [2]. It is very difficult to make the differences between them transparent. On Decnet, for example, the number of operations that operate between nodes running heterogeneous operating systems is a subset of those that work across homogeneous ones [6].

10.4.3 Control

An operating system controls access to and use of its resources. Examples are scheduling the CPU between processes, opening and closing files etc. In a single computer, all the algorithms that the operating system uses are *centralized*, i.e. the final decision is taken in one place only. In a distributed system, a number of nodes can be involved in making a decision. Algorithms where decisions are not concentrated in a single node are said to be *distributed*, i.e. the control of a resource is not concentrated in a single place but rather distributed around the network.

Examples of this were seen in the previous chapter in the discussion on updating replicated files. 'Primary copy update' is a centralized algorithm while 'voting' is distributed. A second example can be seen in the different 'access methods' used on various networks. A star network, where the controller polls each node in turn, is an example of a centralized algorithm: the controller decides which node transmits next. CSMA/CD on the other hand is a distributed algorithm because no single node controls access to the transmission medium.

The normal decision-making process on uniprocessors is centralized. Distributed systems provide an opportunity to develop a different type of decision-making process. One of the main advantages is that the availability of a resource is not determined by the availability of a particular controlling node.

To continue with network access methods as examples, any network which uses polling to control access to the medium is vulnerable to the failure of the *controlling node*. A distributed control algorithm is much more robust, e.g. in CSMA/CD, *any number of nodes* can fail without affecting the availability of the resource, i.e. the transmission medium.

To increase reliability in a distributed system control should be as distributed as possible.

10.4.4 Communication aspects

Distributed systems are based on the fact that spatially separated nodes can exchange information with each other. This section focuses on some of the issues raised in designing a communication mechanism for a distributed system.

10.4.4.1 Message passing

At the lowest level, all processes communicate with each other by exchanging *messages*. A message is a unit of information of any size, sent from one process to another. Messages are sent out over the network in packets, using whatever facilities are provided by the network. A process wishing to transmit information *sends* a message. The destination process picks up the message by doing *a receive*, and at some later stage responds to the sender by doing a *reply* to the original 'sender'. Thus a distributed system that supports message passing must supply *send*, *receive* and *reply* as primitive operations.

There are two basic types of send/receive operations, with numerous variations. These are *synchronous* and *asynchronous* message passing, they are also referred to as blocking and nonblocking primitives. In a synchronous send operation, the sender of the message is suspended, blocked from executing further, until the reply arrives (see figure 10.6a). In the asynchronous case, the sender continues execution and picks up the reply at a later stage by doing an explicit receive operation. A synchronous *receive* operation 'blocks' until a message arrives, while the asynchronous version returns immediately if there are no messages waiting.

Messages take up space and are held in system buffers. When asynchronous communication is used each process on the network can have

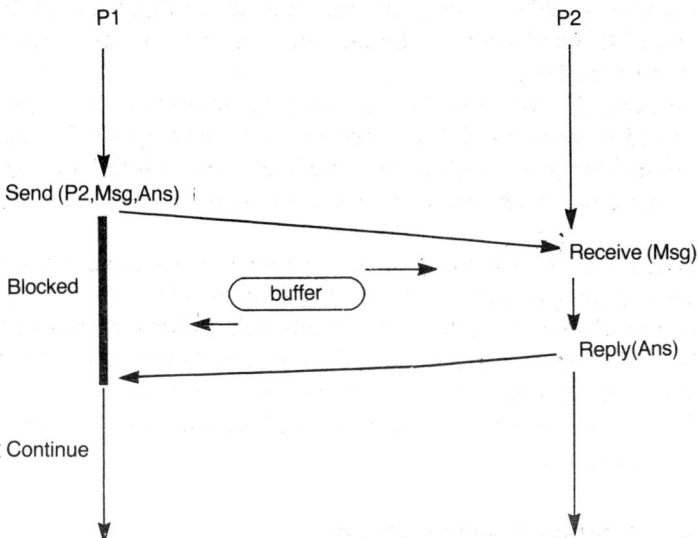

Figure 10.6a Synchronous message passing
Note: The sender is blocked until the receiver replies

P1   P2

Send(P2,Msg)
**Continue
execution**   Receive(Msg)
                        (buffer)
                                                 Reply(Ans)
Send(P3,Msg2)

Receive(Ans)
(buffer)
Pick up reply
later

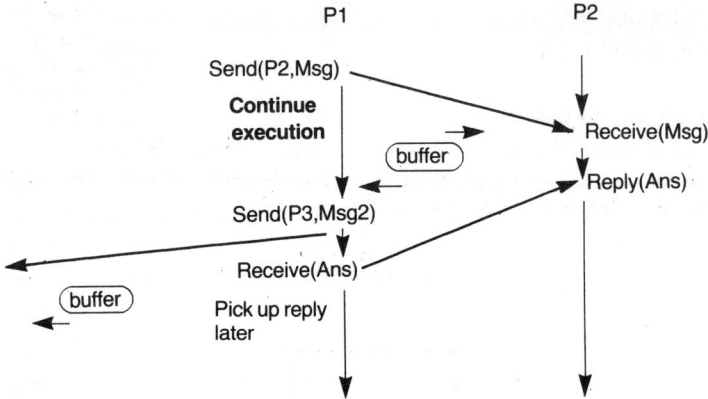

Figure 10.6b   Asynchronous message passing
Note: P1 continues executing after the send operation and picks the reply up later

many messages outstanding at the one time. Message buffers are a finite
resource, so it can happen when using asynchronous message passing that the
supply of buffers becomes exhausted. Asynchronous message passing
demands that the system implements nontrivial *buffer management*
algorithms to cater for this. In synchronous communication on the other hand
there is never more than one message outstanding per process so buffer
management is a much simpler task.

Synchronous message passing is particularly well suited to the client/
server model. A client requiring a server to perform some operations sends it
a message. It is then suspended until the server replies, i.e. the operation is
completed. A server can be written as an infinite loop, waiting to *receive*
requests, processing them and then *reply*ing. Clients are blocked while they
wait for the operation to complete, but a server blocks only when there are no
messages for it, i.e. there is no work for it to do (see figure 10.7).

Synchronous primitives have an additional property other than the ability
to exchange information. When a process invokes a primitive it is suspended
and it remains blocked until the primitive completes. This *blocking* property
of synchronous primitives can be used for synchronization purposes similar to
the way semaphores [10] are used on a uniprocessor. Figure 10.8a shows two
processes synchronizing using a semaphore. When P1 *waits* on the semaphore, *sem*, it is blocked until P2 *signals* it. The same effect, of one process
waiting on another, can be achieved using synchronous send/receive
primitives (see figure 10.8).

Other variations on the send/receive outlined above do exist. A *selective
receive* operation allows the user to select a process or group of processes to
receive from. A *conditional send* will complete immediately, without sending
a message, if the intended receiver is not already blocked waiting to receive a
message. In practice, it has been found that most asynchronous sends are

Client	Server

Send(TimeServer,GetTime,Time)	While TRUE Do
	  Receive (Request)
	  Read_Clock(Time)
	  Reply(Time)
	Od

(Time Server loops for ever receiving requests to read the clock. It does this and replies to the client before looking for the next request.)

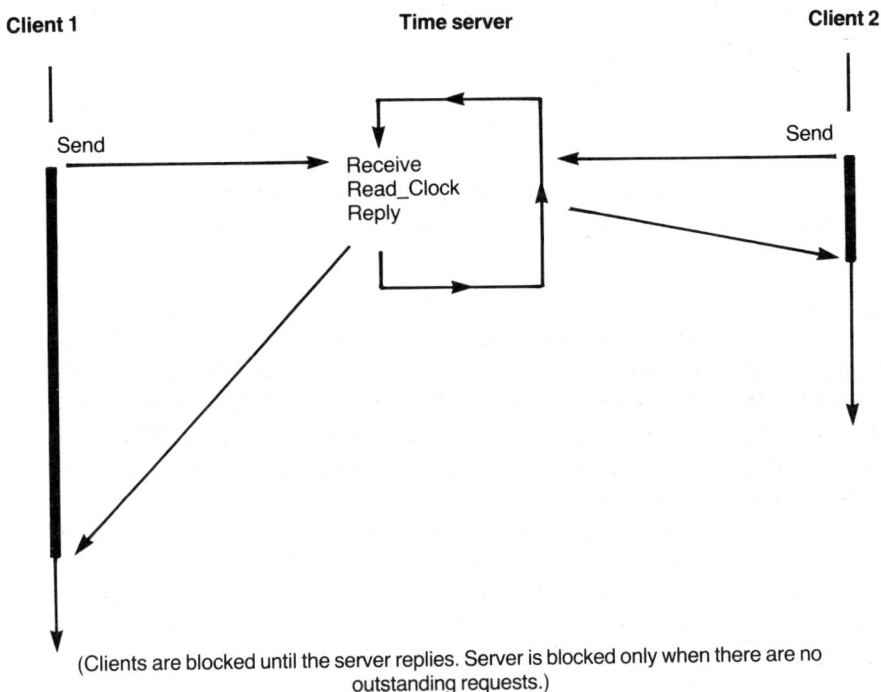

(Clients are blocked until the server replies. Server is blocked only when there are no outstanding requests.)

Figure 10.7   Client/server model using message passing

immediately followed by a receive. For this reason many distributed systems provide only the synchronous versions of the primitives.

10.4.4.2   RPC

The send/receive/reply form of communication bears a very close resemblance to the more familiar *procedure call* used in most programming languages (see figure 10.9). The 'caller/source' is suspended. The 'parameters/message' are passed to the 'callee/destination' which executes. On completion the 'return parameters/message' are transferred back to the 'caller/sender' which then continues execution. A procedure call transfers both *data* and *control* from the caller to the callee.

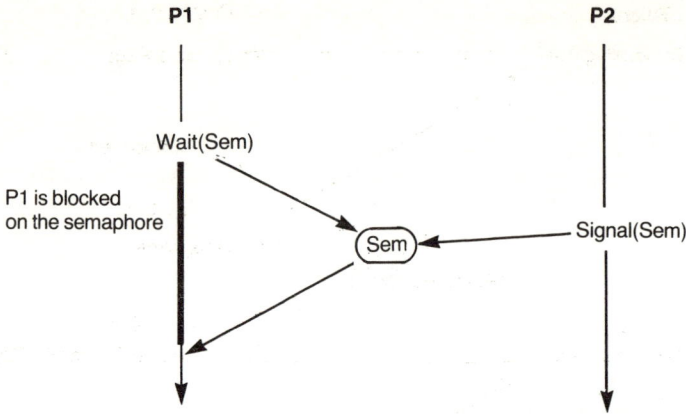

Processes synchronizing using a semaphore **Sem**

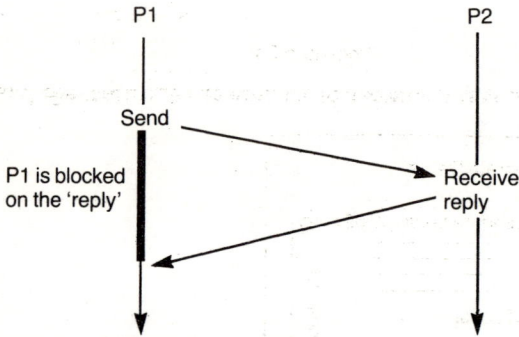

The same effect can be achieved using sysnchronous communication primitives

Figure 10.8   Synchronization

Procedure calls are well understood and widely used as the basic building block for structuring programs in conventional languages. For these reasons there are obvious advantages to be gained if the same concept can be used in distributed systems. *Remote procedure calls* (RPC) [7] are an attempt to extend this concept to the network environment. Programs are still made up of procedures that look and behave just like conventional ones. The difference is that some of the procedures called actually run on a different node than that of the caller (see figure 10.10).

Implementing an RPC   There are two separate aspects to implementing an RPC. Firstly, when a remote call is made, the calling node must be able to locate the node on which the procedure actually runs. Secondly, the two nodes involved must cooperate with each other to exchange parameters. All

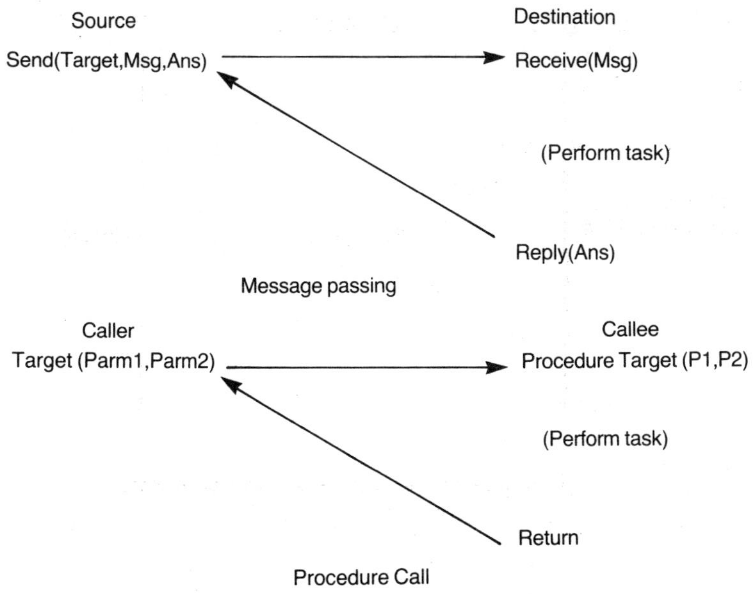

Figure 10.9 **Similarity between procedure call and message passing**

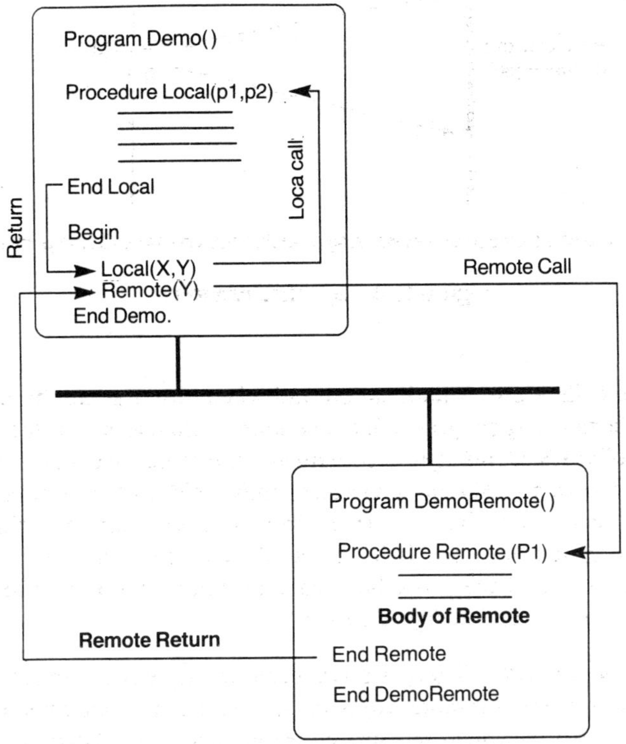

Figure 10.10 **Making a remote procedure call**

this must be done transparently to the user. These two aspects are looked at in turn. Reference [8] describes one implementation of an RPC mechanism. It was implemented as part of the Cedar project [25] and is typical of many RPCs. Its operation is sketched in figure 10.11.

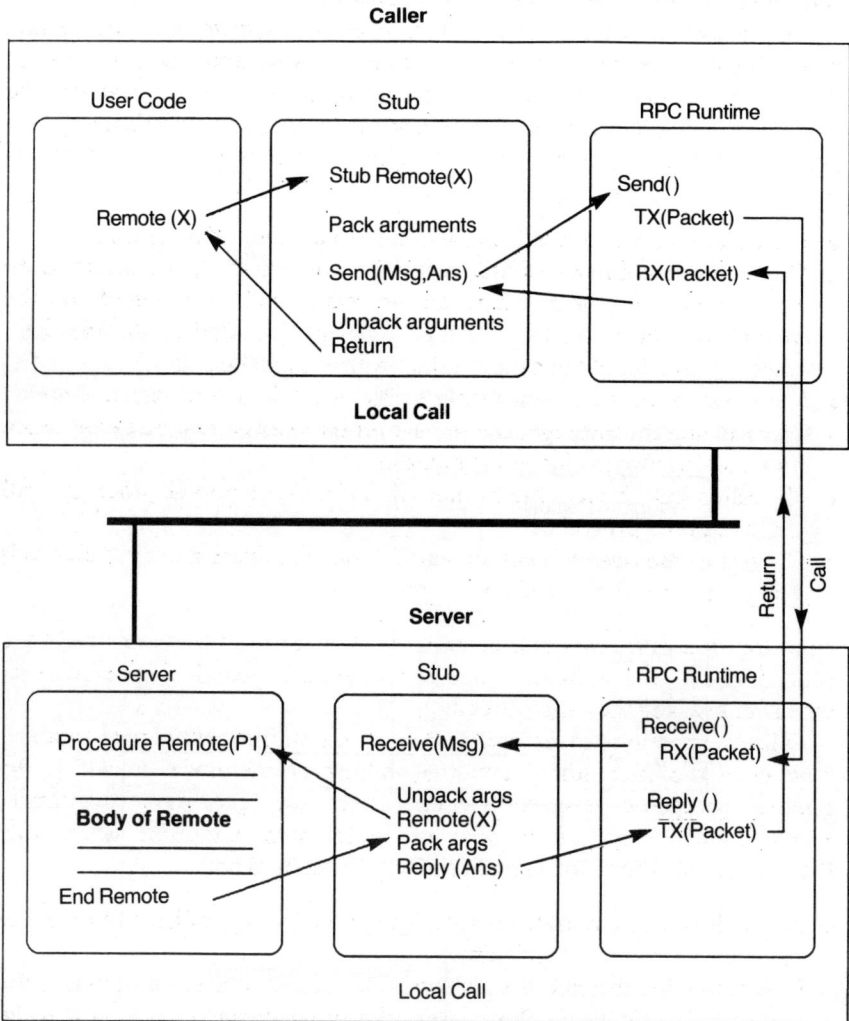

Figure 10.11   Implementing RPC

Each remote call consists of a number of components. There is the caller, or user, code which makes the call and the callee, or server, code which is invoked. Both of these are written in a conventional high level language with no extra facilities provided, just as if they were to execute on the same node.

The other components are a *stub* for the caller, a different stub for the callee, and the *RPC runtime* which executes on all nodes in the system.

The function of the stubs is to pack and unpack the arguments to the call into messages. In addition, type checking can be performed on the parameters as they are being processed. The stubs pass the messages to the runtime which sends them out over the network.

An important point to note is that, given the *definition* of a procedure, producing the code for both stubs is a straightforward and repetitive task. In [8], it is automated and done by a special compiler utility. In practice, the programmer defines the procedure and writes the body of it, while the system produces the corresponding stubs. Invoking a remote procedure works as follows:

- The caller makes a perfectly normal call to a procedure in the stub.
- This stub procedure packs the parameters into a packet, or packets. Both the *address* of the node where the procedure will be executed and the *identifier* of the procedure on that node are included in the message. (Where the caller obtains these values will be explained later.)
- The message is passed to the runtime which sends it to the designated node.
- On receiving the message, the remote runtime calls a routine in the callee stub, passing it to the incoming message.
- The callee stub unpacks the parameters and makes a normal procedure call to the required procedure.
- The results are returned in a similar fashion, culminating in the caller stub doing a 'return from procedure' to the callee.

Note that the caller makes a procedure call and the callee is invoked by a procedure call, the stubs and runtime cooperate to give the impression that the caller invoked the callee directly.

This description leaves one important question unanswered. Namely, how does the user stub know the address of the node on which the remote procedure executes?, i.e., given the procedure invocation, ProcX(Param1,Param2), how does the caller stub determine what node ProcX runs on? There are a number of ways it can find out:

- The address of the remote node can be written into the caller stub when it is generated. This is very inflexible.
- Before making the call, the stub could broadcast to the world, asking the node to identify itself. This causes a lot of traffic and can be slow if the broadcast has to be propagated over a number of interconnected networks.
- The final way is to maintain, somewhere on the network, a table of:

    1 – node addresses; and
    2 – the *remote* procedures that they run.

Nodes wishing to make a procedure available to other nodes put an entry into this table giving their address and the name of the procedure. Nodes wishing to invoke a remote procedure look up the table to see if it is available and if so at what address.

This is in fact what is done in *Cedar*. Cedar includes a network-wide distributed data base, called Grapevine [24]. When a procedure wants itself to be available over the network, its stub calls a routine in the runtime which accesses the data base and makes an entry specifying the name of the procedure and the address of the node on which it resides. On the caller side, the stub gets the runtime to access the data base to extract the address of a node which runs the required procedure. This need be done only once, as the caller stub remembers the values returned and can use them whenever that remote procedure is called again.

The process of a caller locating and attaching itself to a remote procedure is known as *binding*. An analogy can be drawn between binding and the process of a linker resolving labels when linking a program.

Note that it is not necessary to modify a language in any way to cater for RPCs. The entire mechanism can be implemented as a collection of runtime library routines and utility programs.

Semantics of RPC There are a number of differences between local and remote procedure calls.

If the call is to be made between two heterogeneous machines, there may be a problem with the representation of data, e.g. the machines may have different word sizes. One solution to this problem is to have the RPC mechanism convert all data into some agreed network format before transmitting it. Receiving nodes convert the data from this *common format* into their own local one.

A second problem is how to interpret pointers, or more correctly what a pointer refers to. In the absence of a shared address space, an RPC cannot allow pointers to be passed over the network. Thus it is not possible to pass a parameter by *reference* in an RPC.

A more serious problem than either of the above two is that of *failure*. In a local procedure call, the caller and callee fail together. In an RPC, there can be communication failures, or, more severely, the callee can fail leaving the caller suspended. If this happens, the caller may have to be aborted, a situation that *never* occurs in the case of a local call.

After a failed call, the caller is placed in the predicament of not knowing how far the call got before it failed. There are 3 possible cases:

1 the callee failed before it received the call;
2 the callee failed while executing the procedure;
3 the callee correctly completed the procedure but failed before returning the results to the caller.

An additional, less serious, possibility also has to be catered for: the caller failing after making the call but before getting the results.

As the caller has no way of knowing which case holds, the system must provide some minimum guarantees about the exact effect of an RPC. The problem is compounded by the fact that, because of communication errors and attempts to recover from failure, a procedure may actually be invoked a number of times before it successfully completes. Various implementations of RPC define the effect, or semantics, of a call differently. Two common semantics are as follows.

- **Last-of-many** For a single remote call the procedure may be executed a number of times. The results returned are those of the last execution. This scheme demands that operations are performed by idempotent procedures.
- **At-most-once** If the caller receives a reply, then the procedure completed correctly and just once. If no reply is received, or if the caller crashes before getting the reply, the effects, if any, of the procedure are undone. These semantics closely resemble that of an atomic transaction, which completes successfully or not at all.

Thus it can be seen that when failure is taken into account, RPCs do have different *semantics* from local calls where partial failure is not possible.

Finally it is worth pointing out that just as there are many different variations on the send/receive paradigm for communication there are also variations in the operation of remote procedures. Asynchronous remote calls are possible whereby the caller and callee execute in parallel, it being the caller's responsibility to pick up the results later by doing a so-called *rendezvous*.

10.4.5 Languages

The purpose of writing a distributed operating system is to provide support for the development of application programs in a distributed environment. This support can be offered at different levels. Just as block structured languages were developed for writing programs in a structured fashion, languages are now emerging with 'distributed features' incorporated into them, e.g. *DP* [23] and *CLU/ARGUS* [11].

A language can ease the task of writing distributed programs in a number of ways. As well as having facilities for data abstraction, separate compilation, etc. which are used in writing conventional programs, a language can provide built-in *distributed features*. These include the following:

- **Remote procedure calls** An RPC mechanism, as described above, can be incorporated into the language.
- **Transactions** The language can make transactions available as a programming construct.
- **Parallelism/concurrency** Languages such as *ADA* [22] allow for structuring a single program as a number of cooperating processes. On a uniprocessor, these processes cannot exhibit true parallelism, but on a distributed system they can.

The techniques used for implementing these features are the same as those described for an operating system implementation. The disadvantage of this approach is that for programs to avail of these facilities they must be written in a specific language. When support for distribution is offered at the operating system level it is available to *all* users no matter what language they use. Many distributed systems are themselves written in 'distributed languages'.

10.4.6 Application domain

The intended application domain will have a very strong influence on how a system is designed and accordingly on how the above issues are tackled. What is an acceptable solution for one type of use may not be acceptable in another area. As an example take failure and the effects it may have. In a university environment, where implementing *total* resilience may be deemed too expensive, an occasional system failure possibly involving loss of data may be allowed. It will, of course, be unpopular. On the other hand, such loss of data would be totally unacceptable in a banking environment. It should be noted that a bank or other commercial organization, as well as having stricter operational requirements, would also have more money available to pay for it.

As a second example, take hardware redundancy. Again a university, and possibly even a bank, might be prepared to have the system temporarily out of operation, if for instance the transmission medium was cut. This could happen for example if repair or minor construction work was being carried out. The criteria for a LAN to be used in military applications, like connecting command computers in a battleship, are much stricter. The operation environment is much harsher with catastrophes like the severing of a network cable being much more likely. It is in the event of such an occurrence that a military network would be of most use, e.g. to transmit damage reports between various control systems. Accordingly greater emphasis would be placed on achieving continued operation in the face of such disasters than would be in a university. Possible steps to ensure such extreme fault tolerance would be to replicate, or triplicate, the transmission medium.

The real challenge in building a distributed system is to achieve as many of the above features described as are relevant to the application area, ensuring at the same time good system performance.

10.5 EXAMPLES

The previous sections described the problems and issues in designing a distributed system. Algorithms and techniques for solving some of these problems were also described. This section looks at a number of systems that have been implemented and examines how they tackle or avoid tackling the issues mentioned in the previous sections.

10.5.1 The Cambridge Model Distributed System

The first example looked at is one of the oldest and best documented ones [13], namely the *Cambridge Model Distributed System* or *CMDS* for short. CMDS is server-based. It consists of a network, the Cambridge Ring, of heterogeneous computers – mostly micros. Figure 10.12 shows the basic layout. The main components are the *file server*, the *name server*, and the *processor pool*. These are looked at in turn as are the other servers that go to make up the system.

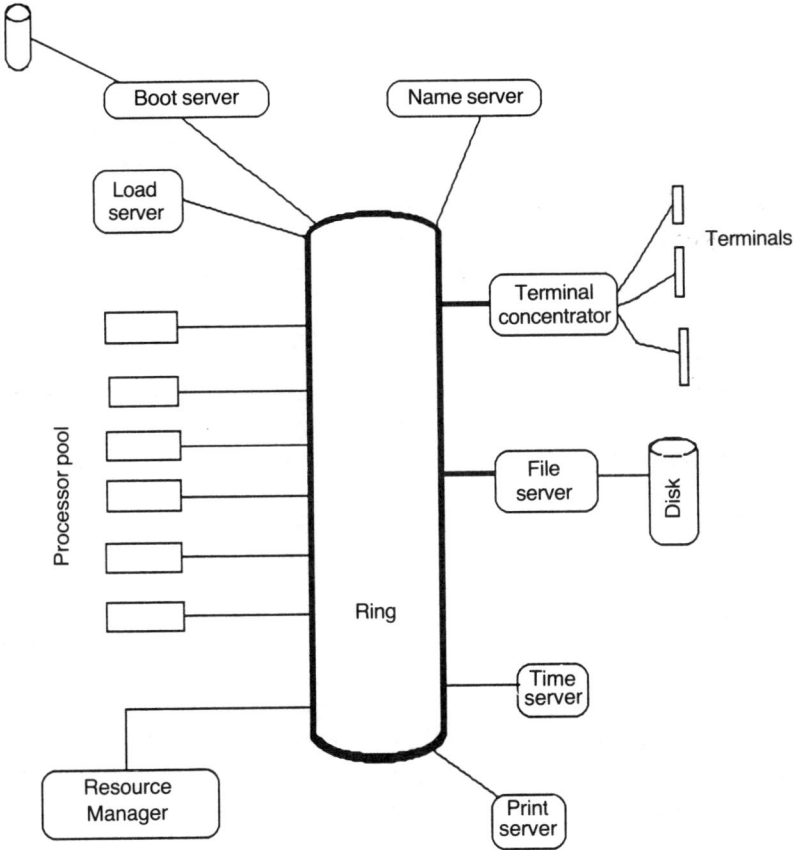

Figure 10.12 The Cambridge Model Distributed System

10.5.1.1 The name server

CMDS is server-based, therefore if a user is to avail itself of any service it must be able to contact the correct server. Servers can reside at any address and a method is required for locating them. This is the function of the name server (NS). It keeps a table of *server names* and corresponding *network addresses*. When a user wishes to locate a particular server, it contacts the NS, specifying the *name* of the server it wishes to communicate with. The NS responds with its *address*. A node wishing to make a new service available informs the NS, which puts an entry for it in the name table. If a service changes its network address, it again informs the NS which updates its entry. (This is similar to the way binding of remote procedures is done in Cedar, described earlier.)

There is, however, one problem with this scheme. How does a user locate the name server itself? This is done by having the NS reside at a fixed and well-known address on the network. All users know this address and by contacting it they can get in contact with any other service. This is a violation of network transparency as the *address* of a resource is embedded in client programs. An alternative way of locating the NS is to have clients broadcast a message asking the NS to reply.

10.5.1.2   The processor pool

Users of the system do not need to have any local computing power, access is via terminals connected to terminal servers (concentrators) and processors are allocated from a common pool. This pool consists of a number of work-stations, mostly 68000 based. Users are allocated these on request, and, once allocated, a processor is dedicated to a user until it is released.

The machines in the pool have no local peripherals. Their only connection to the rest of the system is via the ring. All terminal I/O is routed to a terminal concentrator and all file I/O is to the file server. The ring interfaces used at Cambridge were sophisticated. They implement the 'packed protocol' mentioned in Chapter 5 and data is transferred between the host and the network using DMA. Finally, as the processors have no local disks, the ring interface is also involved in 'booting' over the network.

10.5.1.3   The resource manager

As its name suggests, this server is responsible for managing resources on the system. In particular, it controls the allocation of processors from the pool. Users requiring a processor contact the resource manager (RM). They must specify two things:

- The type of processor they require, e.g. a 68000 or whatever else is available in the pool.
- The software they want loaded into it. This is simply a file on the file server. Users can choose any file they wish but the TRIPOS single-user operating system is the most common.

The RM allocates a machine, if there is one available. The loading of user software is not done by the RM itself but by one of the *load servers* on the network. Its function is to read files from the file server and write them into a processor's memory via the ring interface. On completion of loading, the user communicates directly with the allocated machine.

10.5.1.4 The file server

The Cambridge File Server, (CFS) [14], is a capability-based, centralized file server. It supports transactions on single files and is very similar to the Universal File Server described in [12].

CFS supports two types of objects, *files* and *indices*, both of which are referred to via a capability, called a *Permanent Unique Identifier* (PUID). The PUID contains a pointer to the object on disk, so once it is known an object can be located. Indices are used for holding PUIDs and can be thought of as a one-dimensional array. There is a special *root* index maintained by the system. An object remains in existence as long as its PUID is stored in the root, or in an object which is accessible from the root (see figure 10.13a). Garbage collection is used to remove all other objects.

The operations on indices are as follows:

- insert a PUID into a given slot in an index;
- retrieve the PUID from a given slot;
- delete the PUID at a given slot.

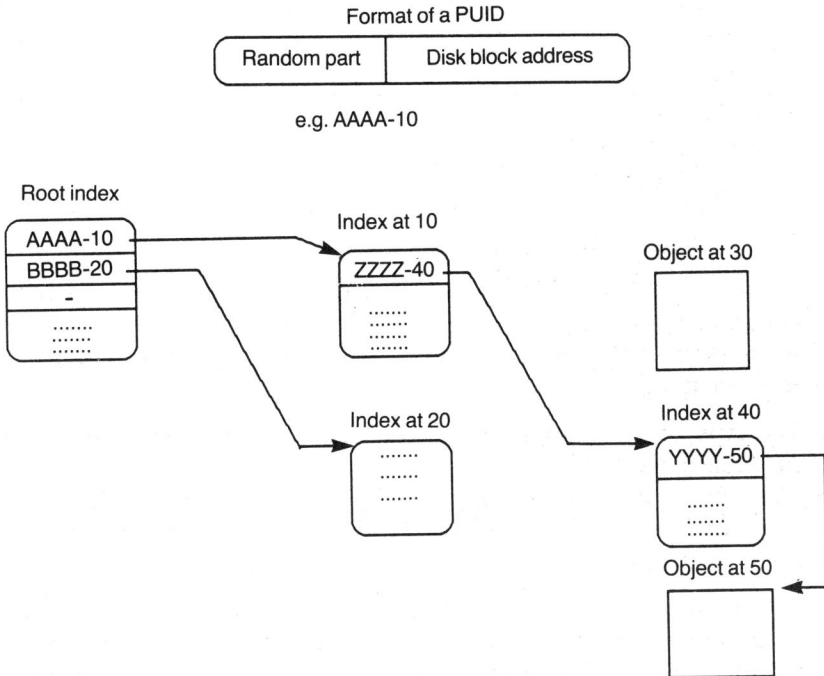

Figure 10.13a PUIDs and indices in CFS
Note: The indices at 10 and 20 have their PUIDs stored in the root so they will not be deleted. The objects at 40 and 50 are accessible from the root, so they will be preserved. The object at 30, however, does not have its PUID stored in the root or in any index that is accessible from the root so it will be deallocated

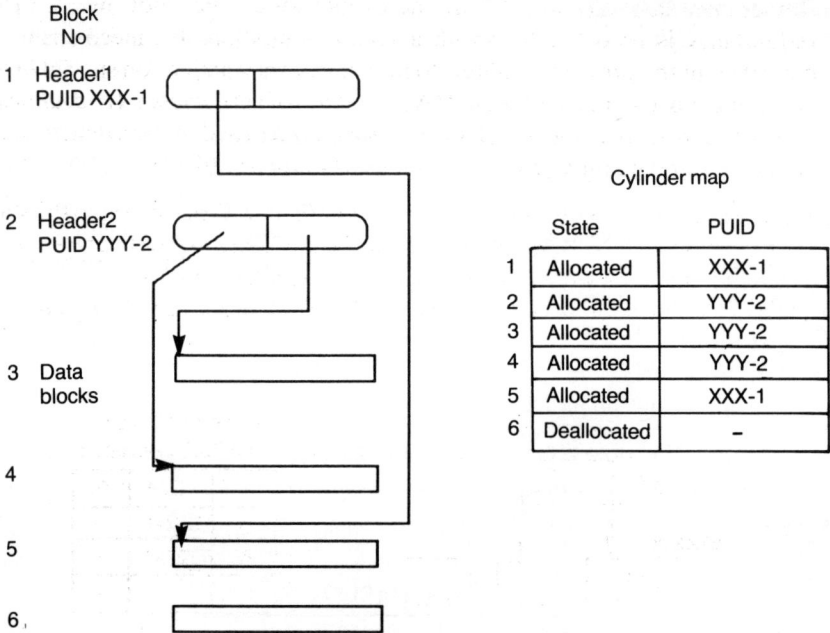

Figure 10.13b   Redundancy in CFS
Note: The cylinder map and file header blocks both contain the same information. If one
is destroyed it can be recreated from the other

Files, on the other hand, are just a sequence of words upon which the usual read/write operations can be performed. There are two types, *normal* and *special* files. Special files are updated atomically, normal files are not. Indices are implemented as special files.

All file system objects are represented by a header block on disk. If the object is small, the header also contains the data. For larger objects, one or two levels of indirection can be used. The PUID actually contains the disk address of the header block, so, once it is known, the object can be accessed directly. Each cylinder also contains a *cylinder map block*, at a fixed disk address. This block has an entry for each block on the cylinder (see figure 10.13b).

The entry in the cylinder map for each block specifies two things:

1 the *state of the block*, as explained below;
2 the PUID of the object to which it belongs. If the block is deallocated this field is blank.

This introduces a level of *redundancy* into the system. If a header block is destroyed, it can be recreated from the cylinder map. On the other hand, if the cylinder map is corrupted, it can be reconstructed from the header blocks.

Remember that all objects are accessible from the root index. This redundancy is used together with a type of intentions list mechanism, as described in the previous chapter, to implement transactions on special files.

Blocks have 4 states: *allocated* (A), *deallocated* (D), *intended to deallocate* (ID) and *intended to allocate* (IA). This state is recorded in the cylinder map. An atomic update then proceeds as follows (see figure 10.14).

1 Data is never written in place but to *shadow blocks*. When doing so the state of the old block is set to 'intended to deallocate', and that of the new one to 'intended to allocate' in the corresponding cylinder map.

2 The cylinder map *followed by* the header block are updated, *in place*, on disk.

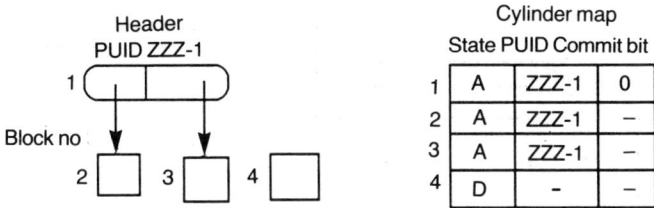

Initial configuration. File contains two blocks (2,3). Commit bit in cylinder map is set to 0

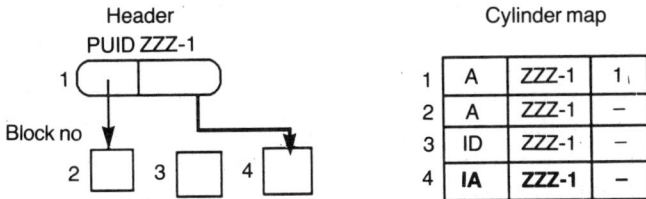

Page 3 is updated. New version is written to page 4.

Cylinder map and header are updated in place. Cylinder map updates are intentions. Setting the commit bit to 1 commits the transaction

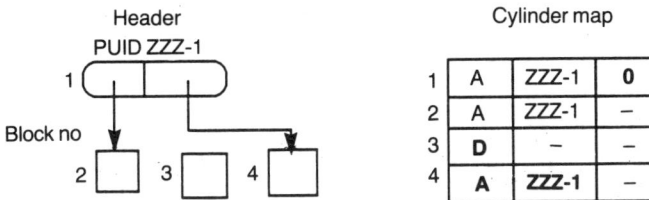

Cylinder map is re-written. Commit bit is reset

Figure 10.14   Atomic update in CFS

3 When this is done, a special *commit bit* in the cylinder map entry for the header block is set, again in place. This effectively commits the transaction and the user can, at this stage, be informed that it has completed.
4 The cylinder map is then rewritten changing all the 'intended to allocate/deallocate' states to 'allocated/deallocated'.
5 Finally the commit bit is reset to indicate that the transaction is actually finished.

Crash recovery proceeds as follows. A crash before the commit bit is set means that the file should be returned to its original state. This can be got from the cylinder map by reversing the intentions:

• State ID goes to A.
• State IA goes to D.
• The header block is changed back.

If the crash occurs after the commit, then the intentions are carried out.

• IA goes to A.
• ID goes to D.
• The header is not changed.

Finally if the cylinder map is inaccessible, it can be recreated from the headers.

In CFS it is possible that a large file will spread over a number of cylinders. In this case the header block points not to the data blocks, but to a level of indirect blocks, which point to the actual data blocks. The algorithm for atomically updating a file still works. All cylinder maps are written first and then the header and the indirect blocks. The commit bit is stored in the cylinder map for the cylinder that the header block resides on.

CFS provides storage for the users of CMDS. Its two biggest clients are the TRIPOS single-user operating system which is the one used on most processor pool machines and CAP, a mainframe with a capability-based file system. Both of these systems have been modified to use CFS.

10.5.1.5 Small servers
A load server, or *Ancilla* as it is known, is an example of what are called *small servers* in CMDS, i.e. servers which run on small dedicated processors to perform simple tasks. They include terminal concentrators, a print server and a time server.

Two important small servers are the Ancilla and the boot server. *Ancillae* or load servers are used by the resource manager to load processor pool machines with user software. It does this by reading the file from CFS and writing it into the processor's memory as previously described. A different technique is used for booting small servers from that used for booting pool machines. They boot directly from the boot server, a machine with its own local disk which contains the code for the various servers.

10.5.1.6 Summary

CMDS is a very early example of a distributed system and many of the ideas used in it have been incorporated into other designs. In particular CMDS makes extensive use of servers. It has been in operation in Cambridge University for a number of years and is used as a teaching machine, as well as for research.

10.5.2 The Newcastle Connection

The Newcastle Connection, or *Unix United* [5], is the name given to the distributed system designed at Newcastle University. It uses the *layered* approach, the underlying operating system being *UNIX*. The aim of the Newcastle Connection (NC) is to make a network of UNIX machines appear to the user to be a single node. All intermachine boundaries are hidden from the user. This is done without any change to the operating system kernel.

For the purpose of this discussion, and the following one on Locus, it is assumed that the reader is familiar with the UNIX [4] operating system, and the file system in particular.

10.5.2.1 Global directory structure

This is the key to providing transparency in the Newcastle Connection. The principle of the UNIX hierarchical directory structure is extended, so that the entire file system of a UNIX node can appear as a subdirectory *anywhere* in a larger global name space. Accessing a file on a remote node then appears exactly the same as accessing a file on a single machine.

Figure 10.15a shows a possible directory structure for a network of UNIX machines. It consists of a 3 nodes, labeled *UNIX1*, *2*, and *3*. Machine and

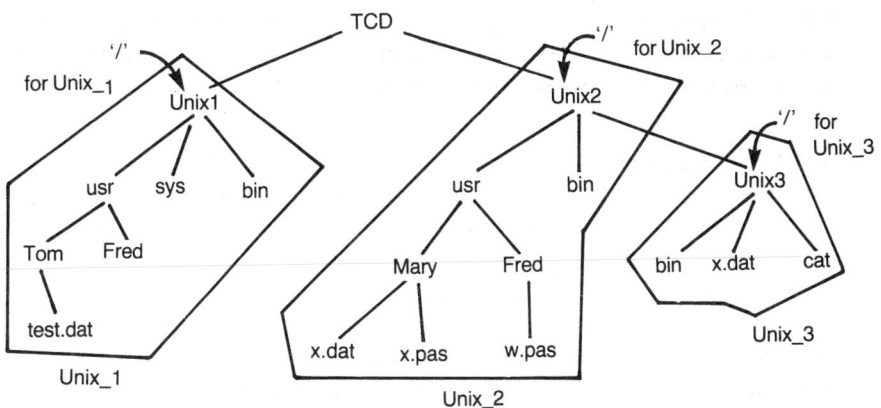

Figure 10.15a The Newcastle Connection
Note: A network-wide directory structure for three nodes. There is a bin directory on each node and Fred has directories on both nodes 1 and 2

Pathname Relative to/usr/Mary on UNIX2	Location Relative to Mary	Absolute PathName from the global root **TCD**
x.pas	current directory	TCD/UNIX2/usr/Mary/x.pas
../Fred/w.pas	different directory on the same node	TCD/UNIX2/usr/Fred/w.pas
../../UNIX3/x.dat	Node_3	TCD/UNIX2/UNIX3/x.dat
../../../UNIX1/usr/Tom/test.dat	on Node_1	TCD/UNIX1/usr/Tom/test.dat

Figure 10.15b   Accessing files in the Newcastle Connection
Note: The table shows the relative pathnames that a user with current directory
"/usr/Mary", on node Unix2, would use to access various files in the global directory
structure shown in figure 10.15a
In Unix, the pathnames start from one of two places: "/", i.e. the root, or relative to the
current working directory, in this case ". ." means the parent directory

network boundaries are transparent to users who treat nodes in the same way they treat directories. Figure 10.15b shows the *relative* pathnames that a user with current directory /usr/Mary, on node UNIX2, would use to access various files in the global directory structure. Note that the naming structure does not reflect the network topology. UNIX1, 2 and 3 could for example be nodes on the same LAN or on different LANs connected by a WAN.

This naming mechanism is similar to that used in Decnet, described earlier, but differs in two important ways.

1 All pathnames are relative, rather than absolute; this means the directory structure can easily be extended.
2 Nodes can appear anywhere in the hierarchy, and not just at the root.

It does however suffer from some of the same disadvantages. A file cannot be moved from one node to another without changing its name and replication is not supported.

10.5.2.2   Remote execution

As well as being able to read and write files across the network it is also possible to *execute* a file which resides on a different node. Most UNIX commands are invoked by typing a file name, followed by the parameters if any. The command cat, for example, is a UNIX utility for concatenating files. It takes a list of input files and appends them to each other. The resulting file is displayed on the user's terminal but it can be redirected to another file using the UNIX redirection symbol >. Thus the command

cat x.dat y.dat

appends y.dat to x.dat and displays the resulting file on the screen. While the command

cat x.dat y.dat>z.dat

writes the result to a new file z.dat.

As an example of both remote file access and execution, take the following command line as invoked by the user, Mary, logged into node UNIX2, with current directory /usr/Mary, on node UNIX2, and the directory structure as in figure 10.15a.

% .. / .. / UNIX3 / cat   x.dat .. / .. / .. / UNIX1 / usr / Tom / test.dat
> .. / .. / UNIX3 / newtest.dat

COMMAND	SOURCE FILES	DESTINATION
Concatenate files	x.dat & test.dat	newtest.dat

The effect of the above command line is to:

- Invoke the copy of the program CAT in the directory TCD / UNIX2 / UNIX3, i.e. execute the copy of the 'cat' program on the node UNIX3. Although Mary is logged in to node UNIX2 the 'cat' program will actually be executed on node UNIX3; this is because in the Newcastle scheme files are always executed on the node that they reside on.
- When cat runs, it takes its I/P from the two files test.dat on UNIX1 and x.dat in Mary's current directory. In both cases this involves reading files across the network.
- The O/P goes to the file newtest.dat which is on the same node as the cat program is being executed on.
- All this is done without the user being aware that any machine boundaries are being crossed.

This single command line shows both the flexibility of UNIX and the manner in which that flexibility has been extended transparently to a network environment in the Newcastle Connection.

10.5.2.3 Implementation

The Newcastle Connection is implemented as a layered system, as shown in figure 10.16. Users who wish to make use of the NC link their programs with a special runtime library. This library sits between the user and the UNIX kernel and handles distribution. In particular, this *connection layer* must take care of all *naming* and other *network*-related issues. This is done by

1 Maintaining additional directories for remote nodes.

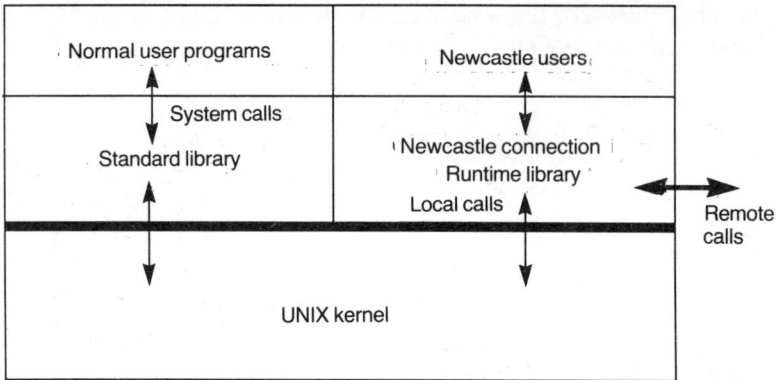

Figure 10.16   The connection layer

2 Intercepting all file handling system calls to determine if a remote operation is being requested.

These two aspects are looked at in turn.

Directories   In the NC, emphasis is very much on transparent access to remote files. To allow for this, the directory structure has to be extended. All nodes in a Newcastle system run standard versions of UNIX, with normal directories. The connection layers on each individual machine maintain additional directories which when viewed as a whole give a single network-wide hierarchical name space. Thus the global Newcastle directory structure is made up of two types of files.

1 **Normal UNIX directories**   These contain file names and *inodes*, a type of pointer which are used to access the file on disk.
2 **Special Newcastle directories**   These contain node names and network routing information used to contact them.

Figure 10.17 shows the portions of the global directory structure from figure 10.15a which are held on the various nodes. Note that no node need hold the complete structure; each has a piece of the overall picture. Certain data is replicated, which means that care has to be taken with updates. The advantage of this method is that it is quite flexible. Nodes can appear anywhere in the hierarchy and it can change dynamically, with nodes being added and removed. This flexibility extends to the global root which may itself become a subdirectory in some larger configuration. (In effect it is possible to include a new node in the same way that a new file system can be *mounted* in conventional UNIX. The root can itself be mounted onto another file system.)

System calls to remote nodes   As previously stated, the connection layer intercepts all file-related system calls. If the call can be handled locally then it

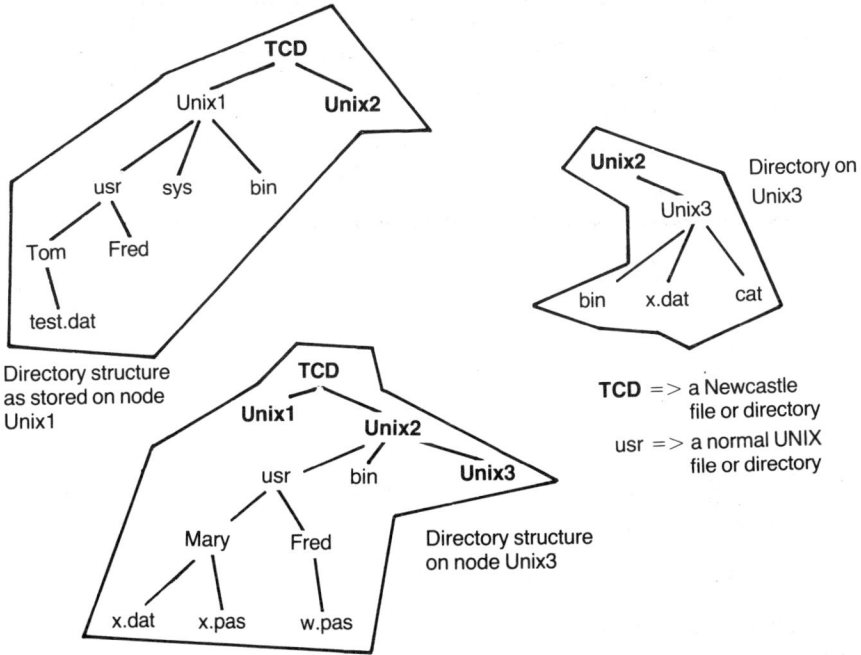

Figure 10.17   Implementation of directories in the Newcastle Connection
Note: Each node stores a fragment of the overall structure. The diagram shows how the
network-wide hierarchy from figure 10.15a might be stored on the three nodes involved.
Each stored its own normal UNIX directories and files as well as special Newcastle
directories which contain information about remote nodes. Note also that there is some
duplication of information

is passed on directly to the kernel, but if it involves a remote node the
connection layer communicates with its counterpart on that node to complete
the call.

In the case of an 'open file' or 'create file' operation, the pathname of the
file is specified by the user. Within the 'connection layer' path names are
interpreted as far as they can be locally, by looking up normal directories. If
part of the name involves a component on a different node, i.e. it is stored in a
special NC directory, then control is passed to a server on that node. The
server completes the interpretation of the remainder of the name and on
completion of the call returns the result to the calling node. In some cases
fragments of the pathname may be passed between a number of nodes.

Thus the rule for interpretation of pathnames is that the local part is
interpreted locally and the remote part is passed on and interpreted remotely.
In the case of a pathname that spans more than two nodes, this process may
need to be repeated a number of times, with fragments of the name being
passed from node to node.

This process of locating a file has only to be done once. When the file is

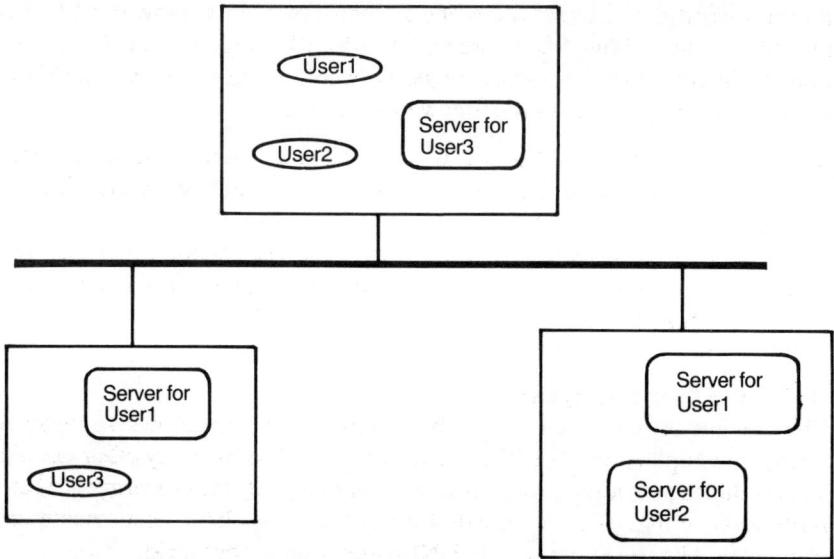

Figure 10.18 Newcastle clients and servers
Note: There is one client per server. A user who accesses files on a number of nodes
will have a server on each node, e.g. User1. Clients and servers can reside on the same
node

opened/created the kernel returns a file identifier (FID). On subsequent file operations, the user passes this FID rather than the file name. As each connection layer keeps a per user table of FIDs and locations, it can determine whether a file is local or not in a single lookup.

Servers The NC uses *servers* in a slightly unusual way (see figure 10.18). There is just one client per server. When a user first requires access to a remote node, a server process is created for it. The server acts as a *representative* for its client. Any file handling requests from the client are carried out by its representative, which returns the results to its client, e.g. in the case of opening a file it returns the FID, or, for a read operation, it returns the data that was read. As far as the kernel is concerned the 'server' process is a normal local UNIX user process.

Communication aspects All network communication is via an RPC described in [19]. Although the system was first implemented on the Cambridge Ring, the protocols used by the RPC are network-independent and can run on top of any network. The information stored in the Newcastle directories is passed to the RPC as routing information.

Administration From an administration point of view, all nodes in a Newcastle network are completely autonomous, each with its own local administrator. To Log in to a UNIX machine, a user must be given a user name and password, i.e. a user ID, by the administrator. In a network of UNIX machines, a user should negotiate an ID with each administrator. In the NC, nodes will continuously receive requests from remote users. Validation of remote users is by either of the following schemes.

- A table of [(host,id) − (local id)] is maintained. So once a user has been validated on one node it can be automatically validated on others if there is an entry for it in the table.
- Alternatively, all unknown remote users, i.e. those not present in the table, can be given the same local ID − e.g. that of a guest with some limited default access to resources.

10.5.2.4 Other developments
The previous section described the basic Newcastle Connection system. Since it was first implemented in 1982 it has been added to by many other people. This includes providing for *diskless workstations* [16], *stable storage* [15] and *replication of files*. The Newcastle Connection is available as a commercial product and has been installed in UNIX sites around the world.

10.5.3 Locus

Two sample distributed systems have been looked at; CMDS, a system built from scratch and the Newcastle Connection which adopted the layered approach. The final example covered is *Locus* [2, 3]. Like the Newcastle Connection, Locus is a distributed version of UNIX but in this case *major* modifications are made to the UNIX kernel. The aims of Locus are:

1 network transparency;
2 increased availability of resources;
3 good performance.

The version of UNIX used is *BSD 4.2* and *upward compatibility is guaranteed*, i.e. any program which runs on BSD 4.2 should also run on Locus. The reverse however is not true.

Locus rejects the server model and instead uses the integrated approach. Each node runs a complete version of Locus, so that any node can function on its own if disconnected from the network.

Efficiency considerations play an important part throughout the implementation. Communication is via a simple RPC and special purpose problem-oriented protocols are used between processes. Extensive use is made of efficient lightweight processes within the UNIX kernel. These kernel processes perform work that could be done at user level. This increases the size and complexity of the kernel but greatly improves overall performance.

At the heart of Locus is a distributed file system, but there is also support for distribution of processes.

10.5.3.1   The Locus distributed file system

The Locus distributed file system supports *network transparency*, *automatic replication*, *synchronization of access* and *atomic updates* to files. These aspects are looked at in turn.

Naming   Network-wide naming is much more sophisticated in Locus than it is in the Newcastle Connection. There is a single hierarchical name space and new nodes, or more correctly new file systems, can be *mounted* anywhere in the file system (see figure 10.19). Unlike in the NC, the root is fixed and cannot itself be mounted as a subdirectory of some other system. Locus users are presented with a truly distributed file system, the directory structure appears as it would on a single node, e.g. there is a single 'bin' directory and users are unaware of what nodes their files reside on. In particular files can be moved between nodes without affecting their names.

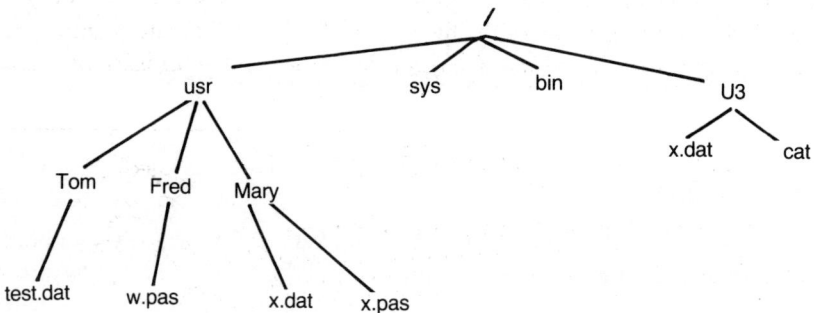

Figure 10.19   Logical directory structure in Locus
Note: Network-wide naming structure appears as if it was for a single node. There is a single root and a node name does not appear in the file name. The diagram shows a possible Locus implementation of the directory structure in figure 10.15a. Note also that there is a single instance of the 'bin' directory, similarly 'Fred' has just one directory

The implementation of naming in Locus differs considerably from the Newcastle Connection. File systems in Locus are known as *file groups* and each node in the system must know about the following:

1 The file groups that are *physically stored* on it.
2 *All* the *mounted* file groups in the global name space.

This latter piece of information is held in a globally replicated *logical mount table* which has one entry for each file group. Any change to the logical mount table must be propagated to all copies. Locus includes algorithms for updating the mount table in the event of any changes in the number of nodes connected or in the network topology.

The way in which pathnames are interpreted also differs from that used in the Newcastle Connection. Interpreting a pathname involves reading the contents of directories. Local directories are read with a conventional read operation. In the case of remote directories the kernel looks up its location in the logical mount table and reads its contents across the network. Thus the rule for interpreting pathnames is that all interpretation is done locally, entries in remote directories being read across the network if necessary.

From the above, it can be seen that it is not necessary for any node to store the entire global directory structure. All a node needs to store is its local directory structure *and* a copy of the mount table. Using that information, any file can be located. This process is, of course, more efficient if looking up directories can be done locally rather than remotely.

Replication To increase the availability of files, Locus has built in support for replication. A *logical file group* may be replicated, i.e. the same file group can be stored at any number of physical sites (see figure 10.20). It is not necessary to have an entry in the mount table for each physical copy of a file group, instead only one site address per group is held and that site in turn knows about all the other instances of the file group. This particular site is known as the *current synchronization site* (CSS) for the group, and other uses for it are

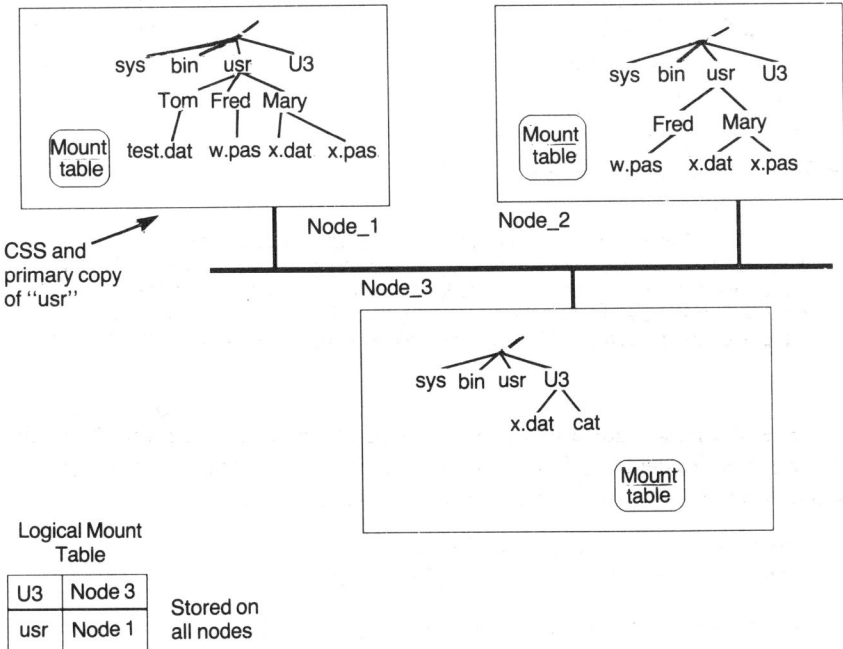

Figure 10.20 Implementing directories in Locus
Note: The diagram shows a possible configuration of the logical directory structure in figure 10.19. The file group rooted at 'usr' is partially replicated on two physical nodes, 1 and 2. The copy on Node_2 is incomplete. The mount table, which is replicated on all nodes, shows a single entry for 'usr', i.e., the address of the CSS for the group. The root is stored on all nodes

explained later. Only one instance of a file group, the primary copy, need contain all the files in that group, others can hold just part of it, i.e. *partial replication* is supported. A file cannot be stored at a site if its file group is not also stored there.

Replication is transparent to the user. Accessing a replicated file is the same as accessing a normal one; the system chooses which physical copy to use. If a replicated file is updated the system ensures that all instances of it are automatically updated, using an algorithm described in the following sections.

Accessing a replicated file   As files are replicated, access to them has to be synchronized. A *centralized algorithm* is used. The *logical mount table* (LMT) contains the address of the CSS for each file group. When a request to open a file is issued, the location of the CSS of its file group is obtained from the LMT. The actual open request is then sent to the CSS. It in turn knows what nodes store instances of its file group. It picks a suitable one, and asks it if it will act as a *storage site* (SS) for the file that is being opened. The SS replies to the CSS which in turn replies to the user at the *user site* (US). The user site interacts directly with the storage site to read and write the file and has no further contact with the CSS. When the file is finally closed, the SS informs the CSS, so that it can update its own state information.

As all open requests go through the CSS, it can carefully control concurrent access to files. The locking rules imposed in Locus are quite conventional, namely *multiple readers* and *exclusive writers*. (An additional type of lock, called *no lock read*, is introduced to speed up accessing directories when searching through a pathname. It allows multiple writers in a restricted fashion.) In keeping with Locus's aim of good system performance it checks if the CSS, SS or US happen to be the same physical site. Optimizations in the code are taken as appropriate.

Availability of a replicated file   Replication is used to increase the availability of a resource. A problem arises in ensuring the consistency of replicated copies if the network becomes partitioned, or copies become otherwise available. Locus after experimenting with a more complicated strategy [3] adopts a simple, centralized, approach to this problem [2].

For each logical file group, one site is designated the storage site of the *primary copy*, i.e. it stores the entire file group. Whenever a file in the group is opened for updating the site that stores the primary copy is chosen as the SS. Any site can be used when reading. In the event of a break in the network, updates are only allowed in the partition that contains the primary copy. A version number is associated with each copy of the file and it is used to identify out of date copies when the network is repaired.

Committing a replicated file   Atomic updates to files are supported *at the SS* using a standard shadow page technique, i.e. the primary copy is updated atomically. The problem then remains to update the other copies. As part of the commit/close, the SS informs the CSS. The SS also informs all other sites that store a copy of the file that a new version is available. These sites then read the updated version, i.e. it is the responsibility of the other sites to update themselves. This propagating of the update goes on in the background and is implemented at the kernel level for efficiency reasons.

The read operation carried by each of the other storage sites uses the same shadow page technique to ensure the atomicity of the update to their local copies.

10.5.3.2 Other issues
The distributed file system is a very important part of Locus but some other features are also worth looking at.

Process distribution   Processes in UNIX communicate with each other via pipes and signals [4]. In Locus these have been extended to operate across a network, allowing remote processes to communicate with each other in the same way they do on a single machine.

In UNIX processes are created using the 'fork' and 'exec' system calls. The Locus versions of these are upwardly compatible with BSD 4.2 UNIX. They have, however, been extended. The Locus versions of this system calls allow a user to specify *which* physical site the new process is to run on. In addition, a new system call 'migrate' enables a user to change the execution site of a process *while that process is still executing*.

This ability to move a process after it has been created is known as *process migration*. An example of its use might be the case of a user who has initiated a very large compilation job. On noticing that all the users of another machine have just gone to lunch he may decide that a better response could be achieved by moving the compilation onto it. This can be done, without aborting the job and losing the work already completed, using the 'migrate' system call. The implementation of process migration is nontrivial and will not be discussed here. Interested readers are referred to [2] for further details.

Optimizations   Several features of Locus violate the principle of network transparency. As well as being able to specify the actual location of a process, it is also possible to locate physical copies of files at designated storage sites. These violations are included to allow a user to optimize the performance of the system.

Heterogeneity   Locus goes some way towards easing the problems encountered when operating in a network of heterogeneous hardware. Locus runs on a number of different hardware configurations including Digital VAX and Motorola MC68000 processors. In keeping with the criteria of network transparency, users of both types of node must refer to a given command file using the same logical pathname, e.g. /bin/cat. Obviously a different copy of the file is required to execute on each processor, i.e. the same name must map onto two different files without the user being aware of it. Locus resolves the difficulty by maintaining what are known as *hidden directories*. For cases such as the one outlined, Locus implements the file, not as an ordinary one, but as a directory. The directory has two entries:

/ bin / cat / VAX

and

/ bin / cat / M68k

containing the correct versions of the file cat for each processor. The directory is 'hidden' in that it is not normally visible to the user, who on inspecting the contents of the directory /bin sees /bin/cat as an ordinary file. When a user executes the file, the operating system automatically picks the correct version.

Locus summary Of the three example systems looked at in this chapter, Locus is the most sophisticated; the entire system looks and behaves like a single UNIX machine. The key to this is the extent to which the network is made transparent. This description has focused on the file system aspects; books with further details of process management etc. can be found in the references.

10.6 SUMMARY

Some of the important issues in distributed computing have been identified, and three sample distributed systems have been examined. The discussion has not been exhaustive, but it has been representative of the type of developments that have been going on in distributed systems. The field is very much in its infancy and rapid developments can be expected over the coming years.

Apart from distributed operating systems, work is also being carried out on *languages* for distributed computing and *distributed data bases*. The issues in both these areas are similar to those discussed in this chapter. The reader should look at the references for further reading.

10.7 REFERENCES

1   Stankovic, J.A.: 'A perspective on distributed computer systems', *IEEE Transactions on Computers*, **C-33**, no. 12, pp. 1102–1115, December 1984.
2   Locus Computing Corp.: *The Locus distributed system Architecture (Edition 3.1)*, Locus Computing Corporation, June 1984.
3   Walker, B., Popek, G. *et al.*: 'The Locus distributed operating system', *Proceedings of the Ninth Symposium on Operating Systems Principles*, New Hampshire, October 1983.
4   Ritchie, D.: 'The Unix time sharing system', *Communications of the ACM*, **17**, no. 7, pp. 365–375, July 1974.
5   Brownbridge, D.R., Marshall, L.F. and Randell, B.: 'The Newcastle Connection', *Software Practice and Experience*, **12**, no. 12, pp. 1147–1162, December 1982.

6   Digital: *Digital's Networks: an architecture with a future*, Digital Equipment Corporation, 1984 (order no. EB 26013·42).

7   Xerox: *Remote Procedure Call*, Xerox Corporation Technical Report, CSL-83-7, 1983.

8   Birrell, A.D. and Nelson, B.J.: *Implementing Remote Procedure Call*, Xerox Corporation Technical Report, CSL-83-7, 1983.

9   Digital: *VAX/VMS Summary Description*, Digital Equipment Corporation 1978 (order no. AA-D0224-TE).

10 Lister, A.M.: *Fundamental of Operating Systems*, London: Macmillan 1979.

11 Liskov, B. and Schiefler, R.: 'Guardians and actions: Linguistic support of robust distributed programs', *Proceedings of the Ninth Symposium on Principles of Programming Languages*, pp. 7–19, January, 1982.

12 Birrell, A.D. and Needham, R.M.: 'A universal file server', *IEEE Transactions on Software Engineering*, **SE-6**, no. 5, pp. 450–453, September 1980.

13 Needham, R.M. and Herbert, A.J.: *The Cambridge Distributed Computing System*, Addison Wesley International Computer Science Series, London: Addison Wesley, 1982.

14 Dion, J.: 'The Cambridge file server', *Operating Systems Review*, **14**, no. 4, pp. 26–35, October 1980.

15 Anywanu, J.A.: 'A reliable storage system for Unix', *Software Practice and Experience*, **15**, no. 10, pp. 973–990, October 1985.

16 Lobelle, M.C.: 'Integration of diskless workstations in Unix united', *Software Practice and Experience*, **15**, no. 10, pp. 997–1010, October 1985.

17 Lampson, B.W., Paul, M. and Siegert, H.J. (eds): *Distributed Systems: Architecture and Implementation*, Berlin: Springer Verlag, 1983.

18 Shrivasta, S.K. and Panzier, F.: 'The design of a remote procedure call mechanism', *IEEE Transactions on Computers*, C-31, no 7, pp. 692–696, July 1982.

19 Traiger, I. *et al.*: *Transactions and consistency in distributed database systems*, IBM Research Report, KJ2555, IBM Research Laboratory, San Jose CA, 1978.

20 Xerox: *Mesa Language Manual*, Xerox PARC Report, CSL-79-3, April 1979.

21 Barnes, J.G.P.: 'An overview of ADA', *Software Practice and Experience*, 10, no. 11, pp. 851–887, November 1980.

22 Hansen, B.: 'Distributed processes: a concurrent programming concept', *Communications of the ACM*, **21**, no. 11, pp. 934–941, November 1978.

23 Birrell, A.D. *et al.*: 'Grapevine: An exercise in distributed computing', *Communications of the ACM*, **25**, no. 4, pp. 260–274, April 1982.

24 Deutsch, L.P. and Taft, E.A.: *Requirements for an experimental programming environment*, XEROX PARC Report, CSL-80-10, 1980.

CHAPTER ELEVEN

OFFICE AND FACTORY AUTOMATION

Part 2 of this book has concentrated on the techniques involved in exploiting the services provided by LANs. This chapter will explore how they can be used in two environments: the office and the factory. The needs of these environments will be examined and some examples of high level protocols aimed specifically at these applications will be looked at.

11.1 OFFICE AUTOMATION

The first application of computers in the office environment was in the area of accounting. The information storage and processing power of the computer was used to automate the tedious task of maintaining company accounts. Their success in this area is due to the fact that the mechanical tasks of posting transactions, performing calculations etc. can be carried out with far greater accuracy and speed by a machine than by a human. This technology has now matured, and all but the very smallest of organizations use computers for this purpose.

The next area to be tackled was that of text handling. Manuals, books, letters and other forms of correspondence are distributed using paper as the medium. During a document's transition from draft version to final form, it may have to be typed and retyped several times. If a similar version were to be created, the process started from scratch. Wordprocessing application programs were an attempt to improve productivity in this area. The document could now be stored on the computer as it was typed and retrieved for subsequent editing.

Both computerized accounting and wordprocessing were forms of office automation, as is any service which uses machines in the office. As this book is concerned with LANs, we will define office automation as services devoted to enhancing office communications through the swift storage, transmission and retrieval of information.

The contribution that LAN technology offers is that of a high speed communications channel with the ability to move digital information swiftly between nodes. By building on this foundation, it can become the primary vehicle of communication in the office.

The transition to the automated office is taking place on two main fronts. Firstly, existing means of office communication are changing to take advantage of advances in technology. Secondly, new architectures are being developed to cope with a completely new strategy for information handling. In the following sections we will examine the most common means of communication (the telephone, letters, telex, etc.) and the effect LAN technology will have on them. We will also look at one proposed architecture for the paperless office.

11.2   OFFICE COMMUNICATIONS

11.2.1   The telephone

The global telephone network is the largest communications network in existence. It allows audio contact with any other telephone user connected to the network. The equipment and lines used in the system were initially designed to carry voice traffic. As the necessary technologies became available, the system evolved from a network carrying analog signals which were manually or mechanically switched to today's system of electronic switches operating on digital links.

In recent years, the connectivity offered by the network has prompted its use as a means of transferring data between computers. Typically this is done using modems which translate between the digital signals emanating from the computers to audible tones which can be transferred over conventional telephone lines. The speeds possible under this regime are limited. For high bandwidth applications, users have to resort to specially leased, high quality telephone lines, with the associated cost penalties.

In its present form, the telephone systems serves the needs of voice users admirably well. But in data applications, it is an expensive and inflexible medium. As the proportion of interoffice communication accounted for by data traffic increases, there is a greater need to provide an integrated (i.e. voice and data) service to cater for the needs of both camps. One of the benefits of integration is that a new range of sophisticated services can be offered. Examples of these include the sending of messages consisting of mixed speech and data, 'calling party identification' where the callee is informed as to who is trying to contact him before accepting the call, directory services etc.

The change over to an integrated service is being performed on two fronts. Firstly, the conventional telephone network is evolving into a network known as the *integrated services digital network* (ISDN) [14]. This is a CCITT standard, specifying an interface through which a user may transmit voice and data using telephone switches. Provision is made for variable amounts of bandwidth to be allocated to the user for different applications.

Another way in which integrated services may be offered is by an *integrated service local network* (ISLN) [15]. In this case, the underlying network is a LAN with interfaces designed for carrying voice traffic. The problem with this approach is that just as the telephone system was designed for voice, LAN technology was developed primarily for data transfer. When carrying speech in a real-time situation such as a telephone conversation, delays in transmitting packets result in a garbled message being received at the other end of the line. For this reason, the LAN used must provide a guarantee that packets will be delivered at regular intervals for the duration of the call. This is not possible with nondeterministic access methods like CSMA/CD and register insertion. The token-passing ring allows for this type of traffic and other customized protocols are being developed specifically for this purpose.

Given the advantages of an integrated voice and data service in terms of the cost savings in cable and the potential for new services, it is likely that the next few years will see the introduction of two kinds of products: telephone systems that offer data transfer facilities and LAN systems that offer voice transfer facilities. These systems will be capable of connecting to wide area networks such as the public ISDN, or the IEEE 802 Metropolitan Area Network (MAN).

11.2.2 Video conferencing

The simplest and most effective means of communicating is the face-to-face meeting. In recent years, video conferencing [5] has become a potential alternative to this. This technique involves transmitting images over a conventional communications channel so that the parties involved can establish full audio visual contact with each other.

Depending on the available bandwidth, these images may be continuous or may consist of freeze frames transmitted at regular intervals. This form of communication is almost as satisfactory as a face-to-face meeting and it removes the need for all parties to be physically present in the same place for the duration of the session. The availability of a high speed LAN as a communications channel with connections to global wide area networks may make this technique a cost-effective option.

11.2.3 Printed documents

Businesses needing to communicate in a formal or recorded fashion currently use two main methods: mail and telex. Conventional mail will distribute printed and typed documents to virtually any location in the world via a network of national PTT authorities. Large companies often devote considerable resources to providing an internal mail service to perform this function. It is a reliable, but slow, service.

For short messages where speed is important, the telex or teletypewriter is used. This system has a more limited coverage, but messages in English character text can be transmitted quite reliably to a large range of destinations in the developed world. As with mail, the noninteractive nature of the communication means that the sender does not have to worry about whether the recipient is available, living in a different time-zone etc.

The reliance of both the above methods on paper as a medium has led to an elaborate range of services being developed to store, retrieve, modify and distribute the individual documents. This encompasses such activities as filing, photocopying, binding etc.

A number of alternative technologies are developing. The first of these is *electronic mail*. Users of mainframe equipment have had access to this facility for a number of years. If one user of the system wishes to send a message to another, he uses a text editor to compose the message and send it to the appropriate user. The next time the addressee logs in to the system, he will be informed of the waiting message.

A similar service can be provided to users of independent workstations connected by a LAN. In this case, the users must contact a mail server which looks after messages held for all registered users of the system. Communication to other organizations could be achieved by linking the LAN via a gateway to some form of wide area network where a similar messaging facility operated. This means of communication offers much more flexibility than paper in terms of ease of distribution, copying, retrieval etc.

Another new means of transmitting printed documents is via the Teletex [7] system. This is a development of the Telex system and is now available in many countries. It operates in a similar manner to telex but offers a more complete character set, higher transmission speed and better error control. For text-only applications, this has the potential to form the interorganizational link for electronic mail systems.

One of the major advantages of paper as a communication medium is that it can store mixed text and graphics messages. Systems are now becoming available to digitize images for storage on, and transmission between, computer systems. In terms of interoffice communications, the normal way to achieve this is using a *facsimile device*. This machine digitizes an image and transmits it as an analog signal over a conventional telephone line to a suitable receiver/printer at the other end. Electronic mail systems of the future will need to allow for communication of mixed information of this type.

11.2.4 Document storage

In the paper office, elaborate systems have been developed for the storage and retrieval of information. In the electronic office, the majority of documents will be stored on magnetic or similar storage media as digital information. Systems must be developed to cope with the long term storage of information together with a facility of easy retrieval of relevant documents.

The widespread use of digitally transmitted and stored information opens up a new range of problems related to legal significance and ownership of documents. The laws of copyright are not sufficiently well developed to cope with problems that may arise in this area. Similarly, some equivalent to a human signature must be adopted if electronic mail communications are to have the same legal significance as their conventional mail counterparts.

11.3   OFFICE AUTOMATION SUMMARY

It can be seen from the above discussion that the transition to the electronic office is taking place gradually. Conventional methods of interpersonal communication are acquiring more functionality and new methods are evolving. The availability of the LAN in the mass market provides a base upon which these enhanced services can be based. A lot of work remains to be done in providing protocols to handle these new needs as well as legislation to cope with their effects. The next section will describe a set of protocols designed by IBM with the paperless office in mind. This is followed by a brief description of the X.400 standard for electronic mail.

11.4   THE IBM APPROACH

In the automated office, LANs will be used to transfer information between users. This information may consist of many different types of data other than simple characters and numerical information. Some types that have been suggested are voice, freezeframe video, facsimile documents, handwritten manuscripts etc. New methods must be developed to transmit, store and retrieve this information.

The approach to this problem adopted by IBM centers around the concept of a 'document'. A family of architectures has been developed to cover their possible contents and means of distribution. The first of these is the *document content architecture* (DCA). This deals with the information that is captured in the document. When dealing with conventional English language text, the use of ASCII or EBCDIC codes provides a sufficient character set to meet requirements. It is envisaged that the documents under consideration here could contain characters from many different sets, e.g. German, French, Chinese, Japanese etc. Because the architecture is open-ended, it is designed to be able to cope with new applications such as graphics, digitized speech, facsimile codes etc. A set of *graphics codepoint definitions* (GCD) have been developed to cover the problem of representing many more graphics than can be uniquely determined by the 256 different bit combinations in a byte. Using this standard, characters unique to different countries can be accommodated without risk of misinterpretation.

Since even simple, text-only documents can exist in many different forms, DCA has been defined in several different levels. The *revisable form DCA* describes documents that contain the actual content of the document together with information as to how it is to be formatted. This will include directives as to centering, footnotes, pagination etc. Documents in this form can be exchanged between users over a network system in such a way that they are easily modified by any wordprocessing system conforming to the standard. In cases where this feature is not required, *final form DCA* is used to express documents in device independent final form. In this case, the document holds the formatted document in a manner which enables it to be reproduced on a variety of devices.

11.4.1 Document interchange architecture (DIA)

Having standardized the contents of documents, the next problem is how to distribute them. The environment envisaged by IBM in this context is that of a large number of workstations, each connected to a *document distribution node* (see figure 11.1). These DDNs communicate with each other to perform safe storage and forwarding of documents through the distribution system. They may also provide storage and processing to maintain document libraries.

The DDNs offer three classes of services: *document distribution services* (DDS), *document library services* (DLS) and *application processing services* (APS). The architecture is so defined that new classes of services can be added as required.

Communication between the various components of the system is achieved using a construct called the *document interchange unit* (DIU). This packet of information is distributed between nodes by a service known as *SNA distribution services* (SNADS) which forms the top two layers of the SNA architecture (see figure 11.2). Each DIU can consist of up to five entities (see figure 11.3) called *prefix, command sequence, data unit(s), document unit(s)* and *suffix*.

The command sequence and data units are used to allow a DDN to give instructions to its neighboring nodes relating to the services required, while the document units relate to the content of the document and a description of its contents. Prefix and suffix fields are used to synchronize sender and receiver and to provide high level error control.

11.4.1.1 Document distribution services
The first class of service provided by a DDN relates to the transfer of documents between users. Documents may be transferred between users asynchronously, i.e. the two parties need not be in session with each other. It

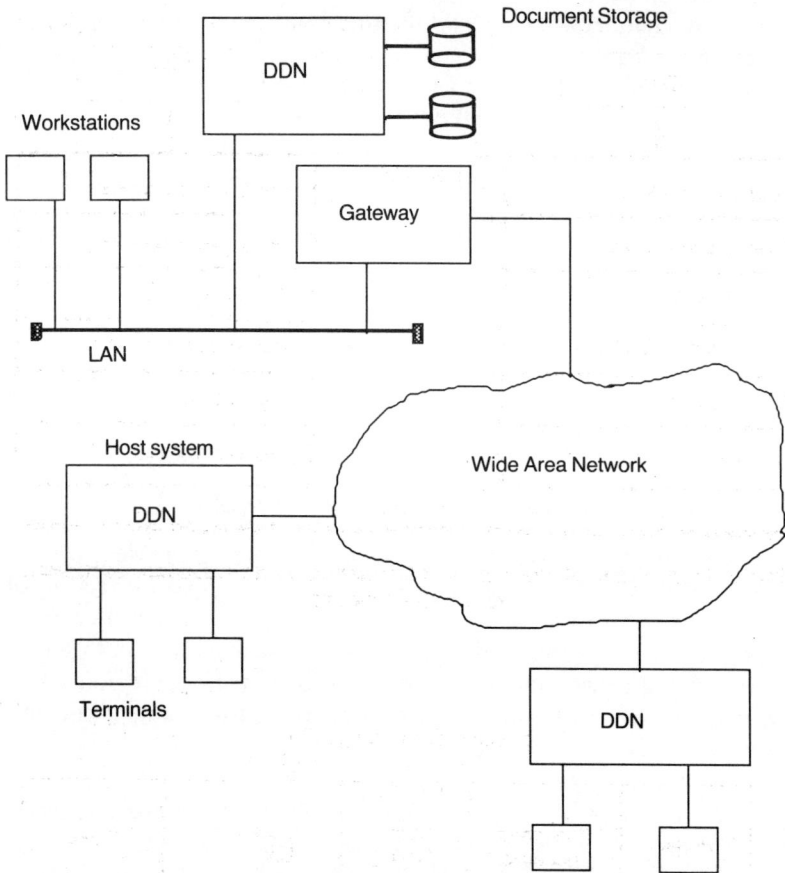

Figure 11.1   Document distribution environment

consists of a set of commands that may be sent either between a user at a workstation and his associated DDN, or between communicating DDNs. Briefly, they are as follows:

1 **Request-distribution**   This causes a document to be transported from a source node to a DDN for distribution to the specified recipients. This document may already be located in the DDN, or it may be transmitted with the request.
2 **Distribute**   Used between DDNs to distribute documents.
3 **Obtain**   Requests a DDN to deliver one or more documents to the requester.
4 **Deliver**   Requests a DDN to transport a document from a DDN to another node immediately. This command can also be used to override the store-and-forward functions of the system.

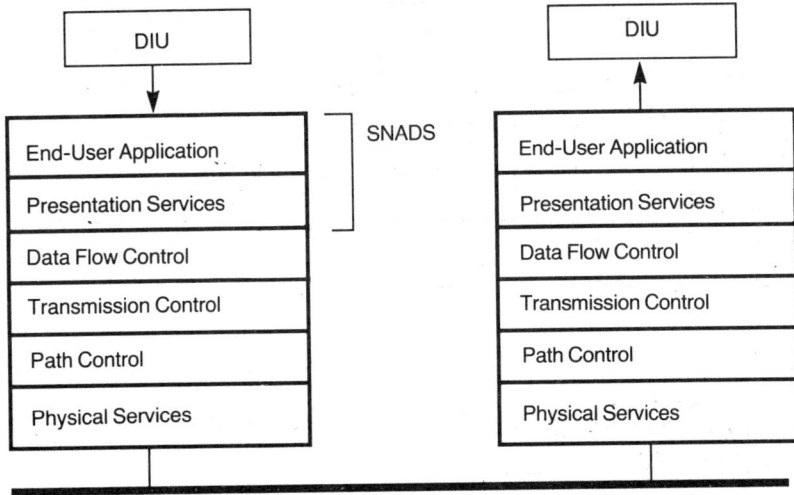

Figure 11.2   Flow of document interchange units between document distribution nodes

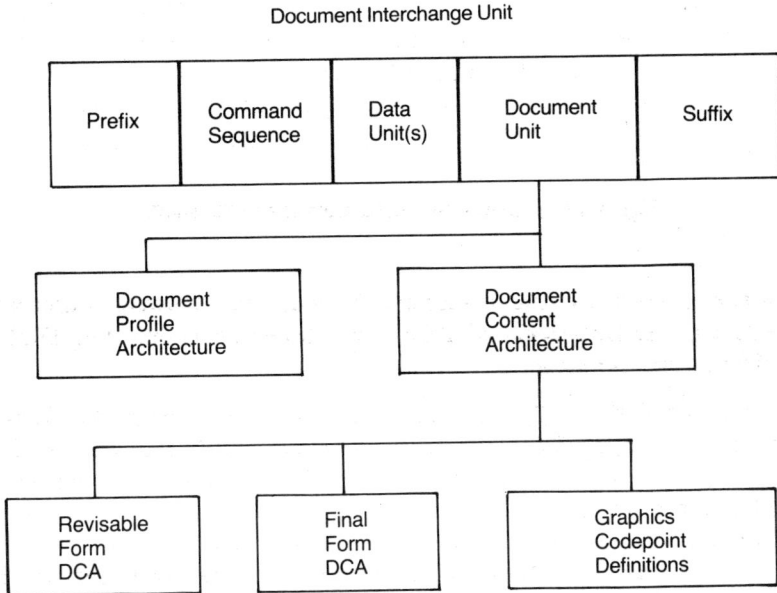

Figure 11.3   Document interchange unit structure

5 **Cancel-distribution, Distribution-status, Status-list and List** Provide control and status information on the progress of the distribution functions.

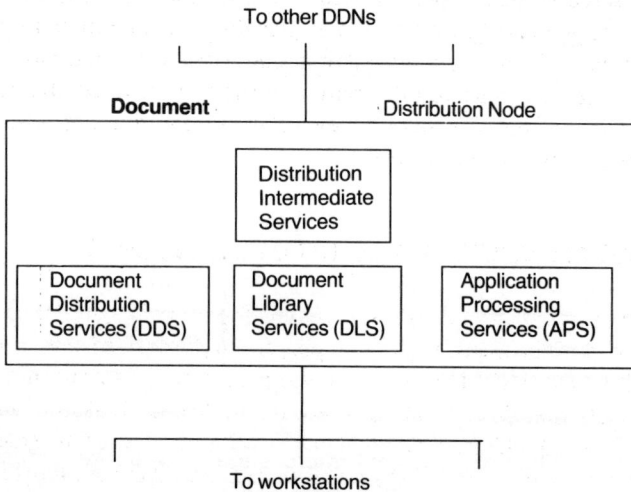

To other DDNs

Document · Distribution Node

Distribution
Intermediate
Services

Document
Distribution
Services (DDS)

Document
Library
Services (DLS)

Application
Processing
Services (APS)

To workstations

Figure 11.4   Services offered by document distribution nodes

11.4.1.2   Document library services

This service provides functions for maintaining a library of documents owned by the system's users. Both the contents of the document and a *profile* describing its contents are stored in such a way that a single document can be owned by many users. In this way, a document distributed to all users sharing access to a single DDN would only exist once in the document storage. A set of commands are defined for storage, retrieval and deletion as follows:

1 **File**   Preserves an identified document in the library for a specified owner.
2 **Retrieve**   Fetches an identified document from the library.
3 **Search**   This command takes a series of operands which describe document characteristics. It creates a named list of references to documents satisfying these criteria for subsequent retrieval.
4 **Delete**   This command removes the link between a user and a document permanently. When all links have been destroyed, the document is purged from the library.

11.4.1.3   Application processing services

This set of services is used to perform operations on documents stored at a DDN. Commands can be issued from workstations that will cause the DDN to transform one of its stored documents in some way. The following commands are available:

1 **Format**   Executes a named formatting process on the identified document.

2 **Modify**   Used to revise document information fields.

3 **Execute**   Requests the DDN to invoke a named program.

The above three classes of service form a foundation for the distribution of documents between nodes on a network. The document content architecture covers the types of information used in documents today, and has scope for accommodating new types of information in the future. In combination, the family of architectures will support new office automation applications that are likely to arise in the near future.

11.5   X.400 MESSAGE HANDLING SYSTEM (MHS)

The IBM family of architectures was developed as a general document transfer and storage facility. It is a proprietary standard and serves the anticipated needs of IBM systems for the near future. At an international standard level, the CCITT set up a group in 1980 to look at the area of 'store-and-forward' electronic mail. They developed a series of recommendations known as *X.400* [16, 17, 18] which were adopted as standards in 1984.

11.5.1   The X.400 model

The X.400 [17] recommendation specifies the model in which user-to user-message transfer is carried out (see figure 11.5). A user interacts with an entity called a *user agent* to prepare a message in a standard form. When it is ready to send, it is submitted to the *message transfer agent* which will be responsible for its delivery to the recipient *user-agent entity* (UAE). This transfer may involve the message being routed through several intermediate *message transfer agent entities* (MTAE).

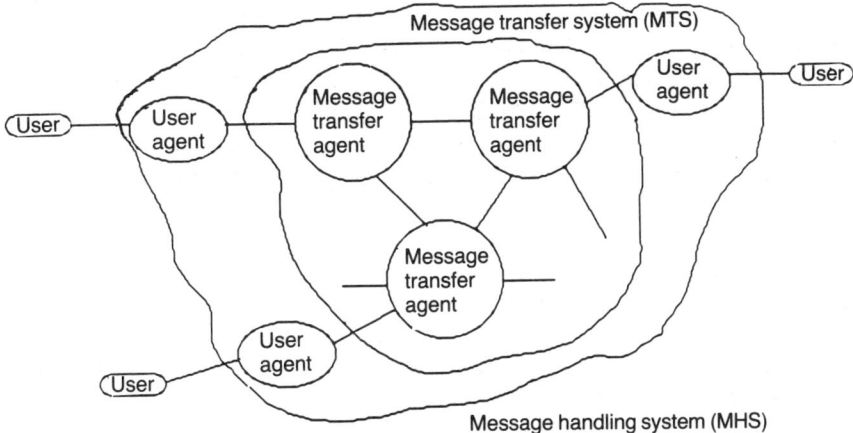

Figure 11.5   X.400 Environment

The interconnected collection of MTAEs is concerned only with the delivery of messages and thus is known as the *message transfer system* (MTS). Since the UAEs are involved in message composition, the combination of these with the MTS is known as the *message handling system* (MHS).

11.5.2 Message content

The format of messages in X.400 bears some resemblance to that of IBM's Document Content Architecture described in the previous section. The message is divided into three sections: Envelope, Heading and Body. The body section contains the information that the user wishes to communicate. The first type of information to be supported was a memo-like document containing text only. The standard will eventually allow the use of telex, teletex, facsimile, videotex and digitized voice to be included in this section.

The heading section describes the type of information contained in the body, and stores other information concerning the attributes of the message. In the case of the simple memo service (known as *interpersonal messaging*

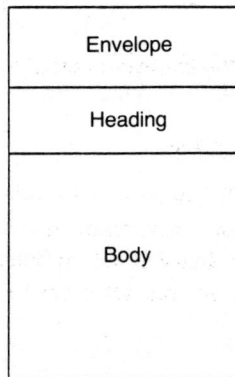

Figure 11.6   X.400 message format

protocol (IPM) [19]), this field will contain such things as the to:, from: and cc: fields of the message as well as other attributes such as the 'sensitivity indication' (e.g. personal, private, company confidential etc.).

The final section is called the Envelope and contains information to enable the message transfer agent to deliver the message to its intended recipient(s).

11.5.3 Relationship to the OSI model

The X.400 standards run as an application layer service, in terms of the OSI model described in Chapter 6. X.400 further subdivides the application layer into two layers: the *user agent layer* and the *message transfer layer*. These embody the functions of the user agent and the message transfer agent respectively. In the case of intermediate nodes used only to route messages, the user agent layer is not required.

Often, a node with a user agent entity is not equipped with a corresponding message transfer entity. In this case, the message transfer layer of the node will be equipped with a *submission-and-delivery entity* (SDE) which will communicate on its behalf to its associated MTE.

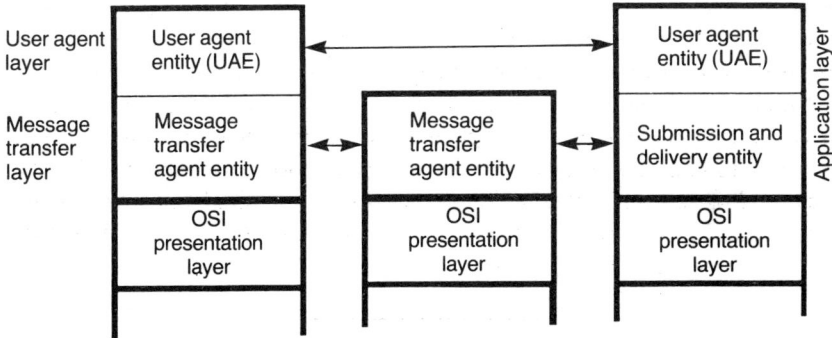

Figure 11.7   X.400 in the context of the OSI model

11.5.4   Applications in LANs

In a LAN environment, it is likely that each node on the system will have a UAE and an SDE. One node, designated the mail server, will contain a message transfer agent entity that will act on behalf of its clients. This node could also be connected via wide area networks to other MTAE.

11.5.5   Summary

It can be seen from the above description that the range and complexity of devices available to assist interpersonal communication are growing. The LAN offers an efficient low-cost way of implementing the communications channel between the equipment involved. If, however, this equipment is to supersede the paper office, appropriate protocols and architectures must be developed to support the transfer, storage, retrieval and distribution of information in a wide range of formats.

11.6   FACTORY AUTOMATION

Another area where automation has a great role to play is in the factory environment. Modern production lines are increasingly being dominated by a

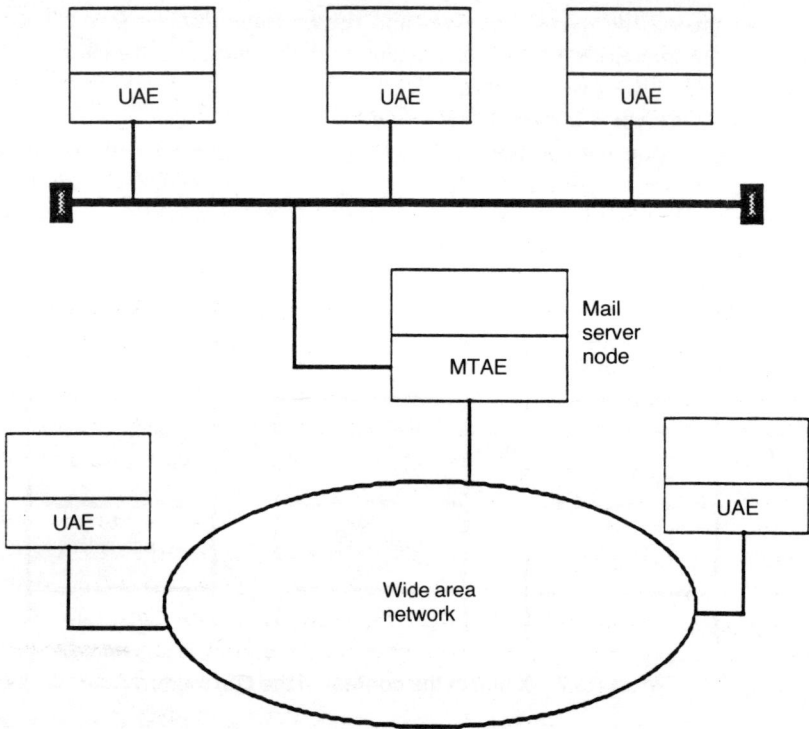

Figure 11.8   X.400 in a LAN Environment

large range of industrial robots, controllers and other computerized equipment. Design of components is often achieved using computer-aided design (CAD) techniques. The handling of materials can be managed by a computer system locating and retrieving parts from a warehouse. Numerical control machinery can perform simple mechanical tasks given appropriate instructions and robots may perform a complex range of production tasks.

All of these facilities form 'islands' of automation, each capable of performing a specific task without any reference to the surrounding environment. There is a great need to integrate the equipment into one coordinated system. In this way, information flow could be achieved from the initial design on a CAD system, through the automated materials handling, through production using automated machine tools and robots and ending up with quality control. The entire process could then provide inputs to the traditional factory applications like materials requirements planning (MRP), ordering, and financial accounting systems. LANs can help in achieving this integration by providing a high speed channel for communications between the different areas of activity in the enterprise. Software to integrate the functions will evolve if a uniform interface exists to all automated systems within the factory.

Typically, both the software and hardware involved in these systems emanate from a diverse range of sources each adopting their own conventions for intermachine communications. Thus, in order to achieve integration a common set of standards is needed to which all will adhere.

11.7 MANUFACTURING AUTOMATION PROTOCOL

In the early 1980s, General Motors began to realize that their car manufacturing operations were not competitive with their highly automated Japanese counterparts. In response to this, they adopted a policy of automating their plants to redress the imbalance. They realized that the equipment required for this purpose would come from a wide variety of vendors and that communication between machinery would be a problem. They further realized that to achieve integrated automation, a widely supported, nonproprietary factory communication standard was necessary.

Standards work on protocols based on the open systems interconnect (OSI) model was being undertaken at the time by the International Standards Organisation (ISO). The standards being produced covered the communications needs of the widest range of applications. This work formed the basis for standardization in General Motors. During 1984, the *manufacturing automation protocol* (MAP) users' group was formed to bring interested users and vendors together to form a broad base of support for MAP.

The MAP standards are essentially an application-specific subset of the ISO protocols designed to meet the needs of factory automation. In June 1985, the MAP users' group released a public MAP specification which summarizes the standards specified by General Motors' MAP version 2.1. This version is current at the time of writing.

11.8 THE ISO SUBSET

The reference model for Open Systems Interconnection specifies a 7 layer model (see Chapter 6) for subdividing communications functions. Each layer offers a number of alternative services, each suited to a particular range of applications. The MAP specification selects a subset of these options for use in the factory automation context.

11.8.1 The physical layer

The operating environment for the physical layer in a factory automation context has a number of distinct characteristics. The network often covers a very large area. Within this area, conditions can be quite harsh in terms of electrical noise and other environmental pollution. Equipment is subject to relocation or replacement at regular intervals. Despite the hostile conditions, reliability is often a crucial factor as breakdowns in the system may lead to financial loss or serious safety risks.

A bus topology using broadband transmission techniques was chosen to be the MAP standard in this area. The use of broadband enabled the large areas involved to be covered by a single network. Other equipment, e.g. security monitoring, could share the same backbone cable, and suitably shielded coaxial cable with passive taps could survive the harsh environment.

11.8.2 The data-link layer

11.8.2.1 Media access

When using the bus topology, a protocol is necessary to control access to the shared medium. The two approaches that could be used are IEEE 802.3 (CSMA/CD) or IEEE 802.4 (Token Bus). In a factory environment, several factors are present which determine the choice. The ability to determine the minimum time to access the network is important for monitoring applications. For a given network configuration, access time on a token bus network is deterministic, whereas with CSMA/CD, this is not the case. Priority traffic is also supported with four different levels in IEEE 802.4.

In the token bus, permission to use the network is passed in a fair manner from node to node on a logical ring. Not all nodes connected to the medium need to be part of this logical ring. Also, once a node has seized the token, there are no restrictions to the type of traffic it can initiate on the bus while holding the token. It is possible to have a configuration consisting of several low-cost, limited function nodes connected to the medium responding to query/response sequences from a full function node that has possession of the token. For example, in figure 11.9, if node A is holding the token, it may communicate with nodes G and F provided that such communication is completed within the maximum token-holding period. In this way, a computer controller could supervize several simple machine tools without the need for each to be equipped with complex network interfaces. It is for these reasons that in the factory floor environment, the IEEE 802.4 token bus access method is the preferred mode of operation.

11.8.2.2 Logical link control

The IEEE standard relating to the logical link component of the data-link layer is 802.2. Three possible classes of service are available: Class 1 – connectionless, Class 2 – connection oriented and Class 3 – an immediate acknowledge service.

The connection-oriented service sets up a virtual circuit between the communicating parties and gives the ability to detect and recover from transmission errors. The connectionless service involves communication using datagrams and can only detect and discard packets with parity errors.

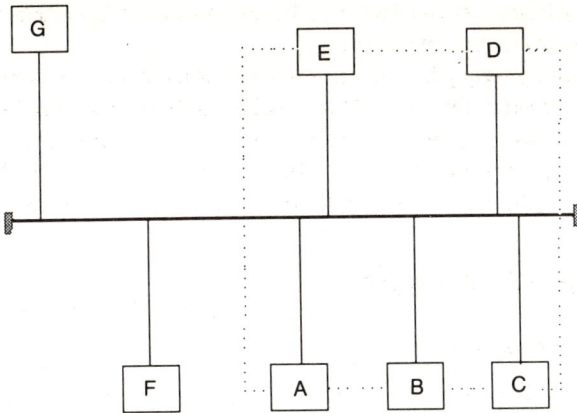

Figure 11.9   Token bus: Nodes G and F are connected to the bus but do not form part of the logical ring

Since one of the assumptions of transmission over LANs is that they have high reliability at the physical layer, the overhead of connection-oriented services was considered unjustified. End-to-end reliability constraints can be satisfied by having a connection-oriented service at the transport layer. Accordingly, Class 1 service was chosen as the standard for the MAP backbone network.

The Class 3 service has its uses when used with fast response programmable devices, but because of the associated higher throughput, it was felt that this feature should only be used on small subnets where message transfer and acknowledgement are critical.

11.8.3   The network layer

This layer looks after the routing of messages from source to destination through intermediate systems. In a MAP context, this may mean routing through separate token bus network segments, or through a wide area network. Performing routing of this kind implies a standardized, hierarchical addressing structure. The need for uniqueness of addresses between multiple organizations is acknowledged.

As with the data-link layer, the ISO network layer standards offer a *connection-oriented network service* (CONS) and a *connectionless network service* (CLNS). In the connection-oriented service, numbered messages are monitored and acknowledged between communicating systems. This guards against the danger of packets being delivered in an order other than that in which they were sent. The connectionless service on the other hand can only detect missing message fragments based on a timeout, following which it discards the entire message. It is this connectionless service that is used in MAP. The burden of packet ordering and detecting errors involving the absence of, or duplication of, entire messages, is left to the transport layer.

11.8.4   The transport layer

One of the overall goals of the MAP suite of protocol subsets is to ensure a reliable end-to-end connection between nodes. This is achieved by delegating the greater part of this overhead to the transport layer. The ISO transport specification gives 5 classes of service from Class 0, which is designed for simple teletex transmission up to Class 4 which has full error detection and recovery control.

Placed on top of the connectionless network and data-link layers, the Class 4 service provides guaranteed delivery, message sequencing and full error detection. The time overhead for this function is concentrated in this layer, with a relatively speedy passage through the lower levels. Accordingly, the MAP group chose the Class 4 service. In certain cases, where speed is of the essence, a Class 2 (multiplexing class) service may be used.

11.8.5   The session layer

Thus far in our treatment of the various layers of the system, the emphasis has been on the reliable end-to-end transfer of packets of unspecified data. The upper three layers, session, presentation and application, are concerned with the interaction and synchronization between the communicating parties. The ISO session layer [10] has been defined with 4 subsets: the *Kernel*, the *basic combined subset* (BCS), the *basic synchronized set* (BSS) and the *basic activity set* (BAS). At the time of writing, only the Kernel service has been included in the MAP 2.1 specification.

This service allows for connection negotiation, establishment and release as well as duplex (2-way simultaneous) data transfer. Facilities for expedited data transfer are also included. As the demands of the higher level services increase, other capabilities such as synchronization, checkpointing, error reporting etc. may be included in the MAP specification.

11.8.6   The presentation layer

This layer is concerned with transforming local data representations into those agreed upon for interchange between nodes. At present, this layer has not been standardized by the MAP users' group. It is expected however that in later versions, the ISO-specified presentation layer [11] will be used.

11.8.7   The application layer

At this level in the layered model, a variety of protocols must be made available to cover the wide range of requirements of communicating systems. Realizing this, the ISO have divided the functionality of this layer [12] into two broad categories. The first of these is called the *common application service elements* (CASE). This consists of a body of primitives that are likely

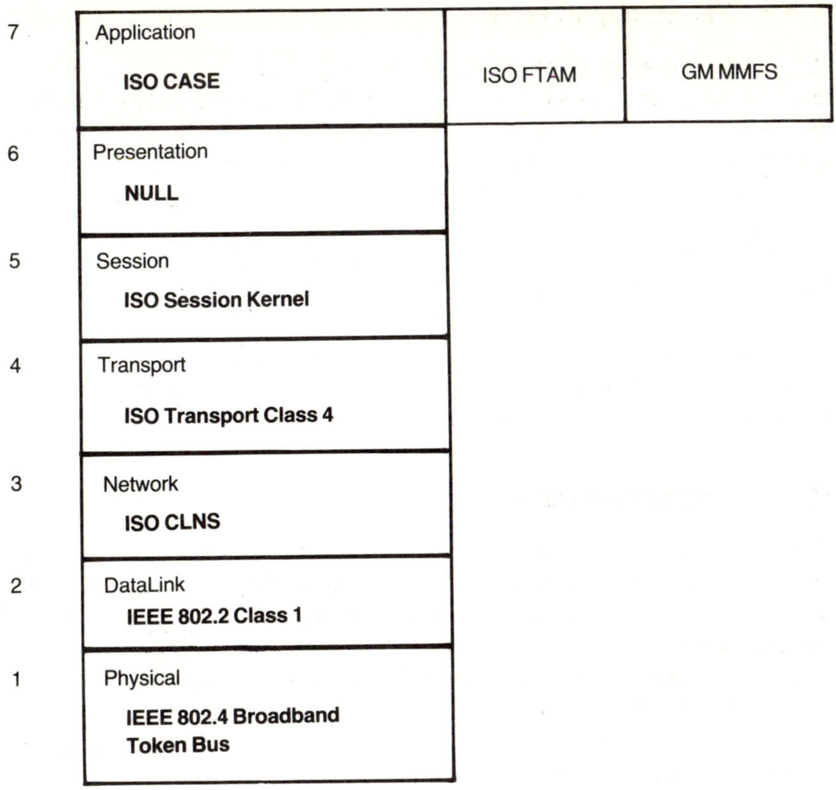

7	Application **ISO CASE**	**ISO FTAM**	**GM MMFS**
6	Presentation **NULL**		
5	Session **ISO Session Kernel**		
4	Transport **ISO Transport Class 4**		
3	Network **ISO CLNS**		
2	DataLink **IEEE 802.2 Class 1**		
1	Physical **IEEE 802.4 Broadband Token Bus**		

Figure 11.10   The MAP subset of the OSI protocols

to be useful in providing any application layer service. Included in this set are calls to connect two parties, abort, and transfer data. The second category of services are called the *specific application service elements* (SASE). These are sets of primitives to be used in conjunction with those of CASE for particular application services. Examples of these sets include the file transfer service, virtual terminal service and job transfer/manipulation service.

MAP as specified in version 2.1 implements a subset of the CASE primitives composed of actions that will establish a connection, release a connection, transfer data and abort. Other synchronization primitives present in the ISO specification are not present in MAP as yet.

As regards specific application service elements, those available to MAP users are file transfer and message passing. These services, coupled with the CASE primitives, provide a good foundation for communication.

The file transfer method chosen is again a subset of the ISO *file transfer access and management* (FTAM). This allows a user to open, read and write files on remote nodes. There is also a limited access to file descriptor information. This means that file attributes can be inspected from a remote location.

One of the main applications in a factory automation setting is the ability to communicate with programmable controllers, numerical control machines, bar code readers and robots. At the time, no standard existed covering this specialized form of message passing. Accordingly, General Motors developed their own, known as *manufacturing message format standard* (MMFS). These protocols are divided into classes for the different applications and support simple message passing and limited file transfer. The primitives in these protocols are highly application-specific, e.g. enter upload/download mode, take/relinquish control etc.

The adoption of this in-house standard was a temporary measure, and it is intended that, in the near future, MAP should migrate to the *RS511 Manufacturing Message Standard* being developed by the Electronic Industries Association.

11.9   ELEMENTS OF MAP NETWORKS

The MAP suite of protocols was developed by a group of interested vendors and users in the factory automation area. These groups already had a large

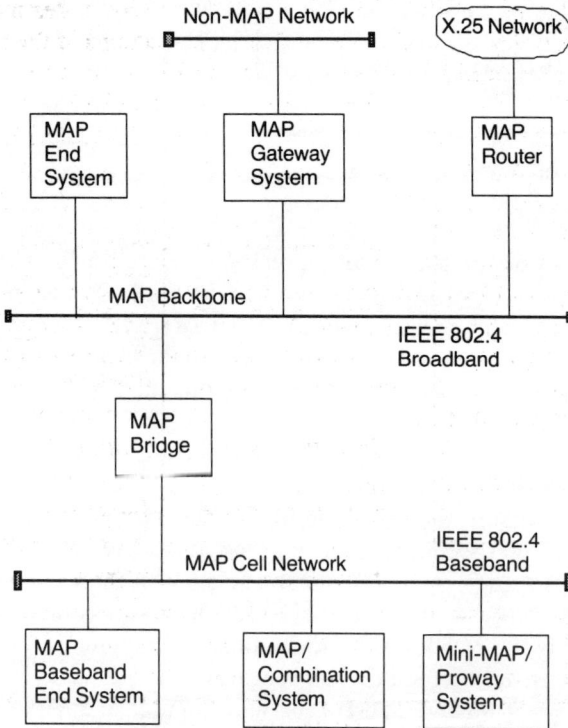

Figure 11.11   MAP architecture

amount of equipment in use conforming to a wide range of standards. The purpose of MAP was to provide a common goal which all would aim towards, without the necessity of discarding all existing equipment. Accordingly, the MAP architecture defines a *backbone* system which will optimally support the ideal MAP system as well as a *cell* architecture (see figure 11.11) to accommodate unusual devices as well as older equipment that does not fully conform to the new standards.

11.9.1 The MAP backbone architecture

The backbone of the system is composed of one or more cable segments conforming to the IEEE 802.4 Broadband Token bus. The main type of nodes connected to these are called MAP End Systems (see figure 11.12). These nodes implement the full set of ISO subset protocols as described above, and are capable of peer-to-peer communication.

Segments of the network are connected together by nodes called *MAP bridges* (see figure 11.13). These nodes are comprized of a proprietary bridge application program running on top of separate data-link and physical layers of the two network segments. Since both subnetworks are using a common 802.2 LLC layer, as well as sharing a single address space, this program has simply to relay packets between the networks. These nodes are useful as a means of extending the backbone, and isolating sections of the network with large amounts of traffic.

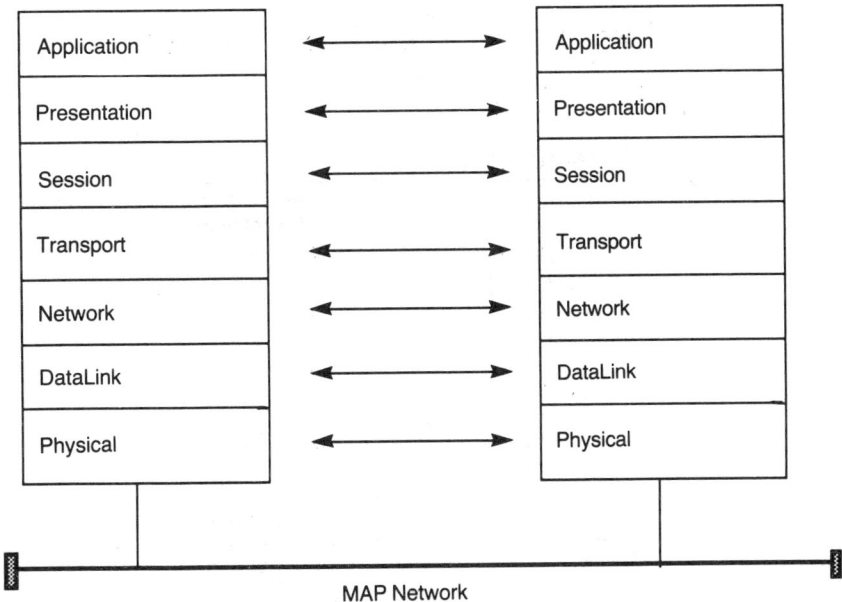

Application	⟷	Application
Presentation	⟷	Presentation
Session	⟷	Session
Transport	⟷	Transport
Network	⟷	Network
DataLink	⟷	DataLink
Physical	⟷	Physical

MAP Network

Figure 11.12 MAP end system

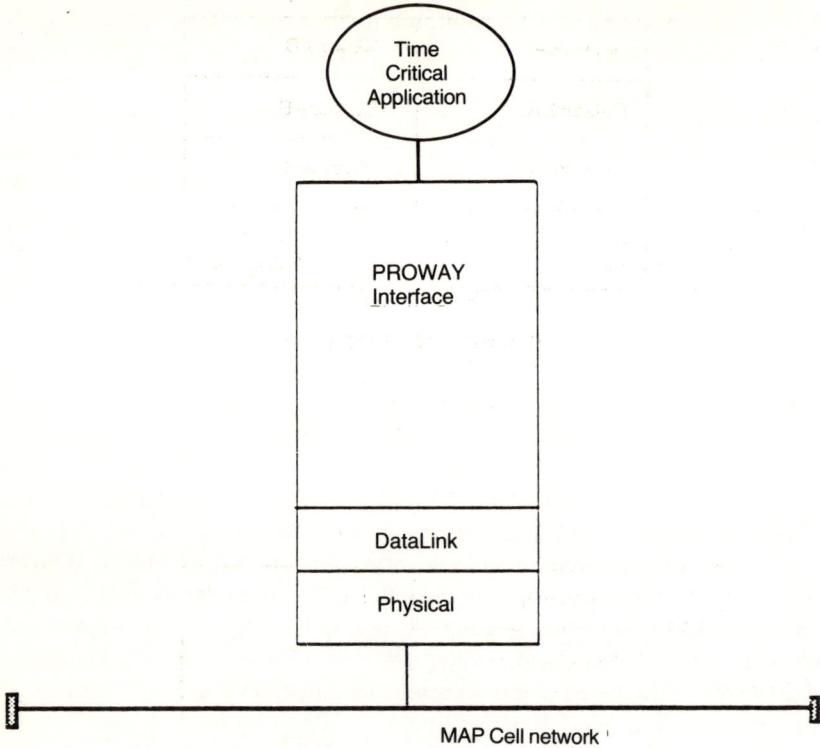

Figure 11.13   PROWAY system

Communication with nodes on other non-MAP networks conforming to the OSI model is achieved through a MAP *router Node* (see figure 11.14). This node implements distinct data-link and physical layers for each connected subnetwork. On top of all of these, a common network layer routes packets between them. Communication between the subnetworks is governed by the ISO *internetwork protocol* (IP). Connection is possible to networks with a wide range of physical and data-link layers, e.g. the X.25 WAN. The existence of the network layer in this node means that addressing schemes need not be the same in both networks.

In order to communicate with non-OSI networks, e.g. an IBM SNA network, a node called a *MAP gateway* (see figure 11.15) is required. This implements all layers of a MAP end system, and the entire layered structure for the foreign network. This allows data to be passed between the systems while satisfying the protocol requirements of each network.

11.9.2   The MAP cell architecture

This architecture is an attempt to accommodate nodes originally conforming to the PROWAY 'standard for industrial and data highways'. The data-link

Network A	Network B
DataLink A	DataLink B
Physical A	Physical B

MAP
Segment A

MAP
Segment B

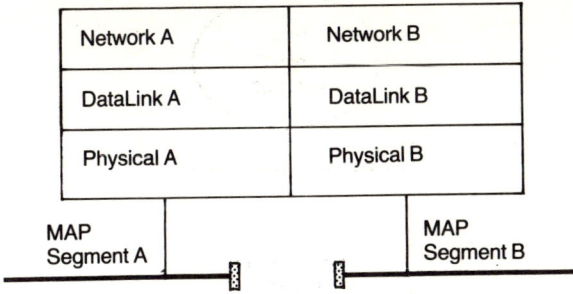

Figure 11.14   MAP router

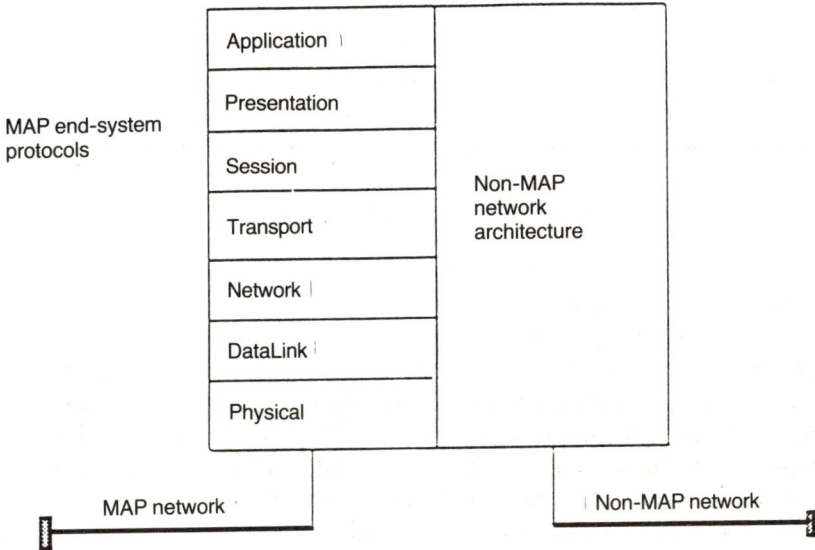

MAP end-system
protocols

Application	
Presentation	
Session	Non-MAP network architecture
Transport	
Network	
DataLink	
Physical	

MAP network   Non-MAP network

Figure 11.15   MAP gateway

layer is IEEE 802.4 baseband as opposed to broadband used on the
backbone. Segments of cell networks are connected to the backbone by the
MAP bridge nodes described above. MAP-end system nodes can operate on
this network if their lower layer is changed appropriately. The other main
types of node on these segments are *MAP/combination* (figure 11.16) systems

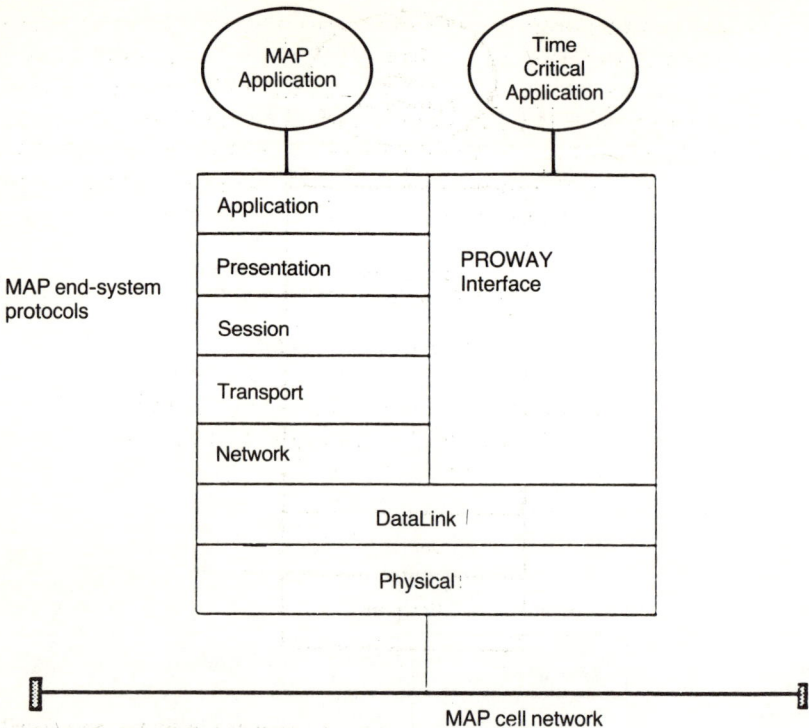

Figure 11.16   MAP/combination system

and *mini-map* (figure 11.17) systems. The latter type of node supports the RS 511 Messaging protocol interfaced directly to PROWAY confirm services. This type of node supports a low cost connection for dumb devices, e.g. sensors, loop controls, bar code readers etc. They can only communicate with other minimap systems or MAP/combination systems and are completely unknown to the MAP network management systems.

   MAP/combination systems on the other hand contain all the functionality of a modified MAP end system as well as that contained within a miniMAP system. The first obvious purpose of these nodes is to form a communications path between all normal MAP end systems and the miniMAP nodes. They can also be used however to give extra functionality for time critical applications. In this case, expeditious data can be sent through the PROWAY layers, while other traffic can proceed as normal.

11.10   SUMMARY OF MAP

The MAP suite of protocols allows for the building of a communications system specifically for use in the factory context. It is based on nonproprietary standards and is backed by a number of major manufacturing concerns. It

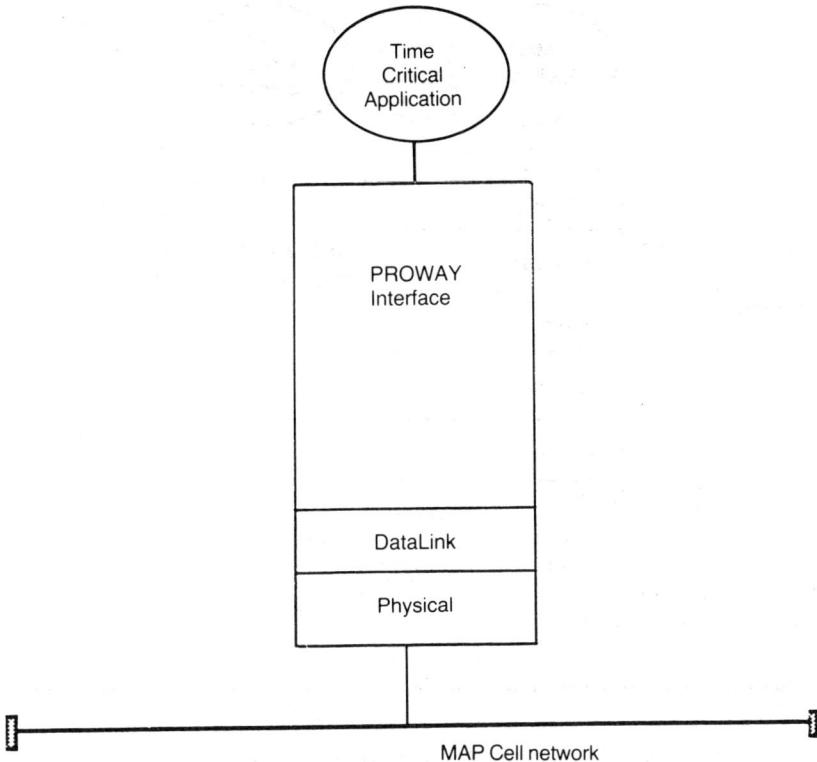

Figure 11.17   PROWAY system

allows for the evolution from an existing base of installed automation equipment into a homogeneous factory-wide network. The application services provided are at present rather minimal, but work is continuing in extending the range and complexity of those offered. Links between it and the office environment will add to its success.

11.11   THE TECHNICAL AND OFFICE PROTOCOL (TOP)

At about the same time as MAP was being unveiled, a group spearheaded by Boeing Corporation was formed to develop a subset of the OSI standards for technical and office applications. The name given to these efforts was the *technical and office protocol* (TOP). In order to be able to communicate between the office and factory environment, efforts were made to be as compatible with MAP as possible.

The differences between the physical environments of the factory and the office are marked. This is coupled with the fact that a different set of vendors are operating in each area. At the time when TOP was conceived, the dominant network system for office applications was Ethernet. Accordingly, the IEEE 802.3 (CSMA/CD) baseband standard was chosen as the preferred physical layer of TOP version 1.0. This provided an upgrade path for Ethernet users and fitted well with the IEEE 802.2 data-link layer. Future developments in this area are likely to accommodate the use of IEEE 802.5 (token ring) as an alternative access method.

Layers 2 (data-link) up to Layer 6 (presentation) are identical in TOP and MAP, and it is only at Layer 7 (application) that significant differences arise (figure 11.18). The applications required in an office environment will be more concerned with nonrealtime information transfer e.g. electronic mail, data base access etc. The only application service specified by TOP version 1.0 is the subset of ISO FTAM file transfer service. Implementation of the CASE is not required by TOP at the time of writing. It is expected that in future versions, an electronic mail facility based on the X.400 standard, discussed earlier in this chapter, will be provided together with a Virtual Terminal Protocol (VTP).

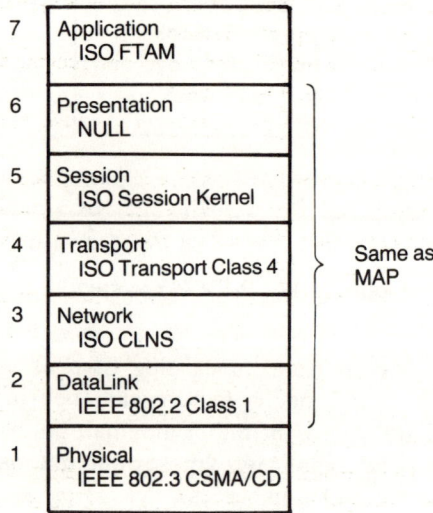

7	Application ISO FTAM	
6	Presentation NULL	
5	Session ISO Session Kernel	Same as MAP
4	Transport ISO Transport Class 4	
3	Network ISO CLNS	
2	DataLink IEEE 802.2 Class 1	
1	Physical IEEE 802.3 CSMA/CD	

Figure 11.18   TOP protocols

11.12   SUMMARY

The introduction of automation into the office and factory environments is bringing great benefits in terms of worker productivity and in the quality of the product/service being provided. Integration of all of the separate services available at present can only be achieved by providing a means of transferring information between them. The LAN hardware provides a high-speed communications channel through which data can be transferred. Higher level protocols are necessary for reliable end-to-end communication and synchronization.

The IBM document interchange architecture addresses the need in a paperless office to distribute, store and retrieve documents containing diverse types of information. The MAP and TOP efforts provide a framework in which software can be developed for the full range of office and factory automation problems.

11.13 REFERENCES

1 *Local Networks and Distributed Office Systems Vol. 2: System Selection and Implementation*, Northwood: Online Publications Ltd, 1982.

2 Schick, T. and Brockish, R.F.: 'The document interchange architecture: a member of a family of architectures in the SNA environment', *IBM Systems Journal*, **23**, no. 1, pp. 220–241, 1982.

3 Stone, R.: *The Push-button Manager: A Guide To Office Automation*, Maidenhead, McGraw-Hill, 1985.

4 Gould, J.D. and Boies, S.J.: 'Speech filing – an office system for principals', *IBM Systems Journal*, **23**, no. 1, pp. 65–81, 1985.

5 Anastassiou, D. *et al.*: 'Series/1-based videoconferencing system', *IBM Systems Journal*, **22**, nos. 1 and 3, pp. 97–110, 1983.

6 Krumrey, A.: 'SNA strategies', *PC Technical Journal*, **3**, no. 7, pp. 40–53, July 1985.

7 Moore, D.J.: 'Teletext – a worldwide link among office systems for electronic document exchange', *IBM Systems Journal*, **22**, nos. 1 and 2, pp. 30–45, 1983.

8 Moore, G.: 'Manufacturing automation protocol – mapping the factory of the future', *IEE Electronics and Power*, pp. 269–272, April 1986.

9 Crowder, R.: 'The MAP specification', *Control Engineering*, pp. 22–25, October 1985.

10 Emmons, W.F. and Chandler, A.S.: 'OSI Session Layer: Services and protocol', *Proceedings of the IEEE*, **71**, no. 12, pp. 1397–1400, December 1983.

11 Hollis, L.L.: 'OSI presentation layer activities', *Proceedings of the IEEE*, **71**, no. 12, pp. 1401–1403, December 1983.

12 Bartoli, P.D.: 'The application layer of the reference model of open systems interconnection', *Proceedings of the IEEE*, **71**, no. 12, pp. 1404–1407, December 1983.

13 Dalrymple, D.: 'LAN standards efforts begin to pay off', *Mini-Micro Systems*, pp. 93–98, March 1986.

14 Roca, R.: 'ISDN architecture', *A. T. & T. Technical Journal*, **65**, no. 1, pp. 4–17, January/February 1986.

15 Falconer, R.M. and Adams, J.L.: 'Orwell: A protocol for an integrated services local network', *British Telecom Technology Journal*, **3**, no. 4, pp. 27–35, October 1985.

16 CCITT Draft Recommendation X.400: *Message Handling Systems: System Model – Service Elements*.

17 CCITT Draft Recommendation X.401: *Message Handling Systems: Basic Service Elements and Optional User Facilities*.

18 CCITT Draft Recommendation X.420: *Message Handling Systems: Interpersonal Messaging User Agent Layer*.

APPENDIX A

DIFFERENTIAL MANCHESTER ENCODING

When transmitting baseband signals, a varying voltage is applied to the medium to represent the data being transmitted. There are many ways of achieving this, but the most common method used in conjunction with LANs is known as *differential Manchester encoding*.

This works by representing bits in the data stream by voltage transitions in the signal. During the middle of each bit time, the signal will change polarity from positive to negative or vice-versa. To determine the value of the bit being represented, the polarity in the first half bit-time is compared with the second half for the previous bit. If they are the same, then a 1 is being represented. If they are opposite, the bit is a zero. Figure A.1 shows three consecutive 1s being transmitted showing that the polarity does not change in crossing the bit boundary. Figure A.2 shows the same diagram for three 0s where it can be seen that the polarity reverses on the boundary.

We have said that a signal transition always occurs half-way through a bit-time. If this transition is absent, a *violation* is said to occur. Figure A.3 shows the two types of violation (positive and negative) that are possible. The presence of one of these violations can be caused by a collision occurring on a CSMA/CD network, or by noise. It may also be deliberately used by the transmitter to signal a boundary in the data stream. An example of this can be found in the IEEE 802.5 token ring network where a set pattern of positive and negative violations is used to indicate the start and end of a packet. If Manchester encoding were not in use, some other means to transmit these boundary markers would have to be found.

The use of Manchester encoding as a signalling technique has a number of advantages. Firstly, when transmitting normal data, a voltage transition occurs in the middle of every bit time. Nodes on a network can use this fact to derive a clock signal from the received bit stream. This minimizes any synchronization problems that may occur. A second benefit of the technique is that each bit transmitted (except violations) has equal positive and negative

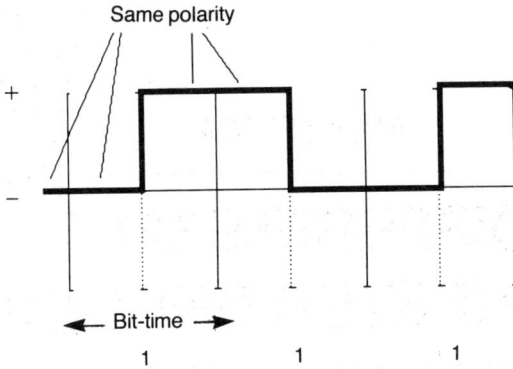

Figure A.1 **Series of three 1s in Manchester encoding. The polarity of the signal does not change between bit times**

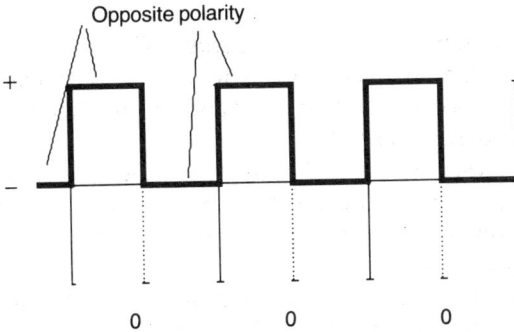

Figure A.2 **Series of three 0s. Note polarity change at between bit times**

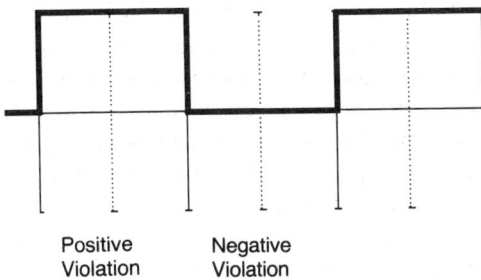

Figure A.3 **Violations of the Manchester encoding system. Note the absence of a transition at the half bit time**

components. This means that a d.c. balance is maintained and no net current flows between transmitter and receiver. This avoids any problems with electroplating at the connection points in the network. The lack of d.c. balance in the code violations will not cause a problem, if every negative violation is balanced by a corresponding positive one.

APPENDIX B

ERROR CHECKING

All communication networks are prone to errors, e.g. data bits may get corrupted during transmission due to electrical noise. Steps can be taken to *detect* and in some cases *correct* such errors. Both rely on including extra 'error control' bits in each packet. Error correcting codes, e.g. Hamming codes, have a large overhead in terms of the number of extra bits that have to be transmitted. On local area networks where the error rate is low it is usual to use 'error detecting' techniques. 'Bad' packets can always be retransmitted if necessary. The two most common error-checking mechanisms are *parity* and *cyclic redundancy checks.*

Parity checking is the simplest technique. An extra bit is sent with each packet. Its value is set by the transmitter so that there are an even number of 1 bits in the packet. The destination checks the number of 1 bits in the packet it receives and if it is not even it knows that an error has occurred during transmission. (Odd parity is also possible where the number of 1s is odd.) Parity checking is a very simple technique and detects errors where a single bit is affected. It is best used with a small packet, e.g. as in the Cambridge Ring.

A more sophisticated technique is a cyclic redundancy check (CRC). This can be used to cover much larger amounts of data and detects multiple errors. The bits to be transmitted are treated as the coefficients of a polynomial. This polynomial is divided, using modula 2 arithmetic, by the CRC generating function $G(x)$. The remainder that is left over after this division is transmitted along with the data. On the receiving side the same procedure is followed, the 'remainder' is again computed and compared with the transmitted value. CRC algorithms can be implemented very efficiently in hardware and, depending on the generating function (G) used, can detect errors with a very high probability.

APPENDIX C

THE TCP/IP SUITE OF PROTOCOLS

One of the nonproprietary protocols mentioned briefly in Chapter 6 is becoming influential in the LAN area. This set forms the ARPAnet network architecture. Of the set, by far the most widely used are the transmission control protocol (TCP) and the internet protocol (IP), collectively known as TCP/IP. This appendix will examine the development of these protocols, and look in some detail at the facilities offered by them.

C.1 HISTORY OF THE ARPANET PROTOCOLS

Research work on a long-haul network began in September 1969. This work was sponsored by a division of the U.S. Department of Defense known as the Defense Advanced Research Projects Agency (DARPA). The network that was developed was known as the ARPAnet and was in regular use by defense contractors and universities by 1971.

Around this time, it became clear that the simple host-to-host protocols in use would be inadequate for use in a network consisting of interconnected packet networks. Accordingly, in 1973, work began on developing a suite of protocols for use in this environment. The interconnection (or concatenation) of a collection of packet switched networks became known as the Internet or the Catanet [1].

The protocols that emerged from this research effort included IP and TCP, as well as a number of application level protocols. Their arrival was timely, given that many of the OSI protocols were still at the discussion stage. This, coupled with the fact that detailed information was easily available to implementers, meant that they were widely adopted.

C.2   THE ARPANET ARCHITECTURE

The layered architecture [2] of the ARPAnet protocols is shown in figure C.1. The lowest layer is known as the network interface layer, and sits on top of whatever communications facilities are offered by the underlying network. This may consist of a long-haul network, a satellite communications link or, more recently, the data-link layer of a LAN. It offers a uniform interface to higher layers and, among other functions, performs addressing and routing over the Catanet. In many ways, it is similar to the network layer of the ISO Reference Model described in Chapter 6.

The next level builds on these facilities to provide an interprocess communication facility between any two processes located in any node on the Catanet. Depending on the choice of protocol for this layer, reliability may or may not be guaranteed. The final layer of the model is concerned with applications services, e.g., virtual terminal, file transfer, electronic mail, etc.

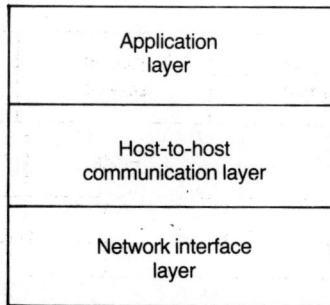

Figure C.1   The ARPAnet reference model

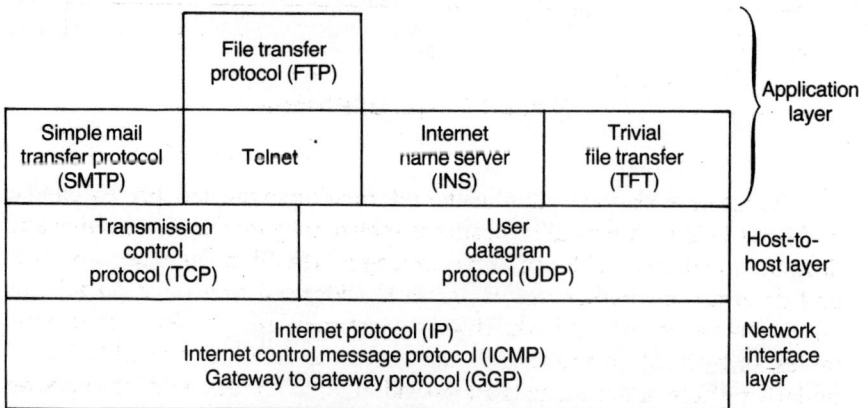

Figure C.2   ARPAnet protocols

The main protocols used in each of the layers described above are shown in figure C.2. This selection is not intended to be complete, as new protocols are added over time, and some are only of interest in highly specific application areas.

C.3 THE INTERNET PROTOCOL (IP)

The protocol used at the network interface layer in the hierarchy is known as the Internet protocol (IP) [3]. It provides a facility for the delivery of datagrams to nodes located anywhere on the Internet. This layer has three main areas of responsibility. Firstly, it provides a uniform interface to higher layers, irrespective of the underlying network in use. Because there may be many different networks in the path between source and destination, the layer must also perform addressing/routing, and, since the networks may have different packet sizes, fragmentation/re-assembly of datagrams.

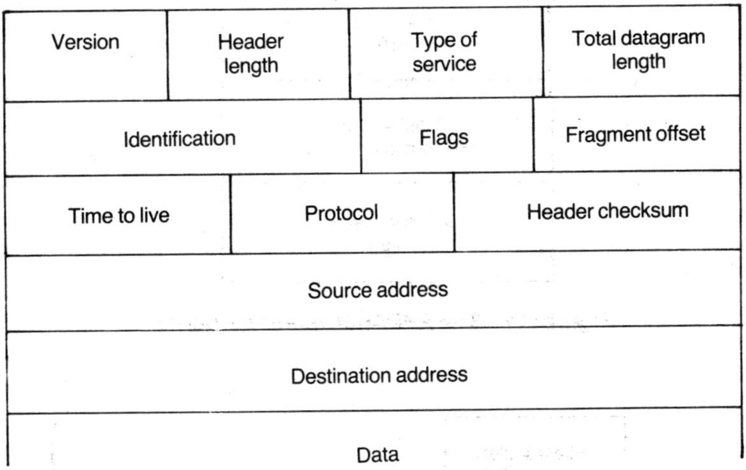

Version	Header length	Type of service	Total datagram length
Identification		Flags	Fragment offset
Time to live		Protocol	Header checksum
Source address			
Destination address			
Data			

Figure C.3   Typical IP header

The Internet protocol adds header information to the data presented to it by higher layers. A typical IP header is shown in figure C.3. The source and destination address fields are 32 bits in length. The IP module inspects these and determines whether the datagram is addressed to a node on this, or another (connected) network. If so, it must translate it (using either static tables, or by a call to a network name server) to an address suitable for the underlying network (e.g., an IEEE 802 address). If it is destined for a node on some other network, it must select an appropriate gateway and send it there instead.

If the network involved in the transfer is incapable of handling the complete datagram in one chunk, it must be broken up, and sent as fragments. A series of fragments of a single datagram can be identified by the unique combination of the source/destination address, protocol and identification fields. The fragment offset, total length and flags assist in breaking it up before transmission and reassembling it on arrival.

The Internet protocol does not provide any reliability features. For example, if an error is discovered in a datagram at any point on its journey, it is immediately discarded without notifying the sender. There are, however, instances where a destination node may send messages to the source informing it of errors. This is done using the internet control message protocol (ICMP) [4]. This uses IP as the transport mechanism, as if it were a higher level protocol, but in fact is a required portion of any IP implementation. A similar error-reporting protocol is used between gateways, and is called the gateway-to-gateway protocol (GGP).

The two main users of the Internet protocol reside in the host-to-host communications layer, and are known as the transmission control protocol (TCP) and the User Datagram Protocol (UDP).

C.4   THE USER DATAGRAM PROTOCOL (UDP)

The datagram facility provided by IP may be used by higher level programs with very little addition in the form of the UDP [5]. In order to allow more than one dialogue to occur at any given time, the UDP extends the Internet address with 16-bit source/destination port numbers. This means that a source and destination of data can be identified by a concatenation of the Internet address and port number known as a socket. These socket numbers are unique within the entire Catanet.

Before handing the data over to the IP module, the UDP will add a header consisting of the source/destination ports, a 16-bit length field and a simple checksum of the data being sent. This service is then used by higher level applications that require a simple datagram service with a low overhead, without guaranteed delivery. Other services that do require guaranteed delivery use the alternative TCP.

C.5   THE TRANSMISSION CONTROL PROTOCOL (TCP)

The basic services provided by the IP are further extended by the TCP [6]. As with the UDP, TCP augments the addressing scheme with port/socket numbers. It also maintains such state information as is necessary to maintain a bi-directional virtual circuit between two sockets on the Internet. TCP transforms the underlying IP datagram facility into a reliable transport mechanism with messages guaranteed to be delivered in the correct order.

Source port	Destination port
Sequence number	
Acknowledgement number	

Header size	Flags	Window

Checksum	Urgent pointer
Options	
Data	

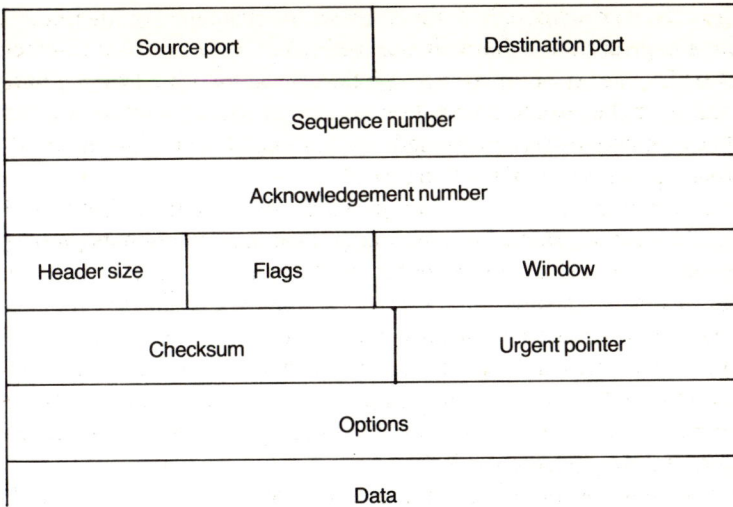

Figure C.4   Typical TCP header

The format of a typical TCP header is shown in figure C.4. This begins with the source and destination ports (as with UDP). The following two fields i.e. sequence and acknowledgement numbers are used for reliability. Each byte in the data stream being transmitted is assigned a number. When a packet is sent, the sequence number refers to the first byte in the packet. The receiver acknowledges, giving the next sequence number he expects to receive. This means that all bytes up to that number have been received correctly and provide a means of both ensuring that data is not lost in transmission, and that it is put together in the correct order.

When acknowledging receipt of a packet, the receiver can use the window field to inform the receiver as to how many more bytes can be accepted over and above the one being acknowledged. This prevents the sender transmitting at too high a rate. As with UDP, a checksum field is provided to detect transmission errors. The remaining fields are used in various ways to control the connection, but will not be discussed further here.

The consumer of this reliable transport service are applications level protocols such as electronic mail and virtual terminal services.

C.6   THE TELNET PROTOCOL

The Telnet protocol [7] makes use of the reliable virtual circuit facility provided by TCP to provide a network virtual terminal (NVT) capability. An NVT is an imaginary device that consists of a keyboard that can generate characters, and a printer of unspecified width that understands a limited number of control codes (e.g. tab, ring bell, etc.).

A Telnet connection consists of full-duplex conversation between two of these NVTs. The characters passed between the two parties use the ASCII character encoding scheme and one of these (character 255) is interpreted to mean 'interpret as command'. When this character is encountered, the following characters are treated as a command. There is a range of commands available to control the connection (e.g. local/remote echoing, interrupt process, etc.).

The user of the Telnet service is responsible for translating the behavior specified by the virtual terminal into actions that are appropriate to the local system. Because of this, the implementation of the Telnet protocol will perform some of the functions provided by OSI's presentation layer. This protocol is often used as a means of remote login to other hosts on the Internet, and is also used by the file transfer protocol (FTP).

C.7   THE FILE TRANSFER PROTOCOL (FTP)

One very common use of networks (local or otherwise) is that of transferring files between systems. One of the ARPAnet protocols used for this purpose is FTP [8]. This works by establishing a Telnet connection between the user and the FTP server. A specified set of commands is available to carry out various connection management (e.g. login, accounting, interrupt), context management (e.g., change directory, specify file structure) and file transfer (e.g., retrieve, store, append) tasks. The data to be transferred travels over a separate Telnet connection and actions on this link are controlled by the server process.

As an example, consider the case where a user on Host A wishes to retrieve a file from Host B. He first establishes a Telnet connection to the FTP server on Host B, and then, using the User, Pass and Acct commands, he identifies himself. This allows the server to look after access and accounting details. Using other FTP commands, he will inform the server of the name, structure and representation used by the required file. At this stage, the user will listen on a given Telnet port on Host A, and tell the FTP server to send the file to that port. It is the server's responsibility to initiate a connection to Host A's data port and send the file to it. As it arrives, the user will store it locally, before terminating the connection.

Hosts implementing these protocols normally set up servers at well-known port addresses. For example, the FTP server on any given host is contactable by making a Telnet call to port 21.

In addition to straightforward file transfer, the FTP protocol also includes commands to direct the data transferred to a particular user as electronic mail. This service is not needed, however, when a dedicated electronic mail protocol is used.

C.8 SIMPLE MAIL TRANSFER PROTOCOL (SMTP) [9]

This applications level ARPAnet protocol provides reliable mail transfer to/from any host on the Internet. It also has the added advantage that it is independent of the transmission subsystem involved in moving the data. For this reason, it can be used on a variety of interconnected networking environments. In a TCP/IP environment, SMTP makes use of the services provided by TCP. This network could be gatewayed to other networks using, for example, the ISO Transport or CCITT X.25 protocols.

The SMTP layer in one node establishes a connection with another SMTP layer located elsewhere on the network. A simple set of commands is available to identify the sender, specify the recipient(s), and transfer the message body. The receiving node may be able to deliver the mail directly to a local user, or it may forward it to yet another node on the route to its ultimate destination.

The addressing scheme used is known as domain addressing [10]. Unlike the IP format, where the hosts on the Internet form a flat, global address space, the SMTP hosts are organized into a hierarchically structured rooted tree. Instead of a simple host name (address), users are specified in the form: "user @ domain-string, where the domain string specifies that host's path from the root. Figure C.5 illustrates how a domain addressing scheme might be organized within a large company that uses several different interconnected networks.

It is important to note that the domain address of a node does not specify the route that the message must take. Each SMTP layer involved examines the destination address, and either delivers it to a local user, or forwards it to a

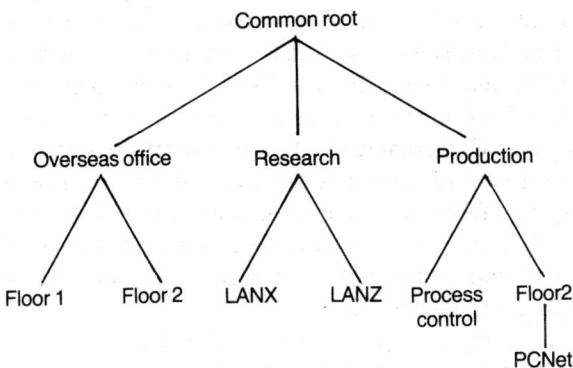

Figure C.5 A typical domain addressing scheme
Mary @ LANX. Research
Patricia @ Floor2. Accounts
Anne @ PCNet. Floor2. Production
Eileen @ LANZ. Research

suitable node. If a message is to be forwarded, the node will delete its address from the 'forward path', and add its address to the 'return path'. If any node is incapable of forwarding the mail, it will know how to return it to the sender.

C.9 CONVERGENCE WITH OSI

As the OSI protocols are beginning to mature, progress is beginning to be made on a convergence of the ARPAnet protocols with those from the OSI reference model. The group of researchers involved in the production of TCP/IP have devised a standard means of providing an ISO transport service using TCP/IP in place of the ISO network layer [11]. This will allow higher level ISO protocols, e.g. X.400 electronic mail, ISO, FTP, etc. to be used in networks employing the TCP/IP protocol set. There is also some progress in passing messages from an SMTP-based mail system to one using X.400.

C.10 EXAMPLE SYSTEM

The diagram in figure C.6 shows a typical Internet involving two LANs (an Ethernet and a Token Ring) together with one WAN using the CCITT X.25 protocol. Since all nodes on each of the networks implement the IP protocol layer, packets can be transferred in a consistent manner between any two nodes on the Internet. If a node on the Ethernet wishes to send a packet to a node on the WAN, it will simply address the packet appropriately. The IP layer in the sending node will send this packet to the corresponding layer on the Ethernet-to-token ring gateway, where it will be forwarded to the token ring-to-X.25 gateway, and from there to its destination node. This occurs without any intervention or special handling on the part of higher level software.

Given this transparent internetwork access, all higher level protocols operate in the same manner regardless of the underlying network con-figuration. Frequently, the IP layer is used in situations where only one LAN is in use, without it being gatewayed to other networks. In this context, the facilities of IP are redundant, but they provide a means of running the higher level protocols, and also offer an option to expand at a later time.

The range of protocols implemented by a particular node is a matter of choice. The only obligatory protocol is IP. In a LAN-only Internet, where the incidence of transmission errors is very low, the features of TCP might be deemed unnecessary for normal interprocess communication and UDP might be sufficient. If application level services are required, a node may choose to implement some combination of FTP, SMTP or any of the other higher level facilities.

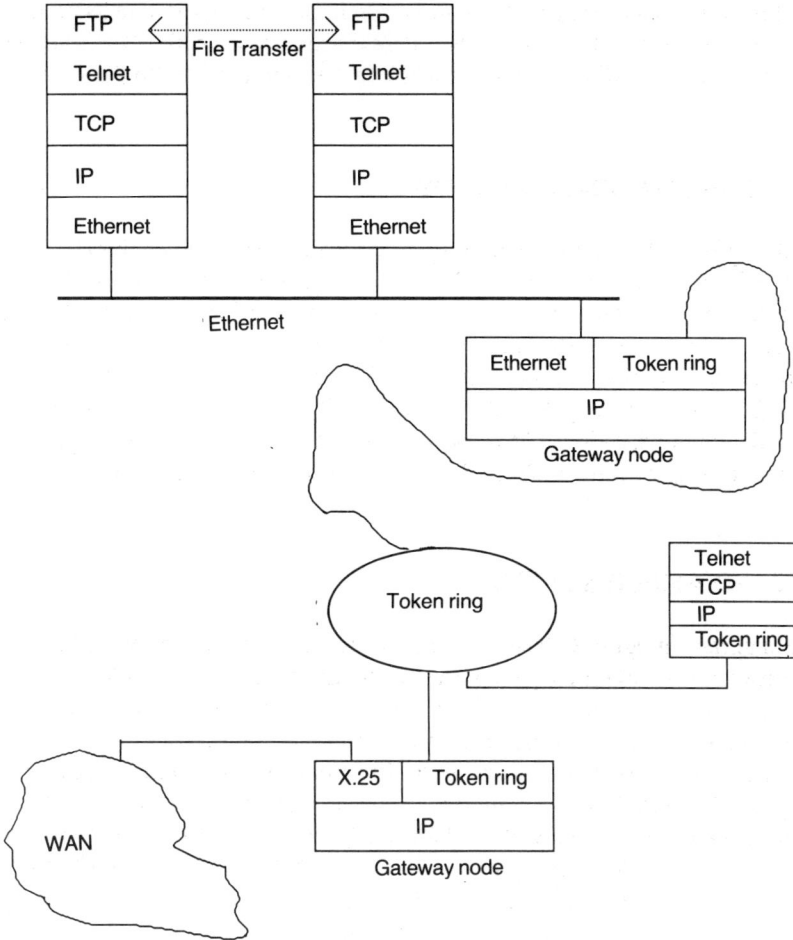

Figure C.6   An Internet

C.11   CONCLUSIONS

The ARPAnet protocols have been in use in one form or another since the early 1970s. Because of this, implementations are available for a wide variety of hardware devices. Although its scope of operation is not as broad as that of OSI, it provides a useful interim solution while the OSI protocols are reaching maturity. Multiple networks can be interconnected with remote terminal access, file transfer and electronic mail available between all attached nodes.

C.12 REFERENCES

1 'The Catanet Model for Internetworking; IEN-48'. In: ARPANET Working Group Internetwork Experimental Note no. 48, SRI International, Menlo Park, Calif., July 1978.

2 Padlipsky, M.A.: 'A Perspective on the Arpanet Reference Model; RFC871'. In: ARPANET Working Group Requests for Comments, no. 871, SRI International, Menlo Park, Calif., September 1982.

3 'Internet Protocol; RFC791'. In: ARPANET Working Group Requests for Comments, no. 791, SRI International, Menlo Park, Calif., September 1981.

4 Postel, J.: 'Internet Control Message Protocol; RFC792'. In: ARPANET Working Group Requests for Comments, no. 792, SRI International, Menlo Park, Calif., September 1981.

5 Postel, J.: 'User Datagram Protocol; RFC768'. In: ARPANET Working Group Requests for Comments, no. 768, SRI International, Menlo Park, Calif., August 1980.

6 'Transmission Control Protocol; RFC793'. In: ARPANET Working Group Requests for Comments, no. 793, SRI International, Menlo Park, Calif., September 1981.

7 Postel, J. and Reynolds, J.: 'Telnet Protocol Specification; RFC854'. In: ARPANET Working Group Requests for Comments, no. 854, SRI International, Menlo Park, Calif., May 1983.

8 Postel, J.: 'File Transfer Protocol; RFC765'. In: ARPANET Working Group Requests for Comments, no. 765, SRI International, Menlo Park, Calif., June 1980.

9 Postel, J.: 'Simple Mail Transfer Protocol; RFC821'. In: ARPANET Working Group Requests for Comments, no. 821, SRI International, Menlo Park, Calif., August 1982.

10 Crocker, D.H.: 'Standard for the Format of ARPA Internet Text Messages; RFC822'. In: ARPANET Working Group Requests for Comments, no. 822, SRI International, Menlo Park, Calif., August 1982.

11 Rose, M.T. and Cass, D.W.: 'ISO Transport Services on top of the TCP; RFC1006'. In: ARPANET Working Group Requests for Comments, no. 1006, SRI International, Menlo Park, Calif., May 1987.

INDEX